W9-DGK-885

CINEMA, COLONIALISM, POSTCOLONIALISM

CINEMA, COLONIALISM, POSTCOLONIALISM

Perspectives from the French and Francophone World

EDITED BY DINA SHERZER

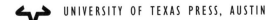 UNIVERSITY OF TEXAS PRESS, AUSTIN

Printed in the United States of America

First edition, 1996

Requests for permission to reproduce material from this work should be sent to Permissions, University of Texas Press, Box 7819, Austin, TX 78713-7819

♾ The paper used in this publication meets the minimum requirements of American National Standard for Information Sciences—Permanence of Paper for Printed Library Materials, ANSI Z39.48-1984.

LIBRARY OF CONGRESS CATALOGING-IN-PUBLICATION DATA

Cinema, colonialism, postcolonialism : perspectives from the French and francophone world / edited by Dina Sherzer.
    p.   cm.
    Includes bibliographical references and index.
    ISBN 0-292-77702-7 (cloth : alk. paper)—ISBN 0-292-77703-5 (pbk. : alk. paper)
    1. Motion pictures—France.   2. Motion pictures—France—Colonies.
3. Motion pictures—Political aspects—Developing countries.   4. Imperialism in motion pictures.   I. Sherzer, Dina.
PN1993.5.F7C4788   1996
791.43'0944—dc20   95-46592

CONTENTS

ACKNOWLEDGMENTS

I wish to thank the authors in this volume, several of whom participated in the "Cinema and Colonialism" sessions that I organized at the 1993 and 1994 International Colloquia on French Studies. I am indebted to all the contributors for their continued interest in and commitment to this project, their excellent papers, and their valuable comments and information. The University of Texas University Research Institute provided a small grant to assist in the preparation of the manuscript. The director of the University of Texas Press, Joanna Hitchcock, and the humanities editor, Ali Hossaini, encouraged this project from its inception and provided support all the way through. Joel Sherzer provided intellectual and technical support.

CINEMA, COLONIALISM, POSTCOLONIALISM

INTRODUCTION

Dina Sherzer

Reflecting on anthropological writings, Clifford Geertz quotes James Clifford, the metaethnographer, as Geertz calls him: "What has become irreducibly curious is no longer the other but cultural description itself."[1] This reflective and deconstructive stance has also shaped postcolonial studies that have examined the nature of visual and verbal representations of the Other, the American Indian, the African, and the Arab created by Western scholars, travelers, writers, and colonizers.[2] This collection of essays is very much in the mode of such studies. It deals with a rich topic composed of multiple realities, past and present, involving France and its colonies, multiethnic contemporary France, and cinematic discourses that have been and are being produced about these realities. More specifically, these essays examine how French cinema has represented the encounter and cohabitation of French individuals and various Others during the colonial era, how French cinema is currently imagining and refiguring France's colonial past, and how it renders and comes to terms with the cohabitation of individuals from the former colonies and French individuals in France. As such, this book is a contribution to postcolonial research, but it also goes beyond that to include another aspect of postcolonialism by offering analyses of films by directors from the former colonies who give their own representation of colonialism and their own presentation of their culture, so that now it is with the lens of the Other that images are constructed.

Resolutely postmodern, these essays interrogate and analyze images of the past and of the present, examine how the images signify, and point out the underlying assumptions behind them and their relationship to historical and cultural facts. Some of the issues raised include: What were the components of the colonial imagination? How was and is the Other represented? What is the nature of the images shown on the screen? What of the past is represented, history or memory? What constructions have been elaborated about the Empire and the metropolis at the time of colonization and after decolonization? What discursive contexts allowed and enabled such cultural constructions to emerge? How are colonial wars represented? Several authors discuss how the films participated in the creation and maintenance of the cultural hegemony of France. Others note the ambiguous messages of the recent films set in the colonies that display an uncanny nostalgia for the Empire. The authors dealing with films set in contemporary France document how the films they discuss participate in the ongoing debate about identity and ethnicity. And the authors who present Francophone cinema document how the Empire writes back, as it were, and bring to the fore the powerful messages of films that intertwine the colonial past with various aspects of African culture that are not often known to the general public.

The scholars who have contributed to this volume are specialists in film studies and teach film at their respective institutions. Their essays reflect their expertise, in that they not only focus on the content of the films but also take into account how narrative and cinematographic techniques such as lack of plot, episodic structure, mise-en-scène, and lighting participate in the creation of meaning. They also pay attention to intertextual relationships that might exist between the films and novels or sociological and cultural documents. In addition, these scholars bring to bear issues of distribution, reception, and spectatorship, which are relevant in that they determine who can make films, who sees them, and how spectators are manipulated to react in specific ways to crucial issues of gender, ethnicity, and identity.

A brief overview of colonialism and the history of cinematic productions in France from 1895 to the present will help to identify the historical context in which the films were made. In a nutshell, here is the story. From the beginning of the twentieth century to World War II, there was not much interest in the colonies on the part of directors, because of the expense involved in filming far away and because of the lack of interest among the French public. When nationalisms began to rise after World War II, during the colonial wars and the period of decolonization (1945–1962), issues related to the colonies were not judged to be appropriate topics for films and would have been censored. Immediately and for several years after decolonization (1962–1975), a reluctance set in that prevented directors from looking outside French borders. Only since the mid-1970s has France dared to examine its colonial past.

During the nineteenth century, France embarked on a series of conquests, annexations, and campaigns of pacification. It conquered Algeria in 1841 after eleven years of warfare; it annexed Tunisia in 1881 and Madagascar in 1885. From 1900 to 1914 the pacification of various colonies continued, agreements were signed with local authorities, and administrative organizations were put in place that imposed French models for schools, hospitals, and the army.[3] Native soldiers were trained to serve France, and in fact they were enlisted to fight in the trenches of eastern France against the Germans.[4] Colonists began developing infrastructures such as ports and railroads, which facilitated the exportation of raw material to metropolitan France. In 1914 France possessed an empire twenty times its size, expanding into Africa, Asia, and the Pacific.[5] These exotic distant lands were a source of profit and contributed to the strength and power of the metropolis. But anticolonial resistance began to be felt as the two societies, one of which oppressed the other, engaged in contact and confrontation and as asymmetries became more and more marked. In the year 1895 Louis Lumière made his first films, and already by 1900 his cameramen brought back documentaries from the colonies. Georges Méliès's 1902 film *Trip to the Moon*, usually read as a precursor of science fiction films, is unconsciously emblematic of the conquering spirit of the time in its scenes of scientists trying to slaughter the inhabitants of the moon, represented as tribal people with body painting and spears, who were resisting the invaders and forcing them to leave.

From 1914 to 1930, France tried to devise a way to deal with the colonies that would best serve its own self-interest. Part of the question to be answered was whether it was better to export the colonies' raw materials to France or to develop industry in the colonies. Nationalism, as well as anticolonial resistance, was on the rise. Meanwhile, French cinema from 1915 to 1929 offered its viewers fictional adventures outside France, in North Africa and in the eastern Mediterranean.[6] Several genres presented the encounter with the Other in exotic lands. The oriental-tales films in the vein of *The Thousand and One Nights*, with revealing titles like *La Sultane de l'amour* (1919), staged brutal, mysterious, and tragic passions with the oriental woman as seductress. The other genre, that of colonial films, used the French colonies of North Africa as settings for such stories as Jacques Feyder's *L'Atlantide* (1921), shot in the desert. An adaptation of Pierre Benoît's best-selling novel by the same title was a huge success and was followed by a series of films shot in Tunisia, Algeria, and Morocco.

Among them was Henri Fescourt's *La Maison du Maltais* (1927), set in Tunisia (see Chapter 2). These films were about adventure, exoticism, and forbidden love. Jean Renoir's *Le Bled* (1929) was a propaganda film that hailed the *mission civilisatrice* of the French and displayed their technical skills. The films from that period did not concern themselves with the political and social problems of North Africa.

From 1931 to 1939, France continued to organize health services and scientific and technical development in its colonies. In 1930, with the advent of the Depression, the difference between rich and poor became more marked, and the colonized intellectuals began to question the presence of the colonizers. The 1931 *Exposition coloniale* celebrated the Empire even as it was already crumbling. In 1937 riots erupted in Meknes and agitations spread in Morocco; in 1938 there were riots in Tunis and other parts of Tunisia. This is the period of the colonial cinema, with Jacques Feyder's *Le Grand Jeu* (1934), Julien Duvivier's *La Bandera* and Edmond Greville's *Princesse Tam Tam* (1935), Julien Duvivier's *Pépé le Moko* (1937), and Pierre Chenal's *La Maison du Maltais* (1938). The films, which took place in North Africa, presented the colonies as the French directors imagined them, as territories waiting for European initiatives, virgin land where the White man with helmet and boots regenerated himself or was destroyed by alcoholism, malaria, or native women. They displayed the heroism of French men, along with stereotypical images of desert, dunes, and camels, and reinforced the idea that the Other is dangerous. They did not present the colonial experience, did not attach importance to colonial issues, and were amazingly silent on what happened in reality. They contributed to the colonial spirit and temperament of conquest and to the construction of White identity and hegemony.[7]

From 1940 to 1945 the soldiers of the Empire fought for France in World War II. As the war ended, nationalisms developed in many countries, and the French sought to repress them and organized military campaigns against them. In 1944 there were troubles in Rabat. The Thiaroye massacre took place in Senegal—native troops coming back from the front requested the money owed to them, and since they seemed to revolt against the French authority and might agitate the rest of the population, the French army killed them. In 1945 there were strikes in Douala and agitation in Conakry. The films that are usually discussed with regard to this troubled period of French history are Jean Delannoy's *L'éternel Retour* (1943), Henri Clouzot's *Le Corbeau* (1943), and Marcel Carné's *Les Enfants du paradis* (begun in 1943 and screened in 1945), which have become classics. From 1941 to 1943, however, several other films—among them *Le*

Pavillon brûle (1941), by Jacques de Baroncelli; *Malaria* (1942), by Jean Gourget; *Mahalia la métisse* (1942), by Walter Kapps; *L'Appel du Bled* (1942), by Maurice Gleize; and *Chant de l'exilé* (1943), by André Hugon— provided French filmgoers diversion from the war. They were tales of love and adultery set in Africa, Algeria, and Indochina, and they staged French characters as the main protagonists, involved in issues that placed the natives in secondary positions, as servants, traitors, or exploited sexual partners. These films displayed the strength and courage of the French working for and developing the colonies and again offered an apology for the colonizer and the colonizing process.[8]

The postwar Fourth Republic extended from 1945 to 1958. In 1946, just after the war, the French government, in a spirit of generosity and equality, declared all the individuals from the colonies to be French citizens and therefore equal to the French from the metropolis. But the gesture was too late and not enough, and little by little France was forced to divest itself of its colonies. Through wars and decolonization the colonies gradually gained their independence. In 1953 riots erupted in Morocco, which was declared independent in 1956. In 1954 the French were defeated in Dien Bien Phu, and Indochina was declared independent. In 1954 the Front de Libération National (FLN) movement began agitating in Algeria, and a series of military campaigns and operations opposed the French army and the Algerian liberation army.

With regard to cinema, 1945 to 1958 was a very active period.[9] France was trying to reorganize itself and its cinema and to ward off the power of Hollywood. At first, directors made films about World War II, such as René Clément's *La Bataille du rail* (1945). Then came Jean Cocteau's *La Belle et la bête* (1946), Claude Autant-Lara's *Le Diable au corps* (1946), and Jean Delannoy's *La Symphonie pastorale* (1946). In the early 1950s, while Indochina was on fire and revolts were erupting in North Africa, Max Ophüls directed *La Ronde* (1950); Jacques Tati, *Les Vacances de Monsieur Hulot* (1951); and Robert Bresson, *Le Journal d'un curé de campagne* (1951). These were safe, very French, apolitical films, comedies on behavior and social rules or the human psyche.

Several directors dared to engage with matters having to do with the colonies,[10] but their efforts were quickly squashed. Chris Marker praised African culture and criticized European imperialism in *Les Statues meurent aussi* (1952). His film was censored. *Rendez-vous sur les quais*, by Paul Carpita (1953), was forbidden because it showed dockers in Marseille refusing to load armaments bound for Indochina as the coffins of French soldiers fighting there were taken off incoming ships. This film has now resurfaced, and its screening was permitted for the first time in 1990. Jean Rouch's *Les Maîtres-fous* (1954), screened in Paris in the Musée de l'Homme, caused considerable controversy. Alain Resnais's *Nuit et brouillard* (1956), which explored the memory of the Holocaust, was censored until the director removed the image of a French policeman in a concentration camp. It was not yet time to bring up topics considered dangerous and taboo. From 1956 to 1958, Roger Vadim in *Et Dieu créa la femme* and Louis Malle in *Ascenseur pour l'échafaud* made their mark with new ideas and heralded the new cinema. Vadim was innovative with Brigitte Bardot and his presentation of a new image of woman, and Malle explored new cinematographic techniques and an interesting sound track. The young critics of the *Cahiers du cinéma* (Claude Chabrol, Jean-Luc Godard, Jacques Rivette, and François Truffaut) were preparing the New Wave. Indochina and Algeria did not appear in cinema during this time.[11]

The period from 1958 to 1978 was the first twenty years of the Fifth Republic, which began with Charles de Gaulle's "coup d'état." War was raging in Algeria and France was in turmoil, on the brink of civil war until 1962 when the Evian accords were signed. The movement that came to be called the New Wave emerged on the French scene in 1958 when the critics of the *Cahiers du cinéma* made their first films, Chabrol's *Les Cousins*, Truffaut's *Les 400 Coups*, and Rivette's *Paris nous appartient*. In 1958 Malle's *Les Amants* and Alain Resnais's *Hiroshima mon amour* also came out, and 1959 was the year of Godard's *À bout de souffle*.

These films were mostly apolitical in that they ignored the Franco-Algerian conflict. In fact, until 1962, "Silence on ne tourne pas" [Quiet there is no shooting in progress] was the rule.[12] "Algeria" was a word that movie directors were told to forget. Censorship was at work, preventing them from choosing topics considered dangerous. In 1960 Godard's *Le Petit Soldat*, dealing with the Algerian problem and torture, was censored; it was not released until 1963. In 1961 Resnais's *Last Year in Marienbad* broached the subject of the relationship between France and Algeria, but in a metaphorical way, using a rape scene to represent France's activities in Algeria.[13]

Adieu Philippine (1963), by Jacques Rozier, timidly alludes to the Algerian war through the story of a young man's vacation before he leaves for Algeria. The same year, Resnais's *Muriel* refers directly but subliminally to the violence and rape committed by the French in Algeria. As Pierre Jeancolas notes, there is a strange silence of French cinema on the subject of decolonization and colonial wars, because viewers preferred to close their eyes; they wanted the past behind them as France was busy entering the consumer society and enjoying an economic boom.[14] The subject of Alge-

ria brought feelings of shame; the war took place not far away like the Indochina war did but in France's backyard. It took an Italian director, Gillo
Pontecorvo, and Algerian funds to make *La Bataille d'Alger* in 1966, a moving film that presented events from the Algerian point of view and did justice to the important role played by women in the actual fight against the
colonizers. In 1965 Pierre Schoendoerffer presented *La 317ème Section*, a
precursor of *Platoon* documenting the heroism of French soldiers fighting
in difficult conditions in Indochina. But the film, a faint echo of the Indochina war fought ten years before, raised little interest. Colonial wars
were doomed topics (*sujets maudits*). French people did not want to be confronted with their past, and amnesia dominated French screens and French
history generally until the 1970s. Films such as *Avoir 20 ans dans les Aurès*,
by René Vautier (1971); *RAS*, by Yves Boisset (1972); and *La Question*, by
Laurent Heynemann (1976) were left in the distributors' drawers for a
long time.

From 1975 to 1980 France and its former colonies continued their relationship in a spirit of cooperation. France helped the newly independent
colonies to develop their infrastructure, trying to keep an important
sphere of influence in the world and an outlet for its products. This relationship with the old metropolis was criticized by some for smacking of
neocolonialism. At this time one could notice a definite change in the
French mentality—it was now possible and tolerable to look at the past
and to begin to assess what had happened. A case in point is precisely the
work of Pierre Boulanger in *Le Cinéma colonial* (1975). In his introduction
Boulanger could write that from 1911 to 1962, 210 films were made about
the colonies, mostly about North Africa, which gave spectators biased,
fanciful representations that are disturbing today. He noted that the films
promoted the myth of aggression; they were apologies for conquest, murder, stupidity, and hatred; and they completely ignored the native populations.[15] It became possible not only to write about the past but also to
make films about it. "Silence on retourne, la mémoire nous reviendrait"
[Quiet, there is shooting in progress again, our memory is returning to
us], an article in *L'Express* states ironically.[16] And indeed, Jean-Jacques Annaud looked at the colonial Africa of 1916 in *La Victoire en chantant* (1976)
and Pierre Schoendoerffer in *Le Crabe-tambour* (1977) reminisced about
World War II, Indochina, and Algeria from the point of view of army
officers who believed in France's mission. Alexandre Arcady's *Le Coup de
sirocco* (1978) showed the traumatism of the Algerian French population
and the uprooting that their resettlement in France provoked. *L'Etat
sauvage* (1978), by Francis Girot, was a scathing indictment of both African

and French racism and of the opportunism and corruption of the French and African authorities in an undetermined African country.

In the 1980s and 1990s the return of the repressed was in full swing. One can speak of the colonial syndrome: just as Vichy continued to haunt the memories, screens, and books of France,[17] similarly colonialism became a topic that was dealt with in many domains, from studies of colonial cultures to research in history and anthropology.[18] Cinema played an important role in this exploration of the colonial past for several reasons. Several directors making their first film in those years happened to have personal experiences shaped by the colonies and by colonial wars and decided to make films on these topics. In addition, it was necessary for French cinema to turn to other places and to innovate. There are now a good number of films that are imaginings and refigurings of colonial culture and life and of colonial wars: for Africa, Bertrand Tavernier's *Coup de torchon* (1981) and Claire Denis's *Chocolat* (1988); for Algeria, Alain Corneau's *Fort Saganne* (1984), Gérard Mordillat's *Salut Frangin* (1989), Gilles Béhat's *Le Vent de la Toussaint* (1991), Brigitte Roüan's *Outremer* (1991), and Bertrand Tavernier's *La Guerre sans nom* (1992); for Indochina, Jean-Jacques Annaud's *L'Amant* (1992), Régis Wargnier's *Indochine* (1992), and Pierre Schoendoerffer's *Dien Bien Phu* (1992).

Even though these films do not purport to be documentaries or truthful renderings of the past, and even though they include many ambiguities, contradictions, and biases, as several of the essays in this volume point out, they are fascinating documents, presenting to French spectators images of the former colonies, of life in the contact zone from a Eurocentric point of view. They capture what *outremer* (overseas) stood for in the minds of French spectators—tropical, exotic places, the desert of *Fort Saganne*, the beautiful blue sea of *Outremer*, the teeming life of the oriental neighborhood of Cholon in *L'Amant*, the haunting beauty of the Bay of Ha Long in *Indochine*, the wide landscapes of Africa in *La Victoire en chantant* and *Chocolat*. They show the colonies as territories occupied successively by several different European countries, and as multiethnic societies where French individuals from different classes and regions lived side by side with native populations under strict organizations and rules that the established hierarchies and asymmetries designed to privilege the French and to exploit the land and the natives.[19] These films provide concrete examples of what colonization meant, i.e., the importation of French traditions through the French military, the French church, and the French administration, which organized and ruled the different countries of the Empire and tried to push aside native traditions.

A postcolonial orientation is definitely a central aspect here; although these films present the point of view of French individuals, they also show the exploitation of the native populations and the privileged life and prejudices of the colonizers, as well as their use of scholarly knowledge to get control of the land they want to conquer.[20] The collaboration of the native elite with the French is made evident, but so are different forms of resistance on the part of the native populations. Viewers are made aware of what has been called "the weapons of the weak,"[21] such as the songs making fun of the Whites by the Africans carrying the two priests and the man praying to Allah but putting on a cross when the priests arrive in *La Victoire en chantant* and the puppet show depicting the story of the Vietnamese princess killing the French officer in *Indochine*. They also see clandestine meetings in *Chocolat* and the rise of nationalism and guerrilla activities in *Le Vent de la Toussaint*, *Outremer*, and *Indochine*, reflecting the powerful will for independence and freedom in the colonies and the bloody military campaigns that France undertook in order to save its Empire. With regard to representation of the natives, in the films of the 1980s and 1990s, in comparison to those of the 1930s, the casting has changed. It is no longer conceivable to have an Arab or an African played by a White actor. Nor is it any longer acceptable to have non-White characters playing roles of inept, ridiculous, or childish individuals. The Other can be a medicine man, can go to French schools, and can speak several languages. The films construct a much more positive image of the Other. And finally these films recall with a definite nostalgia how the French communities felt at home in the lands and territories that they had considered their own, that they had worked hard to develop and to maintain, and how in fact these people often had never set foot in France and were first and really only North African French, Asiatic French, or African French. Indeed, these films are the second wave of colonial films or, really, the only colonial films. They sensitize French viewers to the colonial past, and they have an impact on the formation of a common collective memory of the colonies. Perhaps the salient feature that links all these films is that French directors represent France as embroiled, indeed trapped, as an intruder in other lands and other cultures.

Since decolonization and right up to the present, because of economic and political problems, an increasing number of individuals from the former colonies have settled in France. The contact zone is now in France itself, and immigration, the presence of the Other on French soil, has polarized the country. Individuals of Maghrebian origin called Beur, individuals from African origin called Black, individuals from Vietnam and Cambodia, and French individuals are living side by side within neighborhoods in French cities or on the outskirts of cities where several different ethnic groups cohabit in run-down tenements. Concern with the poverty, marginalization, and modalities of integration of these immigrants and of their children, assimilation or preservation of cultural differences, and notions of identity, national culture, and what Frenchness is have been debated on the political scene and in the press.[22] Cinema participates in this debate as it engages with these touchy aspects of contemporary French life. At the moment, three orientations emerge, which can be classified with the labels Beur cinema, Black cinema, and French cinema. Beur cinema is represented by films made by directors of Maghrebian descent who are living in France, such as Abdelkrim Bahloul's *Le Thé à la menthe* (1984) and Medhi Charef's *Le Thé au harem d'Archimède* (1985) (see Chapter 8).[23] Black cinema is represented by Med Hondo's *Soleil O* (1970) (see Chapter 9) and Thomas Gilou's *Black Mic Mac* (1988). Bahloul's *Le Thé à la menthe* and Gilou's *Black Mic Mac* are fascinating presentations of Maghrebian and Black communities in Paris.

Several French directors have been and continue making films about the Maghrebian and Black populations living in France; Claude Berri's *Tchao pantin* (1985), Gérard Blain's *Pierre et Djemila* (1987), and Cédric Kahn's *Trop de bonheur* (1995) deal with the interactions of Beur and French individuals. Claire Denis's *S'en fout la mort* (No Fear No Die) (1990), Nicolas Ribourski's *Périgord noir* (1988), and Coline Serreau's *Romuald et Juliet* (1988) are films about Black and French individuals (see Chapter 11). Serge Meynard's *L'Oeil au beurre noir* (1988) (see Chapter 8) and Bernard Blier's *Un deux trois soleil* (1993) are about the 3B's, as they are called in France (Black, Blanc, Beur), and capture the multiethnicity of many French cities. Except for Ribourski's *Périgord noir*, the subject of these films is the difficult life of immigrants in tenements, their asymmetrical relationships with French individuals, their negative interactions with French authorities, and the poverty, racism, and unemployment that plague the young people. Denis's *S'en fout la mort* and Gilou's *Black Mic Mac* are particularly interesting documents, sensitive to aspects of the hybrid culture of immigrant populations and mingling elements of the old country and contemporary France.[24] Ribourski's *Périgord noir* and Serreau's *Romuald et Juliet* also present French and Black individuals, but in a very positive utopian tone, with an ironic touch (see Chapter 11).

In the 1960s, immediately after decolonization, the idea of Francophony—a cultural association of countries linked by a common language—began to emerge. It became a reality in 1986 with the inauguration of a regular series of conferences and continues to be so, with the French government actively promoting the conception that France now is no longer only a member of the European community but is also, along with its former colonies, a Francophone country.[25] Concomitantly, the cultures, the literature, and the films from the Francophone world are emerging now as dynamic and creative modes of expression.[26] The Empire writes back, the excolonized peoples express themselves and engage with their past and their present.[27] In cinema, the colonies, which under French domination did not have access to production and distribution possibilities, are now progressively overcoming the considerable difficulties, and several Francophone directors have been able to make films (see Chapters 9 and 10).

Francophone cinema has taken several orientations. One group of films presents the point of view of excolonized people on colonization: *Chroniques des années de braise* (1975), by Lakhdar-Hamina, from Algeria; *Emitai* (1971) and *Camp de Thiaroye* (1988), by Ousmane Sembene, from Senegal (see Chapter 10); *Rue cases nègres* (1988), by Euhzan Palcy, from Martinique; *Mort d'un prophète* (1991), by Raoul Peck, from Haiti, and *Afrique je te plumerai* (1992), by Jean-Marie Teno, from Cameroon. These films, which decolonize knowledge about colonialism and engage with the present as well as the past, are more biting and more committed to showing the evils of colonialism than are the films made by French directors. They focus on African, Martinican, and Algerian history and colonial past, seen through the eyes of those who are the descendants of the victims of colonialism.

Other Francophone films present images and stories set in the contemporary reality of the former colonies: from Martinique, *Siméon*, by Euzhan Palcy (1991); from Cameroon, *Sango malo*, by Bassek ba Kobhio (1991), and *Quartier Mozart*, by Jean-Pierre Beloko (1992); from Senegal, *Touki Bouki*, by Djibril Diop Mamberty (1973), and *Saaraba*, by Amadou Seck (1988). The directors of these films aim at redressing the imbalance that resulted when only images from the West appeared on Francophone screens. Echoing the past and dealing with the present, these films constitute an effort to represent racial and cultural Otherness, which had previously been marginalized or silenced. Francophone directors want to make up for the past silencing of their cultures by the colonizers; their films are the creations of postcolonial individuals who are trying to recover their past and valorize their culture. They use native languages, such as Bambara or Wolof, and present myths, rituals, and beliefs in stories that unfold under non-Western chronotopes. Souleymane Cissé's *Yeelen* (1987), from Mali (see Chapter 10), and Idrissa Ouédraogo's *Yaaba* (1989), from Burkina Faso, are the most representative examples of this new cinema.[28]

The vitality of Francophone cinema also manifests itself in France with the appearance of films that both receive prizes at film festivals and attract a wide public. Examples are the Franco-Vietnamese production by Tran Anh Hung, *L'Odeur de la papaye verte* (The Scent of the Green Papaya) (1993), which was hailed at the Cannes film festival in 1993, and a film on Cambodia by an exiled Cambodian living in France and remembering his country, Rithy Panh's *Les Gens des rizières* (1993). In addition, French directors propose images of Africa as well. For example, Patrick Grandperret based *L'Enfant Lion* (1993) on a children's story relating the friendship between a Black child and a lioness, and Laurent Chevallier is directing a film in Guinea adapting the well-known novel by Camara Laye, *L'Enfant Roi*. Even though these films are isolated examples, they definitely offer other images, other stories, other places, other languages, other gestures, and other customs. They have an ethnographic and cultural appeal for both westerners and contemporary Francophone individuals who have been raised in the Western world and have not known the country of their origin, and finally they valorize cultures that had been despised and silenced during colonization and even during and after decolonization.

I turn now to the essays themselves. They deal with an impressive array of films,[29] which are the products of the cultures of colonialism and postcolonialism, and they address various issues that constitute contemporary postcolonial studies. Postcolonial studies have drawn attention to documents such as films, novels, photographs, and history produced by the colonizers during colonization and examine colonial realities, colonial culture, and colonial ideology as represented in these documents. This is the topic of the essays by Martine Loutfi, Steven Ungar, Nandi Bhatia, and Paul Stoller (Chapters 1 through 4).

As an appropriate opening for the volume, Martine Loutfi, in "Imperial Frame: Film Industry and Colonial Representation," studies the nature of the images of the colonies that were produced by filmmakers. She points out how the images were constructed as representations of the exotic and were concerned not with the reality of the colonial experience but rather with financial profit, propaganda, and escapism—characteristics that enabled them to avoid control and government censorship. In her historical survey of Lumière-Meguish, Feyder, Godard, and Wargnier, she examines the evolution of relationships between the technical and economic evolution of the film industry and the representation of colonial situations. She concludes that film is not only entertainment; it is also propaganda and politics.

In his essay, "Split Screens: *La Maison du Maltais* as Text and Document," Steven Ungar explores a set of fascinating issues that link France, its colonies, colonial expansion, and justification for colonization with notions of identity, hegemony, colonial imagery, and representation. Colonial films, he argues, are packed with messages related to gender, ethnicity, and culture. He then analyzes two different film adaptations of the same novel: Henri Fescourt's *La Maison du Maltais* (1927) and Pierre Chenal's *La Maison du Maltais* (1938), describing and analyzing the differences between them. His essay underscores the necessity for a more detailed analysis of the interwar cinema, which has been viewed until now in a monolithic fashion under the label *cinéma colonial.*

Jean Renoir's *The River* (1951) has been hailed in the French press for its beautiful colors, its superb camera work, and its fascinating presentation of Indian life along the Ganges with its religion and rituals. However, the postcolonial reading that Nandi Bhatia offers in "Whither the Colonial Question? Jean Renoir's *The River*" reveals the orientalist overtones of the film. She documents how Renoir, despite his liberal past and populist beliefs, was expressing the Western position, which presented the Other through stereotypes, and she shows how and why he ignored completely the charged political context of the time.[30]

Paul Stoller, in "Regarding Rouch: The Recasting of West African Colonial Culture," begins by reminding readers of the various discourses through which Arabs and Europeans constructed the African. He then studies how Jean Rouch, in *Les Maîtres-fous, Jaguar, Moi, un noir, La pyramide humaine,* and *Petit à Petit,* mingled poetic lyricism, philosophical content, and political impact to achieve an early and unsettling repudiation of the racist and primitivist foundations of French colonial culture. This is an appropriate essay by an anthropologist, friend of Jean Rouch, and specialist of the Songhai of Niger.

Postcolonial studies concern themselves with recent documents dealing with the colonies. A salient feature of contemporary French culture is that novels about the colonies are being published[31] and, as noted earlier, directors have been particularly attracted by the colonial past. Chapters 5 through 7, by Catherine Portuges, Naomi Greene, and Panivong Norindr, analyze and deconstruct the contemporary images of the colonies produced by French cinema.

Catherine Portuges's essay, *"Le Colonial féminin:* Women Directors Interrogate French Cinema," points out that most of the second wave of colonial films have been directed by women. She examines how these directors draw attention to the roles of female subjectivity and of women in the colonies, the effects of war on women, and women's implication in the conflicts—all subjects that have been marginalized and excluded until now. She explores the significance of history, memory, family, and the focus on interiority in Brigitte Roüan's *Outremer* and Marie-France Pisier's *Le Bal du gouverneur*. She also discusses the significance of Tran Anh Hung's *L'Odeur de la papaye verte*, which, although it is directed by a man, is a film in search of the memories of the past, a reconstitution of maternal gestures, and an evocation of the domestic space in his Vietnamese household.

Naomi Greene, in "Empire as Myth and Memory," focuses on two films, *Le Crabe-tambour* and *Outremer*, and analyzes the questions that they raise concerning the ways in which a bitter and decisive period has been remembered and represented. She shows how these films blur and transform history, since they are more about shattered dreams than about the past, and how they do not represent the most troubling and guilty aspects, but rather express nostalgia for a lost world.

Panivong Norindr, in "Filmic Memorial and Colonial Blues: Indochina in Contemporary French Cinema," captures a current in today's French culture—its fascination, indeed, its love affair, with Indochina—that has resulted in a number of novels and films. After discussing the contact that enabled this type of cultural production, he considers three films—*Indochine*, *L'Amant*, and *Dien Bien Phu*—in order to examine how they establish and mediate historical memory and participate in the construction of a collective memory of Indochina. He concludes that these films sustain and reinforce the founding myths of the colonial presence in Indochina.

The literary and cinematic production of diasporic subjects (descendants of colonized individuals) now in the process of elaborating a Third World cinema is another domain of postcolonial studies. Beur and Black directors in France are part of this development, but some French directors are also participating by representing, like their Black and Beur counterparts, the lives and conditions of Third World diasporic subjects. The essays by Mireille Rosello and Madeleine Cottenet-Hage (Chapters 8 and 9) belong to these categories.

Mireille Rosello, in "Third Cinema or Third Degree: The 'Rachid System' in Serge Meynard's *L'Oeil au beurre noir*," sets the stage for her analysis by raising a number of questions about the concept of Beur identity and culture, the representation of Beurs in the French press, and stereotypes and their functioning in society. The film she studies, which features Smaïn, a very popular Beur comedian, addresses one aspect of contemporary France, the presence of Blacks, Beurs, and French living side by side in cities. She points out how this film is directly implicated in the culture of contemporary multiethnic France, since its director in fact asks how French language and French culture integrate the presence of Black and Beur in their images.

Madeleine Cottenet-Hage, in "Decolonizing Images: *Soleil O* and the Cinema of Med Hondo," presents a typical Third World cinema director, an African individual who has experienced a displacement of culture and language and who, having been able to make films despite enormous difficulties, feels the necessity of addressing African audiences and speaking from their point of view. She analyzes one film, *Soleil O*, which documents the grim postcolonial conditions among African immigrants in France and the effects of their shifting from continent to continent and from place to place, constantly being rejected as Others by the dominant political, economic, and social structure. She notes how Hondo's fragmented narrative techniques contribute to the creation of a sense of instability, movement, and dislocation in the lives of the characters. In addition, she points out the originality and the appropriately hybrid nature of this film, which combines modernity with aspects of traditional African culture.

Another facet of postcolonial studies looks at how individuals from the former colonies take up the pen or the camera to express their version of the colonial experience, thus decolonizing knowledge by proposing their own images, by presenting their own heritage and cultures. John Downing's essay, "Post-Tricolor African Cinema: Toward a Richer Vision," addresses the African manifestations of these issues. He begins with an informative general presentation of African cinema (Africa and North Africa), in which he underscores the variety of themes, structures, and styles, as well as the difficulty that this cinema experienced because of the censorship of African governments, which do not like being criticized. There follows an analysis of several of Ousmane Sembene's films, which, notes Downing, are particularly interesting for their representation of and discourse about women. In his discussion of *Emitai* and *Camp de Thiaroye*, Downing shows that these films are a scathing indictment of colonialism, documenting what French directors hide or cannot show—the brutality of the French army. Downing also refers to *Guelwaar* (1992), a film in which Sembene attacks postcolonial African religion, corruption, and prostitution. Downing moves on to discuss *Yeelen* (1987), a film by Souleymane Cissé that aims to make contemporary African generations aware of aspects of Bambara culture before colonization, African experience, and linguistic and cultural diversity.

Finally, postcolonial studies encompass the examination of issues of gender, race, and ethnicity in colonial and postcolonial contexts. This is the topic of my essay, "Race Matters and Matters of Race: Interracial Relationships in Colonial and Postcolonial Films" (Chapter 11). I examine the development of interracial relationships as more than the inscribing of love affairs and titillating erotic moments in films; in addition, they address questions of race, hegemony, and difference. I use films from the 1930s to the present to document the changes that have occurred as films have moved from condemnation and discouragement of mixed relationships to a more free display of physical attraction and the pleasures of interracial love. Although such unions are not yet widely accepted, shifts in gender roles, more awareness of difference and ethnicity in an increasingly multiethnic society, and sensitivity to how the Other is represented account for the changes in attitudes.

In analyzing representation in films from colonial and postcolonial France and Francophone countries, these essays focus on history, memory, difference, gender, ethnicity, contradictions, and ambiguities to bring out how cinema captures the mood of a country and how films are crisscrossed by various tendencies and issues that were and are agitating or are latent in French and Francophone culture. I conclude with a quote from Henri Rousso that seems to me particularly appropriate to the question of cinema, colonialism, and postcolonialism: "When the time is right, an era of the past may serve as a screen on which new generations can project their contradictions, controversies, and conflicts in objectified form."[32] Perhaps the time has come when images of colonial times are helping France to come to terms with its past and with the issues of diversity and difference.

NOTES

1. Clifford Geertz, *Works and Lives: The Anthropologist as an Author* (Stanford: Stanford University Press, 1988), 133; James Clifford, "Dada Data," *Sulfur* 16 (1987): 162–164.

2. Examples of such studies include Martine Loutfi, *Littérature et colonialisme* (Paris: Mouton, 1971); Robert Berkhofer, *The White Man's Indian: Images of the American Indian from Columbus to the Present* (New York: Knopf, 1978); Malek Alloula, *Le Harem colonial: Images d'un sous érotisme* (Paris: Slatkine, 1981), *The Colonial Harem* (Minneapolis: University of Minnesota Press, 1986); Edward Said, *Orientalism* (New York: Vintage, 1978), *Culture and Imperialism* (New York: Knopf, 1993); Tzvetan Todorov, *The Conquest of America: The Question of the Other* (New York: Harper and Row, 1984); Christopher Miller, *Blank Darkness: Africanist Discourse in French* (Chicago: University of Chicago Press, 1985); Patrick Brantlinger, *Rules of Darkness: British Literature and Imperialism 1830–1914* (Ithaca: Cornell University Press, 1988); James Clifford, *The Predicament of Culture* (Boston: Harvard University Press, 1988); Lisa Lowe, *Critical Terrains: French and British Imperialism* (Ithaca: Cornell University Press, 1992); and Marie Louise Pratt, *Imperial Eyes: Travel Writing and Transculturation* (New York: Routledge, 1992).

3. See Terence Ranger, "The Invention of Traditions in Colonial Africa," in *The Invention of Tradition*, ed. Eric Hobsbawm and Terence Ranger (Cambridge: Cambridge University Press, 1983), 211–262. Ranger documents how these

various institutions are established in Africa, replacing the existing local tribal organization.

4. In *Grand Illusion* (1936), Renoir makes a passing reference to this fact in the form of the Black soldier prisoner with Marechal and De Boeldieu in Germany. In 1984, in *Fort Saganne*, Corneau has a scathing indictment of the treatment of Algerian and Black soldiers sent to the front lines. And in 1990 Tavernier, in *La vie et rien d'autre*, reminds us, somewhat humorously, of the presence of troops from the colonies as part of the French army, when Vietnamese and Muslim soldiers/ diggers request special meals, i.e., rice and no pork.

5. See maps and chronology of France's relations with its colonies from 1814 to 1962 in Denise Bouche, *Histoire de la colonisation française: Flux et Reflux* (Paris: Fayard, 1991), 529–570.

6. I am indebted for this information to Richard Abel, *French Cinema: The First Wave, 1915–1929* (Princeton: Princeton University Press, 1984). In particular, see the section "Arabian Nights and Colonial Dreams," 153–160. See also Pierre Boulanger, *Le Cinéma colonial: De L'Atlantide à Lawrence d'Arabie* (Paris: Seghers, 1975).

7. For more information on the films of this period, see Boulanger, *Le Cinéma colonial*; Raymond Chirat, *Le Cinéma français des années trente* (Paris: Hatier, 1983); Jean-Pierre Jeancolas, *Quinze ans d'années trente* (Paris: Stock, 1983), 250–260; Michèle Lagny et al., "L'Afrique de l'autre," *Générique des années trente* (Paris: Presses Universitaires de Vincennes, 1986); Pierre Sorlin, "The Fanciful Empire: French Feature Films and the Colonies in the 1930s," *French Civilization Studies* 2 (1991): 135–151. Both Jeancolas (253) and Sorlin (143 and 148) discuss how *Itto*, by Jean-Benoît Lévy and Marie Epstein, referred to actual revolts and was sympathetic to the Moroccan people.

8. The scenarios of the films set in the colonies can be found in Jacques Siclier, *La France de Pétain et son cinéma* (Paris: Editions Henri Veyrier, 1981).

9. Raymond Chirat, *La IVème République et ses films* (Paris: Hatier, 1985).

10. In 1951 Renoir directed *Le Fleuve*, a film on India and on British colonizers that was praised for its visual qualities, but critics failed to recognize its biased orientation. See Nandi Bhatia's analysis in Chapter 3.

11. Several essays and a synoptic tableau presenting political, social, economic, and cultural events side by side with films from this period can be found in Jean-Loup Passek, ed., *D'un Cinéma l'autre* (Paris: Centre Pompidou, 1988).

12. "*Silence! on ne tourne pas*" is the title of an article by Sophie Grassin from *L'Express*, 23 December 1988, p. 55, which discusses this issue of censorship during the Algerian war. See also a discussion of the relationship of the New Wave and the war and politics in Jean-Luc Douin, ed., *La Nouvelle Vague 25 ans après* (Paris: Editions du Cerf, 1983).

13. On this topic, see Lynn Higgins, *On Belatedness: New Novelists, New Wave Filmmakers, and the Politics of Representation* (Lincoln: University of Nebraska Press, 1995).

14. Pierre Jeancolas, *Le Cinéma des Français: La Vème République 1958–1978* (Paris: Stock, 1979), 156.

15. Boulanger, *Le Cinéma colonial*, 15–17.

16. A series of articles on this topic appeared in *L'Express*, 29 March 1991,

pp. 36–40: interview with Marc Ferro, "Mémoire: Les tabous et les passions"; Luc Ferry, "Les deux patrimoines"; Jean-Pierre Dufreigne, "Silence on retourne"; and Pierre Solié, "Refoulement collectif: Pourquoi les Français préfèrent occulter les guerres coloniales."

17. On this topic, see Henri Rousso, *The Vichy Syndrome: History and Memory in France since 1944* (Boston: Harvard University Press, 1991).

18. For instance, Jacques Marseille, *L'Age d'or de la France coloniale* (Paris: Editions Albin Michel, 1986); Bouche, *Histoire de la colonisation française*; Jean Meyer et al., *Histoire de la France coloniale: Des Origines à 1914* (Paris: Armand Colin, 1991); Jacques Thobie et al., *Histoire de la France coloniale: 1914–1990* (Paris: Armand Colin, 1990). These books present history through political, economic, and cultural events. On other topics, see Yvonne Knibiehler et al., *La Femme au temps des colonies* (Paris: Stock, 1985); Philippe Franchini, *Métis* (Paris: Jacques Bertoin, 1993); Nicolas Bancel et al., *Images et colonies* (Paris: La Découverte/SODIS, 1993); and a biography of the man who was instrumental in bringing about the abolition of slavery, Nelly Schmidt, *Victor Schoelcher* (Paris: Fayard, 1994).

19. Jean-Pierre Jeancolas, in "La Guerre d'Indochine dans le cinéma français," *Positif* 375–376 (May 1992): 86–91, notes that *Indochine* is the first commercial film that points to colonial exploitation, to French domination and superiority.

20. In *Fort Saganne* the French officer trying to pacify the Sahara is accompanied by a French historian and ethnographer who speaks Arabic and explains the customs of the nomads.

21. James C. Scott, *Weapons of the Weak: Everyday Forms of Peasant Resistance* (New Haven: Yale University Press, 1985).

22. See Julia Kristeva's *Etrangers à nous mêmes* (Paris: Gallimard, 1988), *Lettre ouverte à Harlem Désir* (Paris: Rivages, 1990), and *Nations without Nationalism* (New York: Columbia University Press, 1993); Tzvetan Todorov, *La Réflexion française sur la diversité* (Paris: Seuil, 1989).

23. Along with Beur cinema, Beur literature has also developed, engaging with the same issues as cinema has. See Alec G. Hargreaves, *Voices from the North African Community in France: Immigration and Identity in Beur Fiction* (Oxford, N.Y.: Berg, 1991).

24. *Black Mic Mac* is about Congolese immigrants living in a run-down building who are in danger of being evicted by French health services. They bring a diviner from Africa who is supposed to perform African magic to prevent the expulsion. *S'en fout la mort* takes place in the Paris suburb of Rungis in a setting of concrete and highways, dingy cellars and attics, where Dah from Benin and Jocelyn from the Antilles run clandestine cockfights. This film is a study of the passion for cocks in an atmosphere full of anguish and malaise, reminiscent of the mood of *Chocolat*.

25. There is a dictionary-guide titled *La Francophonie de A à Z*, put together by the Ministère de la Francophonie under the auspices of the Ministère des Affaires Etrangères (Paris, 1990).

26. Such writers as Patrick Chamoiseau, Maryse Condé, René Depestre, Tahar Ben Jelloun, and Abdelkebir Khatibi are widely known. A July 1994 newsletter from the Haut Conseil de la Francophonie sent to cultural and educational offices in the United States and in Francophone countries states the following: "Le dialogue des cultures est devenu l'axe central de nos réflexions depuis plus de 10 ans.

La créativité du monde créole, la vitalité de l'arabofrancophonie, la puissance du métissage africano-francophone répondent à nos attentes." [The dialogue between cultures has been for more than ten years the central focus of our reflections. The creativity of the Caribbean creole world, the vitality of Arabic francophony, the power of the African Francophone mixture are fulfilling our expectations.]

27. See Bill Ashcroft et al., *The Empire Writes Back: Theory and Practice in Postcolonial Literatures* (New York: Routledge, 1989); Françoise Lionnet and Ronnie Scharfman, eds., "Post/Colonial Conditions: Exiles, Migrations, and Nomadism," *Yale French Studies* 82–83 (1993); and Winifred Woodhull, *Transfigurations of the Maghreb: Feminism, Decolonization, and Literatures* (Minneapolis: University of Minnesota Press, 1993).

28. California Newsreel in its series The Library of African Cinema offers several of these films, advertising them as encountering a changing Africa through its changing cinema. For a study of what this film production represents, see Jim Pines and Paul Willemen, eds., *Questions of Third World Cinema* (London: British Film Institute, 1989).

29. The films discussed in the essays either in detail or partially are as follows: For the colonial cinema, Jacques Feyder's *L'Atlantide* (1921); Henri Fescourt's *La Maison du Maltais* (1927); Pierre Chenal's *La Maison du Maltais* (1938); Marc Allégret's *Zou Zou* (1934); Edmond Greville's *Princesse Tam Tam* (1935); Julien Duvivier's *Pépé le Moko* (1937); Jean Renoir's *The River* (1951); and Jean Rouch's *Les Maîtres-fous* (1954), *Jaguar* (1954), *Moi, un noir* (1957), *La Pyramide humaine* (1958), and *Petit à Petit* (1969). For the second wave of colonial cinema: Pierre Schoendoerffer's *Le Crabe-tambour* (1977) and *Dien Bien Phu* (1992); Jean-Jacques Annaud's *La Victoire en chantant* (1976) and *L'Amant* (1992); Euzhan Palcy's *Rue cases-nègres* (1988), Claire Denis's *Chocolat* (1988); Brigitte Roüan's *Outremer* (1991); and Régis Wargnier's *Indochine* (1992). Postcolonial cinema is represented through the films by Claude Berri (*Tchao pantin*, 1985), Medhi Charef (*Le Thé au harem d'Archimède* [Tea in the Harem], 1985), Gérard Blain (*Pierre et Djemila*, 1987), Serge Meynard (*L'Oeil au beurre noir*, 1988), Nicolas Ribourski (*Périgord noir*, 1988), Coline Serreau, (*Romuald et Juliet*, 1988), Thomas Gilou (*Black Mic Mac*, 1989), Claire Denis (*S'en fout la mort* [No Fear No Die], 1990), Jean-Loup Hubert (*La Reine blanche*, 1991), Mathieu Kassovitz (*Métisse* [Café au lait], 1993), and Cedric Kahn (*Trop de bonheur*, 1995). And the films of Med Hondo (*Soleil O*, 1970), Ousmane Sembene (*Emitaï*, 1971, *Camp de Thiaroye*, 1988), and Souleymane Cissé (*Yeelen*, 1987) have been chosen as instances of postcolonial African Francophone cinema.

30. Renoir already demonstrated a certain colonial blindness in his 1929 propaganda film *Le Bled*, which mostly hailed the colonial enterprise and did not pay attention to the indigenous populations.

31. Some such novels are Regine Deforges, *Rue de la soie, 1947–1949* (Paris: Fayard, 1995); and Alain Dugrand, *Les Craven de l'Oncle Ho* (Paris: Grasset, 1995).

32. Henri Rousso, *The Vichy Syndrome*, 5.

Imperial Frame

O N E   *Film Industry and Colonial Representation*

Martine Astier Loutfi

Examining films as the products of an industry is an important comple-
ment to examining them as personal artistic expressions. It entails consideration of the technology that existed and the financial and political conditions that prevailed at the time the films were produced and distributed.[1]
By taking some examples from film history it is possible to show that this
approach deepens our understanding of the relationship between France's
colonial past and the representation of that past in French cinema.

When, in 1895, the Lumière brothers dispatched cameramen to North
Africa or Indochina it was with the intention of bringing back images of
the world. The places figuring most prominently in the Lumière catalog[2]
are Russia, Sweden, and China; an occasional image from Algeria appears—for example, from President Loubet's visit there; some other shots
are titled "Coolies in Saigon" or "Ashantis Negroes: Men Dance."[3] Only
about sixty documents dealing specifically with North Africa are stored
among the more than 1,500 Lumière items at the Cinémathèque in Paris.
What we see in these images are events of the time and mostly local
scenes, illustrations of places made popular by the current travel literature.

Felix Mesguich, one of the Lumière cameramen, gave in his memoirs a
candid account of what he was looking for and how he worked.[4] During
his travels he was guided by the search for exotic scenes. In North Africa it
is "the oasis," with the recurring sight of columns of riders on camelback
leaving toward Timbuktu or "the divine atmosphere of the captivating and
mysterious" Sahara.

But Mesguich, because he was filming and not photographing, needed movement. Capturing movement was the great innovation, the technological breakthrough brought about by the Lumière machine, and movement was what the viewers were demanding. Since the Lumière device had limited mobility and could do only short, one-minute takes, Mesguich, like other operators, used his machine in the most efficient way: he filmed events that were already staged events, such as official visits, or he himself often staged scenes that he wanted to film.

In Biskra, for instance, he wanted to film a fantasia. He hired a *goum* of local troops serving in the French army at seven francs per man. During the filming, two men were accidentally killed. The families of the victims asked for two thousand francs in damages. Mesguich left Biskra in a hurry since he did not know whether his company would pay. The company did pay later, five thousand francs, Mesguich writes. This anecdote signals clearly that, from the beginning, the authenticity of cinematic shots was a troubling question. The practice of using local people as actors in supposedly authentic events seems to have been widespread in the early years of cinema. Raoul Grimoin-Sanson, a pioneer of North African filming, recalls how he arranged with a French general to film a fake battle involving some two thousand men on horseback.[5] Obviously, the reality of the world that was supposed to be communicated through films was manipulated and what the audience saw was a spectacle in which document and performance were inextricably intertwined. Images of the colonies were built in accord with the ways in which they were already perceived, essentially as a representation of the exotic. Soon, oriental fantasies were re-created with painted backdrops in the studio by Pathé Company. Ali-Baba and similar imaginary adventures were casually intermixed with views of real landscapes from the colonized countries, leaving the viewer with a confused and exhilarating impression that the colonies were the land of adventure and fantastic deeds.

Although explicit political considerations seem to have been quite absent from these early colonial films, the images that they portrayed certainly contributed to the shaping of a French popular vision of the colonized lands and people that was favorable to French interests. But the main concern of film companies was financial profit. Early on, the part of the burgeoning industry that proved profitable and remained so until the 1930s was film exhibition. Exhibition was "the major profit center of the organization."[6] Production, as long as the public kept coming to the shows, was considered by French film entrepreneurs to be secondary. Most of the films they showed were produced in the United States. At the end of World War I, "production was fragmented, its return on capital uncertain.

Distribution and exhibition were enormously and reliably profitable."[7] Given this basic orientation, it is not surprising that the industry devised means of cutting production costs, such as using backdrops and studio sets rather than filming on location.

In 1921, when Jacques Feyder was trying to fund the production of *L'Atlantide* and to finance filming on location in North Africa and the Sahara, Pierre Benoît, the author of the novel on which the film was to be based, told him: "Do not make the silly mistake to go to the Hoggar. It is miles away (au diable) and very inhospitable. I can assure you that there are some very nice spots in the Fontainebleau forest."[8] The Gaumont producer objected to the high cost, and so he issued multiple warnings about the sand getting in the camera and the film melting because of the heat. "What is the desert? A backdrop," he said repeatedly to Feyder. Feyder finally succeeded, however; the film was shot in Algeria, and it eventually became an artistic and box office triumph.

But the Algerian location, aesthetically accomplished and attractive though it was, did not do much to illuminate the colonial situation of Algeria. In fact, it diminished the rather elaborate political background given by Benoît in the novel. The film remained more exclusively on exotic and pictorial ground. In particular, it is the sentimental, adventurous part of the plot that Feyder developed, while downplaying the opposition between Berbers and Arabs and the search for an elusive proof of the Touaregs' supposed former Christian religion. Both of these latter themes were important in shaping the colonialist policy, and Benoît had woven them skillfully into his plot.

Feyder's film, of course, upheld the basic worldview of the colonial system: the superiority of the White man fighting against horrible dangers to conquer a nearly empty land and to bring some wretched natives the benefit of French civilization. But the immediate message that the spectators and the critics took from the film was twofold. First, *L'Atlantide* was a French film as beautiful and as well made as any American film. In the context of a Franco-American rivalry for the domination of the French film market, the film was an object of national pride. The second part of *L'Atlantide*'s message was the attraction exerted by the immensity of the desert, the sun, "the pure air"—as a commentator wrote in *Cinémagazine*. He added: "I am sure that this film will give to many the desire to leave our limited horizons."[9] Escapism, as well as colonialist and nationalist propaganda, was a direct product of the "real" Sahara displayed on the screen for the first time.

Following this accomplishment, Feyder filmed another Benoît novel, *Le*

Roi lépreux, in Indochina. A production company, Indochine Films and Cinema, was set up, and Feyder went to Saigon and Cambodia in order to survey possible shooting sites. The film was never made; Indochine Films disappeared, but Feyder brought back a diary and a film document of his travels. A photograph of him in a white colonial outfit, riding on an elephant's back, figured on the cover of *Cinémagazine* in May 1927. The filmed document concerns mostly the temple of Angkor, a favorite place, since Loti, of the tourist trade in the French colony. There are also pleasant images of buffalo, rivers, and village life amid the rice paddies, representing a peaceful and timeless atmosphere. The reality of the incessant indigenous revolts leading to the formation of the Vietnamese Communist Party of Ho Chi Minh in 1930 was unknown or ignored and remained outside the filmic discourse on French Indochina.

Many documents were made over the years to present life and events in the colonies to the French public. The Pathé Company specialized in newsreels and shorts, the documentaries that were presented before the feature film. François Truffaut showed in a devastatingly ironic sequence of *L'Argent de poche* how the conventional and pious comments on images of life in the colonies that were presented in these documentaries were irreverently received by their audiences. Nevertheless, the fact that this kind of documentary pretended to describe a real world, not a fictional one, and that such documentaries continued to be made until Dien Bien Phu (1954) shows how lengthy a process of indoctrination the French cinema presented and the French public endured. Titles are quite evocative of the content of the documentaries: *Saigon, Pearl of the Orient, Perfumed Hills of the Moïs Country, Princesses of Angkor. Imperial Ports-of-call*, made in 1939, follows the French fleet along its voyage to Saigon. Each stop is in French-controlled territory, and Saigon is depicted as the ultimate and glorious achievement of the universal French Empire.[10]

This enduring colonialist filmic discourse was not countered significantly for reasons that can be ascribed less to the power of the discourse itself than to the nature of the French film industry. In French literature at the time, some famous writers—among them Pierre Loti, Anatole France, and André Gide—made some strong anticolonialist statements, testifying against the abuses or the ill-conceived policies of colonial expansion. Nothing comparable seems to have happened in the cinematic world. The financial constraints and the long delays between the idea for a film and the establishment of a production team may have contributed to keeping talented and politically aware directors such as Jean Renoir, Jacques Feyder, or Marcel L'Herbier in the safe territory of existing and commonly accepted colonialist ideology. Jean Renoir made one silent film in Algeria, *Le Bled* (1929). It was sponsored by the French authorities to celebrate the centenary of the conquest and received lavish subsidies. In the film the beauty of the land and the colony's activities are presented through a melodramatic bourgeois plot that concludes with the hero finally settling down, happily, for good, in Algeria. Since Renoir was subsequently to make very political films, it is possible that this film was strictly a money-making project. It may also be that Algeria's colonial situation was not perceived to be of a political nature.

The expression of potential anticolonialist sentiments in French films was seriously limited by the progressive development of an official state-aid and censorship system. At the time of *"l'Empire triomphant,"* before 1940, there was no official state censorship; usually it was the local authorities who were responsible for policing exhibition of scenes that might offend morality or threaten public order. Censorship was then "quite liberal and light-handed."[11] For filmmakers shooting on location in North Africa or Indochina there was the obligation of getting permission, if not outright financing, from the local colonial authorities. This was the case for *Le Bled* and later on for Léon Poirier's Saharan productions, which were well supported—but also closely controlled—by Marshall Lyautey, the all-powerful French resident in Morocco.

Military authorities seem to have exerted a particularly detailed and very narrowly defined type of censorship of colonial films: *Le Grand Jeu* (Feyder, 1934) was cut several times by the censors. One cut was that of the reply "The Moroccans are defending their land."[12] Films that were classified as representing demoralized or seedy aspects of French life never received visas for distribution in the colonies. Such was the case of Marcel Carné's *Quai des Brumes* (1938). The character of the former legionnaire in the film was viewed as presenting a degraded image of the French military. The idea of creating a national cinema regulated through governmental institutions has existed in France since the 1930s. Successive legislations elaborated by the Popular Front, the Vichy State and the Gaullist government resulted in the establishment of a system of controlled production and exhibition of films in France. Government agencies, whether it was the COIC (Comité d'organisation de l'industrie cinématographique) of Vichy or the CNC (Centre national du cinéma), created in 1946, combined financial incentives and censorship powers. The Commission de contrôle, part of the CNC, screened films but also approved preshooting projects. It suggested cuts and banned public releases as well, until the 1970s, when it was abolished under the weight of social protest relating

mostly to the banning of erotic material. Government agencies were especially important in the distribution of public funds, under the labels *"prime
à la qualité"* or, later on, *"avance sur recette."*

The complex and powerful state system that protected and supported
the development of the French film industry exerted enormous economic,
artistic, and political influence. The weight of the political control is obvious in the fact that during the 1950s, when anticolonial movements dominated national life, French films totally avoided the subject. It is difficult to
evaluate the effect of self-censorship in a system where essential financial
support hinged on approval by bodies such as the Ministry of Information.
In 1952 and 1960, the years most marked by the turmoil of colonial and
national conflicts, the censors were also most active in banning films.

War films dealing with the life of French soldiers in Indochina were
censored even after the end of the conflict. In 1955 a proposal for a film
called *Patrouille sans espoir* (Patrol without Hope) was presented to the
commission. It was a film dealing with the life of ordinary soldiers during
the Indochinese war; the Ministry of Defense asked that the film be re-
titled *La Patrouille de l'espoir* (The Patrol of Hope). The filmmaker, Claude
Bernard-Auber, finally settled for *La Patrouille de choc.* Although he had
planned to end the film with the annihilation of the French soldiers abandoned by the commanding officers and the politicians, he was obliged, in
order to obtain the *visa d'exploitation,* to reverse the message completely
and to end with the ultimate rescue of the patrol. Also in 1953, a film by
Paul Carpita, *Rendez-vous sur les quais,* was totally banned. It dealt with the
dockers' strikes in Marseilles, which opposed the loading of ships destined
to be sent to the war effort during the conflict in Indochina. Scenes
showed the strikers holding large signs reading: *"Paix au Vietnam"* (Peace
in Vietnam).[13] Since the film primarily evokes the hopeful spirit of the
workers, in the mode of the Popular Front of 1936—quite innocuous in
1955—one may assume that the ban was caused by the evocation of a by
then old colonial conflict or, more probably, by possible association with
the events in Algeria that were beginning to unfold.

The Algerian war raised the level of official censorship, not only during
the war (1954–1962) but later on as well. Even such a conventional American war movie as *Lost Command,* by Mark Robson, made in 1966 from a
novel by Jean Larteguy, was banned. The often-noticed fact that the war in
Algeria had inspired little cinematic comment has been attributed to the
weight of various forms of censorship.[14] French cinema dealt with the war
in oblique ways—by allusion, as in *Ascenseur pour l'echafaud,* by Louis
Malle (1958), or through a fable, as in *Combat dans l'île,* by d'Alain Cavalier

(1962); *Muriel*, by Alain Resnais (1963); or *Adieu Philippine*, by Jacques Rozier (1963)—all of these made after the war, "cinema of a posteriori."[15] *The Battle of Algiers* (1966), an Algerian/Italian film and probably the best known internationally on the subject of the war, was banned in France until the early 1970s.

Jean-Luc Godard made *Le Petit Soldat* in 1960 while the OAS (rightist organization opposed to Algerian independence and the French government policies) was leading terrorist actions in Algeria and in France. It was a film "about torture," wrote François Truffaut at the start of filming.[16] This was the burning political and moral topic in France: *La Question*, the revealing book by Henri Alleg, had been clandestinely published and distributed by Editions de Minuit in 1958. It gave vivid descriptions of the means used by the French services to obtain information. After its clandestine publication, debates raged over the degradation of human values that the use of torture implied, over the strategic necessity of using torture for military intelligence, and over the attribution of responsibility for using it first to the FLN Algerian forces, to the French services, or to the OAS militants.

In this context the censors considered the Godard project a provocation. The very idea of the film seemingly came from the fact that officially all discussions and a fortiori images dealing with torture were forbidden.[17] Godard, the ultimate provocateur, filmed in Geneva the story of Bruno and Veronica, troubled agents of the OAS and the FLN who fall in love but are both tortured—he by the FLN and she by the OAS. The film shows the confusion and lack of moral or political direction at the time. Godard refrains from judging his characters. He does not side with torturers from the Left or the Right. The political message is nihilist, emphasizing the destructive absurdity of political engagement.

Nevertheless, the film was considered extremely controversial and it was banned. A member of parliament demanded that Godard, who is a Swiss citizen, be expelled from France. It was proposed that if the producer attempted to sell the film abroad under Swiss nationality his producer card would be taken away from him.[18]

When the ban was finally lifted in 1963, the war was over and the torture debate had subsided. The film was judged disappointing by the critics. Because it had been banned and because of Godard's reputation, it was expected that *Le Petit Soldat* would give a realistic and politically significant interpretation of the conflict. "Outmoded," wrote one critic; "an insult to all the victims whose sufferings have not been purely intellectual," wrote another.[19] The delay of public release imposed by the censorship on *Le*

Petit Soldat had in fact completely transformed the nature of the film. Conceived in 1960 as a personal statement about moral anarchy, it was read in 1963 as politically insensitive and obsolete. Godard's attitude and views had also very much evolved; in 1963 he was becoming more politically engaged, filming the antimilitarist *Les Carabiniers.*

The disappearance of censorship and the distancing of events in terms of time and political importance have facilitated evocations of the French colonial past in films that have been made since 1962. But the film industry is not liberated from the demanding rule of financial profit-making, despite the generous system of *avances sur recettes*, which helps the producers in their more artistic or commercially difficult enterprises. The prevailing system of coproduction associating television networks and international financing groups with each other promotes films with huge popular appeal. Broad topics that supposedly transcend national cultural (and language) barriers and limit potential controversies are desired. *Indochine*, the 1992 film by Régis Wargnier, which won the 1992 Oscar for Best Foreign Film, exemplifies the use made of the French colonial past in recent cinema. The producer, Eric Heumann, was the initiator of a project to film *Madame Butterfly* in Vietnam. From the *Butterfly* story there remains, in the film, the love affair between a young Asian girl and a colonial officer. This is the crux of the film, to which all the other elements are attached. Although the colonial situation is presented—there are scenes depicting the corruption of the system, the exploitation of the indigenous population, and the harshness of the penal camps—the film remains a romantic melodrama. Dramatic images of Poulo Condore, the forced labor camp, or the escapes of the lovers are framed by the beauty of the natural landscapes, the age-old temples, the exotic bustle of Asian streets. The political is incidental, a background element to the characters' story. The scenario, written collectively, owes much to Erik Orsenna and Louis Gardel, who were successful novelists of the "Empire nostalgia" in France in the 1980s.[20] The very title of the film underscores the attachment to the colonial past. The word "Vietnam" connotes a historic military defeat and failed policies. The word "Indochine" places the whole episode in a time frame that is safely remote and definitely closed. This is quite obvious at the end of the film. The negotiations in Evian for independence are skillfully bypassed by the scenarists in order to show the always beautiful Catherine Deneuve, framed by Lake Geneva, talking with her adopted grandson. His biological mother—Vietcong-turned-Vietnam-negotiator—has refused to see him. He tells Deneuve: "Ma mère, c'est toi" [You are my mother]. This scene shows the final destiny of the young man as his choice to be a

Frenchman, regardless of his divided cultural identity. It also closes the story of l'Indochine/Vietnam, as if nothing of interest could happen there from that moment on. At the end of the film it is to the eternally peaceful beauty of France that the viewer is returned, away from a turbulent and devious past. In this postcolonial film the same safe discourse prevails that is found in colonial films: personal story, exotic landscapes, adventures in the past tense. In *Indochine* the lavishness, and cost, of the production implied the necessity and expectation of an international commercial success. In order to achieve this success, the filmmaker emphasizes the Frenchness of the story. Deneuve, the embodiment of French beauty on the international screen, is endlessly costumed in the most exquisite clothing. The decors and the settings, villas and cafés, are those that Frenchness often connotes abroad, as are the sex scenes, the adultery, and other wicked cynical deeds. The film plays as a cliché French window for international viewers.

Also, the film is kept stylistically and thematically detached from American Vietnam films, as if Vietnam for France was a different land, another history. It is important for Wargnier to assert his difference while positioning his work at the same level of big productions like the films of Francis Ford Coppola or Oliver Stone. By refraining from allusion to the obvious and complex United States involvement in the ending of the French colony, Wargnier keeps the Indochina/Vietnam story safely fragmented and apparently depoliticized. However, when Camille, the adopted princess who had earlier turned Vietcong militant, rejects her son, there is the clear suggestion that the Vietcong/Communists were dehumanized, transformed into military/political machines. This is a message that the French, the Americans, and the Oscars Academy understood.

A superbly illustrated book published at the time when *Indochine* was released[21] begins with the words "Once upon a time there was Indochina." This emblematic introduction could also serve as one concluding remark on the French colonial/postcolonial film discourse: a ritual formula, playing on mythical imagination and diverting attention from a potentially painful political consciousness.

NOTES

1. See Richard Abel, *French Cinema: The First Wave, 1915–1929* (Princeton: Princeton University Press, 1984). Also, Alan Williams, *Republic of Images: A History of French Filmmaking* (Cambridge: Harvard University Press, 1992), and Susan Hayward, *French National Cinema* (London: Routledge, 1993).

2. J. Rittaud-Hutinet, *Le Cinéma des origines* (Seyssel: Editions du Champ Vallon, 1985), 12.

3. Nos. 743 and 564 in *Catalogue général des vues positives des Etablissements Lumière*.

4. Félix Mesguich, *Tours de manivelle: Souvenirs d'un chasseur d'images* (Paris: Grasset, 1933).

5. Pierre Boulanger, *Le Cinéma colonial* (Paris: Seghers/Cinéma 2000, 1975), 21.

6. Williams, *Republic of Images*, 53.

7. Ibid., 83.

8. Quoted in Charles Ford, *Jacques Feyder* (Paris: Seghers, 1973), 17.

9. Boulanger, *Le Cinéma colonial*, 38.

10. *Les Cahiers de la Cinémathèque: Souvenirs d'Indochine* (Perpignan: Institut Jean Vigo), no. 57 (October 1992), 9.

11. Hayward, *French National Cinema*, 38.

12. Boulanger, *Le Cinéma colonial*, 110.

13. In Chantal Chabert, "Au-delà des quais, y-a-t-il l'Indochine," *Les Cahiers de la Cinémathèque*, 47.

14. See Pascal Ory, "L'Algérie fait écran," in *La Guerre d'Algérie et les Français*, ed. Jean-Pierre Rioux (Paris: Fayard, 1990), 572–581.

15. François Truffaut, *Correspondance: 1945–1984* (New York: Farrar, Strauss, Giroux, 1990), 140.

16. Ory, "L'Algérie fait écran," 577.

17. See Jean-Luc Drouin, *Godard* (Paris: Rivage/Cinéma, 1989), 125.

18. See Truffaut, *Correspondance*, 150.

19. See Robin Buss, *The French through Their Films* (New York: Ungar, 1988), 110.

20. Eric Orsenna, *L'Exposition coloniale* (Prix Goncourt) (Paris: Seuil, 1984); Louis Gardel, *Fort Saganne* (Paris: Seuil, 1980). This novel has also been adapted for the screen.

21. *Indochine*, photographs by J. M. Leroy, text by Eric Orsenna (Paris: Ramsay Cinéma, 1992).

Split Screens

TWO   La Maison du Maltais
                   *as Text and Document**

                   Steven Ungar

BETWEEN IDEA AND IMAGE

French national identity remains linked to the remains of an *idée coloniale* grounded in a belief that certain overseas territories and their inhabitants were part of—and, in effect belonged to—France. Explicit expressions of this idea were essential to conceptions of an imperial French state between the mid-nineteenth and mid-twentieth centuries. Yet it should surprise no one that mention of an *idée coloniale* still elicits emotion more than thirty years after France's ouster from the last of the overseas territories it had occupied.[1] For while the historical reality of France as a colonizing state ended with the 1962 Evian accords, which legitimized the political sovereignty of an independent Algeria, traces of a residual *idée coloniale* persist. These traces are discernible in the affect surrounding current debate over the impact of foreign workers on unemployment and immigration and in renewed calls by some for "La France aux Français" (France for the French) that echo the militant right wing of the 1930s.[2] They appear as well in the fate of the *harkis*, who left their native Algeria for France after siding with the *colons*, and in the generation of young Beurs, who reject the cultures of their North African parents as well as those of the France in which they were born.

Unresolved debate over the past thirty years suggests that a clear sense of the colonial idea's long-term impact on national identity in France has yet to be determined. It also suggests that the persistence of a belated *idée coloniale* can be traced less in terms of explicit political objectives than as the feelings of collective affiliation and allegiance theorized in recent years in terms of nation-ness (Homi K. Bhabha), imagined communities (Benedict Anderson), and the affective life of national cultures (Ernest Gellner).[3] Eric J. Hobsbawm provided an intriguing approach to the related phenomena of affiliation and allegiance when he studied how—mainly in Europe and other so-called developed regions—affect transposed proto-national feelings of belonging onto the macro-political scale of nations and states.[4] Of particular relevance to my remarks on *l'idée coloniale* is Hobsbawm's sense of how such transposition evolved over two phases or moments: first, in the parallel trajectories of colonial expansion and Third Republic France between 1870 and 1940; and second, in more recent considerations of national identity under the looser category of the postcolonial. Extending Hobsbawm's model fully toward the present, one might assert that the resurgence in debate surrounding *l'idée coloniale* during the thirty years following France's ouster from Algeria grew from the gap or slippage of affect between Hobsbawm's two phases. Deprived of a concrete object or entity after 1962, *l'idée coloniale* devolved into untimeliness as a nostalgia increasingly removed from historical reality. Whereas some welcomed this untimeliness, the same slippage between affect and reality served for others as a figurative space of longing and regret for the impossible return to a previous condition.

The trajectory of the colonial idea in France coincides in large part with the Third Republic between 1870 and 1940. As studied by Raoul Girardet, this trajectory extends back to France's 1830 entry into Algeria and forward to the 1962 agreements that ended *l'Algérie française.*[5] Over the final three decades of the nineteenth century, a minority—vocal but not really a *parti colonial* in a strict sense—lobbied for the benefits to be gained by industry, commerce, and French society in general by bringing the ambitions of individual businessmen, statesmen, and soldiers into line with republican ideals. After early advocates of the colonial cause found themselves dismissed as victims of a fantasy more suited to the American West than to the concerns of most Frenchmen, it became clear that the best way to overcome resistance among cautious politicians was to promote the conquest and occupation of foreign territories among a general population whose conversion to the cause of colonial expansion supplemented the consensus expressed directly through politics.

By 1900, an infrastructure of state and private institutions sought to ensure that popular perception cast the colonies as essential to the overlapping concerns of France's national politics, military, and economy. This infrastructure included the Groupe Colonial lobbies established in the

Chambre des Députés (1892) and Sénat (1898) to influence bills favorable to the colonial cause, the Ecole Coloniale established in 1889 that taught future administrators the finer points of *les sciences coloniales,* and the Union Coloniale Française financial consortium founded in 1893 to monitor existing as well as new ventures related to the overseas territories. Conversion extended as well from politics, finance, and commerce to education. By 1920, Minister of the Colonies Albert Sarraut spoke openly of a sustained effort to promote better understanding of France's colonial domain in the press and at all levels of the educational system: "It is absolutely indispensable . . . that a systematic, serious, and constant propaganda of word and image have an impact in our country on each adult and child. . . . We must improve and broaden in our primary schools, *collages,* and *lycées* the narrow teaching that is provided at present of our history and the constitution of our colonial domain."[6]

The trajectory of the colonial idea from 1871 to the Exposition Coloniale Internationale held at Paris in 1931 can also be traced through efforts to convey the material benefits of colonial expansion to a growing population of consumers in France whose desire for employment and capital drew them increasingly from rural provinces to urban industrial centers. Strategies of display promoted a fascination with exotic otherness at world's fairs and universal expositions starting with the Great Exhibition of the Works of Industry of All Nations held at London in 1851. (In France, the first large-scale universal exposition was held in Paris in 1855.) In the words of Robert W. Rydell, such display sought to make mass consumption "unthinkable apart from the maintenance and extension of empire" linked to an evolved modernity.[7]

A striking aspect of the campaign to promote colonial expansion occurred in constructs of otherness that reached the fabric and detail of everyday life in commercial advertising in the print cultures of newspapers, illustrated magazines, posters, and billboards. The Black soldier on the box of Banania and the turbaned male portrayed sporting a goatee on the Café Arabica label ostensibly promoted the sales of a breakfast drink and coffee.[8] Yet there is little doubt that these figures—as well as dozens of others—also hawked an exotic otherness that promoted the interests of colonial expansion. In the case of Y'a bon, the *tirailleur sénégalais* whose portrait promoted Banania breakfast drink as a means of nourishing the youth of a resurgent new France, marketing followed the model of the *petite mythologie du mois* analyzed in the 1950s by Roland Barthes. For Barthes, the mythology operated as a two-tiered communication in which an explicit first-order sign fashioned from a signifier and signified served, in turn, as the signifier in a second sign system that tempered explicit meaning with connotations linked to ever-increasing consumption and expenditure. That many turn-of-the-century images such as Y'a bon asserted a bellicose chauvinism underscored the human resources in the hundreds of thousands contributed by the colonies in support of France's military ambitions.

A grand-narrative approach to the history of colonial expansion in Third Republic France might be expected to relate the conquest, possession, and administration of foreign territories in conjunction with economic gain and political prestige. In particular, it might account for how the idea of Greater France (la plus grande France) developed from individual forays and ventures into campaigns promoting expansion and rule.[9] Redirecting Girardet's work on l'idée coloniale toward a history of material practices might explore instead the extent to which France's evolving relations with the overseas territories it occupied between 1871 and 1962 can be traced in representations that conveyed images of these territories and their inhabitants to a public that included readers of newspapers and novels, filmgoers, and visitors to the World's Fair. Such representations serve less to determine force or significance than as a means of composing a general climate of attitudes linking an evolved idée coloniale and practices that targeted elite and popular cultures in light of attitudes toward foreignness, the exotic, and the picturesque. Herman Lebovics has noted rightly that the critical issue is not simply to correct misrepresentations of difference grounded in racist assumptions, but to analyze how and why they come to be and persist.[10] Because the representations in question ranged in medium from painting and photography to illustration, film, and graphics, l'idée coloniale was constructed very much as the archive of an imaginaire colonial produced in France from the turn of the century to the late 1930s and thus well within the 1871–1962 duration analyzed by Girardet.

In fact, Girardet recognized the interplay between idea and image when he argued that affect and the imaginary inscribed the colonial idea cherished by politicians and industrialists within beliefs and allegiances at the level of collective mentalities: "A page from a serialized novel, an adventure story for children, or a text of polemical writing can thus be considered more indicative of certain kinds of attitudes or behavior than the assertions of a statesman or the speculations of a political philosopher."[11] The interplay of image and affect on which Girardet saw the colonial idea to be grounded helps to account for a persistence that extends past 1962 toward the present. At the same time, neither Girardet's idée coloniale nor what I have referred to above as the archive of an imaginaire colonial should be equated with the direct transposition of history into images. Rather than a means of direct access constructed out of documents in a preexisting archive, the materiality, production, and circulation of the *imaginaire colo-nial* make it much more than a transparent window onto the past.

The goal of the pages that follow is to supplement Girardet's work on *l'idée coloniale* by analyzing representations of France's colonial presence in the Maghreb territories of Morocco, Algeria, and Tunisia. I draw my examples from film and, in particular, from an interwar corpus of *cinéma colonial* whose popularity during the 1930s coincided with the first decade of sound film, the Popular Front government under Léon Blum, and the final decade of the Third Republic.[12] My choice of decade is also meant to test a prevailing view that the 1930s represented the apotheosis of the colonial idea in France: "At the very summit of the State the years 1930 and 1931 loudly and clearly proclaim an 'imperial' French doctrine that seems to have found its definitive formulation. But these years also correspond, for the whole of the national community and relative to the preceding period, to a marked broadening of what could be called colonial consciousness."[13]

By 1930, advocates of colonial expansion understood the need to defend their cause against growing resistance. From abroad, such resistance coincided with the first wave of what was to evolve two decades later into full-blown decolonization. At home, it grew from economic instability precipitated by worldwide depression. The problem was that insight concerning the need to revise popular attitudes toward France's colonial possessions often clashed with an outmoded rhetoric whose ring was increasingly hollow. In his opening remarks, "Address to the Visitor," in the *Official Guide* of the 1931 Colonial Exposition, André Demaison acknowledged that colonization's heroic period had ended and that to colonize had come to mean to deal (*faire commerce*) in ideas and materials with beings who were affluent, free, and happy. In a striking passage that asserted paternalism at its most blatant, Demaison ended his appeal to lofty sentiments as follows:

> A bit of advice: in front of what is foreign or native, do not laugh about things or people that you fail at first to understand. The mocking laughter of certain Frenchmen has made more enemies for us abroad than cruel defeats or demeaning treaties. The ideas of other men are often your own, but expressed in a different way. Think of it. May the most elevated and most French joy inspire you, dear Visitor, and may it stay with you after these visits.
>
> Before entering, I can provide you with no better watchword than that of Maréchal Lyautey, the great Frenchman of such lofty human conceptions: "In this Exposition must be found, along with the lessons of the past, the teachings of the present as well as those of tomorrow.

One should come out of this Exposition resolved to make oneself better, broader, greater, stronger, and more adaptable.[14]

Demaison's remarks show the gap between an idealized civilizing mission and the very real imbalances and inequalities that made colonial expansion possible. Despite claims that colonization had evolved from a tool of war to a great effort of peace, the illusion of enlightenment was difficult to sustain. Good intentions rang increasingly hollow, to the point that they were inextricable from a civilizing mission that was increasingly retrograde. By the time Maréchal Louis Hubert Lyautey, the pacifier of Morocco and its *résident général* between 1912 and 1925, described the goal of colonization in 1931 as that of winning over the farouche hearts of the savanna and the desert to a belief in human kindness, such idealism barely corresponded to the economic and political realities of an evolved colonial expansion.[15] What the 1931 Colonial Exposition sought to display and *le cinéma colonial* to portray as an appreciation (*mise-en-valeur*) of the overseas territories occupied by France soon eroded under the force of a decolonizing process marked in phases over the next sixty years by the end of the Third Republic under Vichy, the progressive ouster of France from overseas territories it had occupied, and the ongoing malaise surrounding a "postcolonial" France subject to chronic crises of identity. After the fact, it is instructive to retrace the genealogy of this erosion-to-come during a 1930s decade that many at the time took to be the high point of an imperial France.

CAPTURED ON FILM

Those in France who saw North Africa in the 1920s and 1930s almost always saw it on film. Yet because what they really saw was projections on a screen in a movie theater in France, the North Africa that they saw was less perceived than imagined. Alongside other accounts and media ranging from fiction and the press to painting, advertising, and photography, the moving picture images of what has come to be known as *le cinéma colonial* produced a fascination with exotic otherness visible in the success of commercial features from Jacques Feyder's *L'Atlantide* (1921) to Léon Poirier's *L'Appel du silence* (1936) and Julien Duvivier's *Pépé le Moko* (1937). Fascination was a prime effect of larger-than-life images that misrepresented the local peoples and foreign places they purported to show by conveying attitudes toward the exotic that described in detail without analyzing or contextualizing, "so that the end product [was] curiously romanticized and distorted, as in a photograph viewed too close up."[16] To approach *le cinéma colonial* from the perspective of fascination is also to consider the extent to which the appeal—ideological as well as commercial—that these films held for French audiences enhanced other efforts to promote a popular climate supportive of colonial expansion. Along these lines, Pierre Sorlin has studied sixty-two feature films of the 1930s set in North Africa in order to account for why the French were "so fond of 'their' Empire."[17] Building on the work of Sorlin, Girardet, and others, I want to explore how various representations of the colonies promoted the interests of expansion as it reflected back onto French national identity over the final two decades of the Third Republic. My immediate objective is to analyze a number of images related to France's overseas territories and their inhabitants. In so doing, I am looking less to determine the ironies and inconsistencies surrounding these representations than to argue for the persistence of attitudes toward normalized difference that are assumed to have disappeared long ago.

Of the 1,305 commercial films produced in France during the 1930s, fewer than 100 portrayed their central story as occurring outside *l'Hexagone*. Among the latter, more than half were set in North Africa. Morocco led the way as the site for 17 films, followed by Algeria with 7 and Tunisia with 3.[18] As a set, these films featured déclassé protagonists in the mold of the rebellious loner type likely to join the Foreign Legion. Conceived primarily as artistic and/or commercial entities, these films drew on and recast deep-seated attitudes toward race, gender, ethnicity, and religion that audiences at the time could hardly fail to recognize. In so doing, they conveyed images of difference consistent with practices of a first cinema in which relations with difference were one-directional.[19] The representation of difference in *le cinéma colonial* was typically built on a sense of the exotic cast through atmosphere and local color in images of teeming Kasbahs, desolate plains, mountains, and desert enhanced by native character types ranging from shifty go-betweens to women in various veiled and unveiled states. Exoticism also appropriated difference by normalizing the sights and sounds of otherness into functions of the cultural chauvinism.[20] The sound track over the opening credits of Julien Duvivier's *Cinq Gentlemen maudits* (1931) mixed chants of workers in the leather-tanning pits of Fez and passages of orientalized themes composed by Jacques Ibert. The romance and adventure that promoted affective identification on the part of the spectator, to the detriment of the more complex realities of colonization, also conveyed attitudes on which the colonial idea was grounded.

The deflection of difference toward the exotic also heightened the appeal of an escapist cinema that projected into a foreign setting the domestic problems of a France whose economy and politics were anything but stable. It is no mere coincidence that the male protagonists in *Le Grand Jeu, La Bandera,* and *Pépé le Moko* all fled to North Africa in order to escape crime or scandal in a France to which they never returned. Pierre Leprohon has identified the phantasmatic function of an exotic cinema whose objective was less one of conveying authentic images of the colonies than of providing the Frenchman with noble actions or satisfying a need for drama and passion that life in France did not provide on an everyday basis.[21] In this sense, the tension between the affect of expectations brought by the spectator to his or her experience of the film and conventions of verisimilitude grounded in elements of entertainment and ideology made *le cinéma colonial* a complex popular measure of attitudes toward the colonies and the exotic. The tension between affect and verisimilitude is, of course, limited to neither *le cinéma colonial* nor to film. Yet what emerges from Leprohon's work on the convergence of aesthetic practice and historical occurrence is a sense that, far from being marked by necessity as a support of normalized difference linked to colonial expansion, the exotic was potentially open to appropriation in a number of ways.[22] To reconsider interwar *cinéma colonial* in its plurality and polyvalence is, then, not merely—following Lebovics—to correct the misconceptions of a monolithic practice. It is also to search for signs of resistance and counterpractice from which decolonization was to emerge during and after the final decade of the Third Republic.

REVISING DIFFERENCE: *LA MAISON DU MALTAIS*

When Pierre Chenal referred to his 1938 feature, *La Maison du Maltais*, as "mon petit Sternberg," he probably had in mind the German director's successful 1930 classic, *Morocco*, in which a world-weary Marlene Dietrich meets up with French Foreign Legionnaire Gary Cooper.[23] With all due respect to Chenal, it is difficult today not to see his "little Sternberg" in more complex terms. Where other *cinéma colonial* films, such as *La Bandera, Le Grand Jeu,* and *Pépé le Moko*, had portrayed losses of identity on the part of White males who found death after fleeing from France to North Africa, Chenal recast loss in the fatal mismatch between Matteo, a Maltese storyteller (played by Marcel Dalio) and Safia (played by Viviane Romance), a prostitute from Marseilles. The two first meet in the native market of Sfax when Safia retrieves a dress that Matteo has picked up from the ground, where it had fallen after Safia accidentally threw it from a balcony. Transfixed by the beauty of this stunning woman who suddenly enters his life like a princess in one of his stories, Matteo follows her and watches over her. Touched by this *petit ange gardien* (little guardian angel) who spoils her with tenderness, Safia finds Matteo's devotion a pleasant break from the harsher treatment by men to which she is accustomed. Even when Safia involves him in the theft of a wallet, Matteo refuses to believe that she is capable of evil. Sobered by the fate of her friend, Greta, who dreams of returning to her native Westphalia but instead dies of tuberculosis in a hospital ward in Sfax, Safia lives for several weeks with Matteo in the house of his father—hence the film's title—at the desert's edge.

Back in Sfax, Safia learns that she is pregnant. Elated by the news, Matteo tells Safia that he is leaving to fish for sponges off the island of Djerba to earn money that will secure their future. In fact, Matteo has agreed to be part of a smuggling operation. When he is arrested and fails to return as expected, his father curses Safia for having caused his son's death and throws her out of the house. Fearful that she will be abandoned and desperate to ensure the future of her child, Safia accepts an invitation to go to Paris with a French anthropologist, Chervin (Pierre Renoir), who found her wandering in the desert after Matteo's father threw her out. She leaves for France with Chervin just as Matteo returns, too late to stop her. When Safia bears Matteo's daughter in France, she raises the child as if Chervin were the father.

Three years later, Matteo arrives by train in Paris. Knowing only that Safia is somewhere in the city but unaware of exactly where or how she lives, he joins a gang of petty criminals in hopes of finding her. One day in the Parc Monceau, Matteo tells his favorite story of the pink and the white pearls to a group of children, unaware that one among them is Jacqueline, his daughter by Safia. After the girl retells the story to her parents that night, Safia knows that Matteo is in Paris. Using a false name in order to keep the matter from Chervin, Safia hires a private detective, Rossignol (Louis Jouvet), to locate Matteo. Because she does not want to jeopardize the privileges that she has earned for her daughter by raising her as Chervin's child, Safia deludes Matteo by meeting him in a hotel, where she pretends to work as a prostitute, and by saying that her pregnancy did not come to term.

Unknown to Safia, Rossignol has followed her to the hotel, overheard her conversation with Matteo, and discovered that she is the wife of Chervin. After Rossignol comes to blackmail her and claims falsely to represent Matteo, Safia sells a ring to buy his silence and tells her husband that it was stolen. Chervin learns the truth about the ring, confronts Safia,

and says that they can no longer remain together. Safia returns to the hotel—ironically named the Eden Hotel—where she deluded Matteo.
When he shows up that night drunk and accompanied by a rowdy group of
friends, Safia confesses that she has been raising their child as the daughter
of Chervin. Matteo realizes all that Safia has sacrificed for her daughter,
goes to Chervin, and reconciles him with Safia. Validated in his love for
Safia and Jacqueline, yet ashamed at the sufferings that his actions have
caused, Matteo puts on his "native" shirt and turban before praying to
Allah and shooting himself in a symbolic return to Sfax and his father's
house.

What makes *La Maison du Maltais* something more than an exotic melodrama—"my little Sternberg"—is Chenal's skill at staging difference and
hybridity. Matteo is first shown in the native market in Sfax, seemingly at
ease as a storyteller who exudes a childlike belief in his stories. Three encounters in the film's opening scenes modify this initial portrait. The first
is between Matteo and a docker friend (Gaston Modot) with whom he
later works and whose invitation to him to fish for sponges off the island of
Djerba will precipitate Safia's departure for Paris. The second encounter is
with his father, Ibrahim, who chides Matteo for wasting his life in idleness.
The third is the initial meeting with Safia.

The first two encounters represent options of assimilation and tradition
that depart from the values of colonial wage labor embodied by Matteo's
French docker friend, as well as from the Islamic faith of his father. Re-
sponding with particular force to his father, Matteo says that those who
work have nothing to do and that he prefers to listen to the birds sing
while he awaits his princess. When Matteo starts to work in the port after
meeting Safia, he extends a conventional division of labor driven by gender according to which the male who works provides for the female who
does not, in the sense that the domestic labor she performs is considered
part of a casual economy without clear wage value. Matteo seems also not
to notice that since meeting him, Safia has stopped working (is no longer a
"working girl"). Significantly, only Safia's female friends and fellow prostitutes seem to notice this. As her landlady, Rosina (Fréhel), puts it with
irony, "Madame est devenue honnête" [Madame has become respectable].

Matteo's sense of Safia is so much a product of his initial vision of her as
a princess that he seems more or less unaware that she works as a prosti-
tute. When Matteo first sees Safia, he cannot keep from staring at her.
Hardened by profession to such looks, Safia mocks Matteo good-naturedly,
"Ma parole, c'est un muet. Merci quand même" [My word, he's a mute.
Thanks all the same], before nodding to her breasts and saying, "Ah! ça,

mon bébé, c'est les grenades du jardin d'Allah!" [Ah! these, baby, these are the pomegranates of the Garden of Allah!] Matteo seems blind as well to the fact that Safia is White and that this whiteness might lend her a certain exoticism among prostitutes in the native sections of a colonial port such as Sfax. Safia's whiteness is an exception to the rule in colonial films of the period, according to which the White French male—Gabin as Pierre Gilieth in *La Bandera* or as Pépé in *Pépé le Moko*—takes up with a native woman. In *La Bandera*, the native woman is played by a White French actress, Annabella. In *Pépé*, the role of Ines, the dark and exotic "Gypsy" who loses Pépé to Mireille Balin's White Parisian, Gaby, is played by Line Noro. Finally, it is significant that such crossovers do not weaken the negative portrayal in *La Maison du Maltais* of hybridity (*métissage*) that remains more or less constant throughout *le cinéma colonial*. Chervin seems never to doubt that he is the biological father of his daughter, Jacqueline. Only during the final confrontation prompted by Matteo does Chervin reveal anything like a hint of irony by referring to Jacqueline in the third person.

When Matteo starts working in the port to support himself and Safia, he also sets into motion a transition in personal identity whose implications he understands only later in Paris, after he has adopted some outward signs of assimilation. This transition can be traced through clothing. When he works in the port of Sfax, Matteo exchanges the turban and billowing shirt that he had worn in the market for shirt, slacks, and leather jacket. From an outfit coded by convention as "native" and/or "exotic," the transition to the *évolué* (civilized) clothing elides the marks of difference and essential otherness to which the turban and billowing shirt had pointed. A similar transition occurs when Matteo arrives in Paris and exchanges his "native" garb for a "French" suit. Later he asks to borrow a more elegant outfit for his rendezvous with Safia and even wears a black tuxedo for a night out on the town with his gangster friends.

The transition of identity marked by clothing is complicated in the scene at the Parc Monceau. After his companion goes off to woo a woman nearby, Matteo is shown in his "French" outfit telling his favorite story to an audience of children. The scene extends earlier moments in the market at Sfax and during the idyll with Safia in the house of Matteo's father. Even when he is dressed "*en bon bourgeois*," the seemingly Westernized Matteo cannot help revealing his "native" identity and presence in Paris to a Safia whose assimilation in the role of the worldly Madame Chervin proves to be less stable than she had hoped. Matteo fails to cross cultures in Paris because the appearance of assimilation equated with clothing is never anything more than a means of locating a Safia whose apparent return to her native national culture includes a rise in region, class, and cultural milieu. (At one point, she reveals to Chervin that she is auditing courses at the Sorbonne on the positivist philosophy of Auguste Comte.) But in what sense other than by birthplace is Safia French? In Sfax, she had been—so to speak—downwardly mobile as part of a marginal community in a colonial port. She is White and says that she is from Marseilles, but her name is unusual and exotic. Assumptions of identity linked to physical appearance are thus tempered by a name that is explicitly non-French and coded as exotic. One wonders also at the nature of Safia's attraction to Matteo, whose devotion to Islam does not negate the fact that as the son of a Maltese father, he is neither Arab (Tunisian) nor French.

A final gap between appearance and reality is the source of a cruel moment in Paris when Matteo's gangster accomplices tell him that they have found Safia and she is waiting for him in their hangout. As Matteo rushes down the stairs, he sees a shapely leg sticking out around a corner. What he finds, however, is not Safia but a female mannequin dressed in veil and "native" garb. Knowing that Matteo was pining over a woman (the word used in the film is *poule*, a derogatory slang term for a prostitute) whom he had come to Paris to find, the gang members assumed that she could be nothing other than non-White.

A SILENT ORIGIN

La Maison du Maltais followed the formula of romance and exotic setting used in a range of *cinéma colonial* films from *Morocco* to *La Bandera* and *Pépé*. Yet, as with G. W. Pabst's *L'Atlantide* and André Hugon's *Sarati le terrible*, the 1938 version of *La Maison du Maltais* was a remake with sound of an earlier silent film. Chenal's remake and its 1927 predecessor, directed by Henri Fescourt, were both adapted from Jean Vignaud's novel of the same title. But differences in plot, characterization, and tone between the two films were striking and significant.[24] From the start, the silent version of *La Maison du Maltais* cast Matteo as a hybrid (*carrefour de deux races*) conceived in the union of a Maltese father and a young Bedouin. Matteo's story is very much an account of his attempts to contend with the fate of his father, whose renown as a sponge fisher was ended by the scandal of an interracial marriage that made him a prisoner in his house:

> Old Matteo had said goodbye to the sea, to the world, to everything. . . .
> He was still expiating a mistake, one that went back twenty-six years;
> this mistake, brought back from the South, had at the time a sixteen

year old body and a saffron skin. Unforgettable scandal in the Maltese clan! Despite the indignation of the parish, despite the mockery of his friends, the fisherman had brought to his house the young Bedouin, Massouda bent Lakdhar, and Matteo had been born.[25]

Matteo's devotion to Islam in the silent film is, in part, a form of revolt against the Christian faith of a father turned by shame against his wife and son. Fescourt portrays the identity of his Matteo with an emphasis on a Maltese ethnicity and culture that are neither Arab (Tunisian) nor French. Along the same lines, Malta and Tunisia are sites where encounters between Europeans, Maghrebian Arabs, and Jews are frequent and perhaps less threatening than they might be if they occurred in France. Unlike Chenal's preference for the Kasbah, Fescourt stages the first encounter between Matteo and Safia when she arrives in Sfax from the South. After the sound of footsteps awakens Matteo from a nap in a quiet spot near the port, he notices a young girl passing by him in the company of a chaperone and concludes that she has come to Sfax to work as a prostitute. (These suspicions are corroborated when Matteo learns that Safia has fled from Kerkenah to escape humiliation after her lover, Sheik Hadj-Hamou, had forsaken her to marry someone else.) After Matteo comes to Safia's aid several weeks later and she laments the circumstances of her life in the city, he vows to help her leave Sfax. Yet Matteo's devotion to Safia overcomes neither the Islamic tradition that subjugates women to the will of a forceful master nor the advantages of the *roumis* (Christians) whose wealth Matteo could never rival.

Matteo's desire to please Safia leads him to steal pearls that his father kept hidden in his house. The prized pearls represent not only capital that the elder Matteo had accumulated during his career as a sponge fisher, but also the identity that he had sacrificed by the scandal of hybridity. Matteo's theft betrays a symbolic as well as a material inheritance, while it extends the hybridity that had destroyed the father's life. The irony is enhanced once Safia realizes that the material goods she craved were only a means of obtaining an even broader freedom:

On our island, I used to push a plow, braid alfa-grass, set octopuses out to dry in the sun. But I was free because there [*chez nous*] women go out in public without a veil. The death of my father drove me here to Sfax. But I wanted to leave this stinking city, I told you so, and you vowed to get me out! Have you kept your word? You tie me down like a goat to a post. Now I am a prisoner! And I know what fate you have in store for me. I have been told . . . you expect one day to shut me up in the Bab Djebli, in the house of the Maltese, as your father did to his Bedouin. I do not want this. I would rather die right away, kill myself with my own hand.[26]

When Matteo's father catches him in the act of stealing more pearls, Matteo runs to Safia, only to discover to his horror that she has left Sfax without him. Forsaken by his father and abandoned by his lover, Matteo realizes that his theft had brought him only despair. He vows vengeance on Safia by swearing to seek her out and bring her back, even if it means crossing the universe on his knees. As in Chenal's film, Fescourt has Matteo follow Safia to Paris. But unlike the remake, in which Matteo's attempted assimilation leads to self-destruction, the silent version portrays a Matteo driven by vengeance grounded in a stable sense of his identity as a Muslim male. Once in Paris, Matteo uses the "inherited" pearls to establish himself among those dealing in jewels and precious metals. The pearls that he sells allow him to fill his bags with the money he hopes will allow him to win back Safia. They also draw the attention of Chervin, a major Parisian dealer who asks Matteo to become his partner and assume control of the company while he works out a personal matter. Ever on the lookout for Safia, Matteo intuits that, like someone fishing in the waters off the coast of Tunisia, he has netted his tuna and needs only to find the right place to throw his harpoon. When Chervin asks Matteo to buy a necklace for his mistress, Matteo is unable to hide an uneasy curiosity concerning the recipient, whom Chervin seemed to keep in a golden cage: "Being the eunuch of the harem," he thought, "I should have the right to know the pasha's favorite."[27] The comment seems glib. Yet it is anything but superficial because it shows that—for Fescourt—Ibrahim, Matteo, and Chervin exemplify the extent to which restrictions imposed by men on the free circulation of women transcend ethnic and racial specificity.

After Chervin's mistress turns out to be Safia, Matteo hardens his resolve to destroy her by ruining her lover. To this end, he invests heavily in risky ventures that threaten the consortium created by his partnership with Chervin. Safia comes to Matteo to learn the true motives of his actions, but he humiliates her. When the investments fail and Chervin kills himself, Matteo carries a small trunk from his room in Paris to the house in Neuilly that Safia had shared with Chervin. Inside the trunk are the clothes that she wore the first time Matteo saw her in Sfax. Matteo enters the house, orders her to put on the clothes in the trunk, and literally carries her off for the return trip via ship to Tunisia. Once they are back in the native section of Sfax, Safia veils herself before throwing herself at Matteo's feet and begging him one last time to let her be his slave in the Kasbah. He turns away without answering:

> Safia felt that it was all useless and that she had to yield to her destiny. She arose. Like a soldier, Matteo raised the almond green trunk on his shoulder and they walked toward the House of the Maltese. The lock was rusted, the heavy key turned with difficulty; then Matteo leaned against the heavy door to make it yield. When it was open he spoke to Safia for the first time since their arrival in Sfax. He ordered, "Enter."
>
> Safia went in without turning around, her shoulders hunched as if the doorway threatened to crush her.
>
> And Matteo closed the door behind her—forever.[28]

The striking differences between the two versions of *La Maison du Maltais* involve gender and religion. Fescourt cast Matteo as totally devoted to Safia. Yet even after she laments the circumstances of her life, Matteo fails to see that his oath to take her away from Sfax will not give her the independence she wants because it will obligate her to him. Matteo's blindness to this truth is borne out when he takes her departure for Paris with the British *roumi* (Lord Hansley) she had met in the Kasbah as an infidelity that he must avenge. In so doing, Fescourt's Matteo reverts to the role of the dominating male whose desire to bring "his" woman to submission contrasts with the self-destructive Matteo portrayed by Chenal for the purposes of melodrama. It is unclear whether this reversion by the first Matteo was meant to convey native authenticity or whether it attempted instead to exploit the success of Rudolph Valentino's sheik persona of the period. Along with the fact that Fescourt shot his film on location in Tunisia (Chenal built the set of his Sfax Kasbah at the Paramount studios in Joinville), it suggests that significant aspects of cultural difference portrayed in the silent original were elided in the remake for the sake of ensuring a safer commercial appeal grounded in exotic melodrama à la Sternberg's *Morocco*. Three examples substantiate the range of these elisions.

Fescourt's Sfax is portrayed as multifaceted and multiracial to a degree that goes well beyond local color. In doorways illuminated by a single candle, prostitutes of all shapes, colors, and races attract potential customers into rooms whose walls display portraits of His Highness the Imperial Bey and President Gaston Doummergues, cut out from illustrated magazines, while seawater and lamb bones serve as the preferred fetishes among Africans and Bedouins. Matteo's friend, the Sudanese Blanchette,

who speaks only pidgin French, likewise runs a stand where visiting foreigners are as likely to be offered a bargain on "hot" pearls as a shoeshine:
"Ti parles franci, ti parles angli un petit peu. Ti parles macaroni. Ti mon-
tres mouquères de la Kasbah aux étrangers. La livre sterling, c'est bon, ti
sais, mon ami." [Ya talk Frenchie, ya talk a little Engli. Ya talk Macaroni. Ya
show Kasbah women to the foreigners. The Sterling Pound is good, ya
know, my friend.] [29]

Fescourt's Paris is likewise filled with displaced foreigners. After an initial contact suggests a hotel in the Marais, Matteo finds himself passing
storefronts whose shingles bear the names Shirman, Aaron, Sonnemberg,
and Bonner. Inside the Café Carrefour, where pearls are sold and traded,
he is struck by a list of names—"Eschmann, Cadir, Brekof, Hamara"—on
a mounted panel, under which letters etched in gold record that those
people had died for France. Matteo is unable to restrain a subtle smile as
he wonders what France might have meant to them:

> They had died in order to conserve their scales and magnifying glasses,
> these people come from every distant horizon. Matteo, crossroads of
> many races, could not understand anything else! Their fatherland was
> this café with its marble tables, this counter, and this pyramid of
> stacked oranges: each one fashioned his fatherland to the measure of
> his interests. [30]

Matteo's obsession with Safia extends from romance to nation. Vignaud
describes Matteo's fatherland as having neither the dimensions of a café
nor the area of a country, but instead the body of a woman: "Safia, the lost
province! In order to locate and reconquer her, Matteo was ready to spill
his blood on every battlefield." [31] Only once in Fescourt's film does Matteo's Westernized persona display any kind of vulnerability. The moment
occurs after Matteo has set into motion his plan to destroy the pearl consortium in order to ruin his rival, Chervin. As in the scene at the Carrefour
when Matteo sees the commemorative plaque honoring those who died
for France in World War I, isolation is the rule. This time, however, it is as
though Matteo feels obliged to reassert to himself an identity in essential
estrangement from Safia, Chervin, and others in the consortium:

> He had bought a phonograph and records with the kinds of processed
> Arab melodies [aux airs simili arabes] that are piped into moviehouses
> every time that a camel or a veiled woman comes forward on screen.
> The twang of the machine transported him to Sfax . . . next to a bucket

of crabs and a glass of boukha on the narrow channel, on the shore of
the glittering sea in front of which he had sworn to bring back Safia.
And he raised his arms to repeat his oath.[32]

The passage shows the extent to which the marks of identity grounded
by Fescourt in gender and religion are tempered by Matteo's need to
evoke self-consciously and from afar his native environment. It is no little
irony that Matteo simulates this transport back to Sfax by means of sound
technology and that the sounds in question are borrowed from the interplay of sound and image in silent film. Whereas Fescourt elsewhere portrays Matteo as stable in his sense of self, Matteo's desire to simulate Sfax
in Paris suggests that, even if only for a moment, his resolve is vulnerable.
The scene of Matteo's reversion to a nostalgic evocation of his Tunisian
homeland provides the most complex staging of fragile identity in Fescourt's silent version of *La Maison du Maltais*. Its elision in the sound remake illustrates the extent to which aspects of gender and religion linked
to identity in the initial screen version were recast by Chenal as melodrama and as a vehicle to promote the career of Viviane Romance.[33] Beyond explicit concerns with commercial marketing, comparisons of the
two versions of *La Maison du Maltais* suggest that other films of the period
likewise conveyed difference in ways that complicated received images of *le
cinéma colonial* as a monolithic and unified practice:

> What emerges from this filmography, beyond the ever-present popular
> image (*image d'Epinal*), is the feeling of an inextricable situation built
> on attraction and repulsion, but henceforth well enough established so
> that one was able to present the moment when complex intercultural
> exchanges, the only problem tackled without daring to contend with
> that of political and social conflicts, began to question in a serious way
> the effects of colonization on the colonized. It was time.[34]

AFTERWORD

Interwar *cinéma colonial* was almost exclusively a first cinema produced by
and for Europeans. Even so, comparing the silent and the sound versions
of *La Maison du Maltais* provides a sense of what was at stake for French
filmmakers and spectators in images that set commercial and aesthetic
concerns against an evolved *idée coloniale* over the final two decades of the
Third Republic. When they are considered after the fact, the two versions
of *La Maison du Maltais* extend a genealogy of representations that ac-

counts for a slippage between an orientalist desire for masterful understanding and a countervailing desire for experiences of otherness grounded in travel narratives by writers from Gustave Flaubert to Isabelle Eberhardt. This slippage—extended in film from word to image—promotes a split that decenters both the speaking/viewing subject and his or her discourse.[35] Marc Augé recognizes a similar ambivalence in the wake of an orientalist tradition when he refers to the residual forms of an ill-defined bad conscience as it afflicts ethnographers who "would prefer not to concern themselves with the conditions under which those they study are directly or indirectly colonized, dominated, or exploited."[36] After the fact, the role of interwar *cinéma colonial* as text, practice, and document has yet to be fully inscribed within the genealogy of representations that continue to elicit strong affective responses grounded in a collective desire for otherness charged with ambivalence (Augé's "ill-defined 'bad-conscience'") and irresolution. My remarks on the versions of *La Maison du Maltais* by Chenal and Fescourt provide a point of departure for a fuller understanding of interwar colonial cinema for which issues of film genre and technology supplement the inextricable links between cultural practices and French national identity during the final two decades of the Third Republic.

*This essay was researched and written with support from the Obermann Center for Advanced Studies at the University of Iowa. It is dedicated to R. S. Draper and Ran Kohn.

NOTES

1. References to *la France d'outremer* following France's ouster from its former colonies are designated as DOM-TOM—*départements d'outremer* and *territoires d'outremer*, respectively. The DOM include Guadeloupe and Martinique, in the Caribbean; French Guiana, off the coast of Venezuela; and the island of Réunion, in the Indian Ocean, off southern Africa. The TOM include French Polynesia near Tahiti; New Caledonia; Wallis and Futuna; and an expanse of largely uninhabited islands and mainland known as French Antarctica. St. Pierre and Miquelon (off the Atlantic coast of Nova Scotia), as well as Mayotte (near Réunion), function more or less as *départements*. These references are taken from Mort Rosenblum, *Mission to Civilize: The French Way* (New York: Anchor, 1988), 10.

2. See Pierre Birnbaum, *La France aux Français: Histoire des haines nationalistes* (Paris: Seuil, 1993).

3. See Homi K. Bhabha, *The Location of Culture* (New York: Routledge, 1994); Benedict Anderson, *Imagined Communities: Reflections on the Origins and Spread of*

Nationalism, rev. ed. (New York: Verso, 1991); and Ernest Gellner, *Nations and Nationalism* (Oxford: Blackwell, 1983).

4. E. J. Hobsbawm, *Nations and Nationalism since 1780: Programme, Myth, Reality* (New York: Cambridge University Press, 1991), 46.

5. Raoul Girardet, *L'Idée coloniale en France, 1871–1962* (Paris: La Table Ronde, 1972; rev. ed. Paris: Hachette "Pluriels," 1991).

6. Quoted in Jacques Marseille, *L'âge d'or de la France coloniale* (Paris: Albin Michel, 1986), 5.

7. Robert W. Rydell, *World of Fairs: The Century-of-Progress Expositions* (Chicago: University of Chicago Press, 1993), 62.

8. Jean Garrigues, *Banania: Histoire d'une passion française* (Paris: Du May, 1991). See also John Mendenhall, *French Trademarks: The Art Deco Era* (San Francisco: Chronicle Books, 1991).

9. See, for example, "L'expansion coloniale" in Maxim Petit's *La Troisième République* (Paris: Larousse, 1936) and the informative account of the expression's genealogy in Herman Lebovics, *True France: The Wars over Cultural Identity, 1900–1945* (Ithaca: Cornell University Press, 1992), 67.

10. Lebovics, *True France*, 61–62.

11. Girardet, *L'Idée coloniale*, 12.

12. Recent studies with major iconographic materials related to colonial France include Eric and Gabrielle Deroo and Marie-Cécile de Taillac, *Aux colonies* (Paris: Hors Collection/Presses de la Cité, 1992), and Nicolas Bancel, Pascal Blanchard, and Laurent Gervereau, eds., *Images et colonies: Iconographie et propagande coloniale sur l'Afrique française de 1880 à 1962* (Paris: La Découverte, 1993). I retained rather than translated the French expression for two reasons: first, in order to emphasize the coherence among a discrete set of films set in North Africa and produced while France occupied Morocco, Algeria, and Tunisia; and second, in order to distinguish these films of the 1930s from more recent practices, such as those analyzed elsewhere in this collection of essays.

13. Girardet, *L'Idée coloniale*, 176.

14. André Demaison, "Adresse au visiteur," in *Guide officiel de l'exposition coloniale internationale* (Paris: Mayeux, 1931), 20.

15. Hubert Lyautey, "Le sens d'un grand effort," *L'Illustration*, no. 4603 (23 May 1931).

16. David Proschaska, "The Archive of *Algérie imaginaire*," *History and Anthropology* 4 (1990): 374. See also Proschaska's *Making Algeria French: Colonialism in Bône, 1880–1920* (New York: Cambridge University Press, 1990) and Lebovics, *True France*. I am grateful to David Slavin and David MacMurray for pointing me to the work of Proschaska and Lebovics.

17. Pierre Sorlin, "The Fanciful Empire: French Feature Films and the Colonies in the 1930s," *French Cultural Studies* 2, no. 5 (June 1991): 136.

18. These figures, based on Raymond Chirat's catalog of French feature-length films of the 1930s, are cited in Geneviève Nesterenko, "L'Afrique de l'autre," in Michèle Lagny, Marie-Claire Ropars, and Pierre Sorlin, eds., *Générique des années 30* (Paris: Presses Universitaires de Vincennes, 1986), 127. Pierre Boulanger counts 210 narrative films (*films de fiction, à trame romanesque*) shot either totally or in part in North Africa from 1911 to 1962. According to Boulanger, 24 were shot

in Tunisia, more than 80 in Algeria, and about 100 in Morocco (Pierre Boulanger, *Le Cinéma colonial: De "L'Atlantide" à "Lawrence d'Arabie"* [Paris: Seghers, 1975], 15).

19. My remarks on interwar *cinéma colonial* as an instance of first cinema are indebted to Paul Willemen, "The Third Cinema Question: Notes and Reflections," and Teshome H. Gabriel, "Towards a Critical Theory of Third World Films," in *Questions of Third Cinema*, ed. Jim Pines and Paul Willemen (London: British Film Institute), 1–29.

20. Tzvetan Todorov, *On Human Diversity: Nationalism, Racism, and Exoticism in French Thought*, trans. Catherine Porter (Cambridge: Harvard University Press, 1993), 264.

21. Pierre Leprohon, *L'Exotisme et le cinéma: Les "Chasseurs d'images" à la conquête du monde* (Paris: J. Susse, 1945), 204.

22. My remarks on the polyvalence of the phenomenon of "cinematographic invasion" as an ideological formation build on (and depart from) the insights of Nwachukwu Frand Ukadike, *Black African Cinema* (Berkeley: University of California Press, 1994), 35.

23. Chenal remains a figure in French film whose work has yet to receive the serious study it deserves. Born Pierre Cohen in 1904 in Brussels, he grew up in Paris, where one of his classmates at the Lycée Buffon was the future film historian Jean Mitry. His feature films include *La Rue sans nom* (Street without a Name) (1933), based on Marcel Aymé's populist novel of the same name; *Crime et châtiment* (Crime and Punishment) (1935); and *Le dernier tournant* (1939), adapted in collaboration with Charles Spaak from James M. Cain's *The Postman Always Rings Twice*. Fleeing to South America during the Occupation, Chenal returned to France after the Liberation and had a final success with *Clochemerle (The Scandals of Clochemerle)* (1948) before dropping out of the film industry in the 1960s. Alan Williams refers to Chenal as Philippe Cohen, in *Republic of Images: A History of French Filmmaking* (Cambridge: Harvard University Press, 1992), 240.

24. My remarks on the first version of *La Maison du Maltais* are based on a text illustrated with photos from Fescourt's film and published by the Librairie Plon in conjunction with the Société des Cinéromans-Films de France. The same series includes an illustrated text of Vignaud's *Sarati le terrible*, based on the 1922 film directed by Louis Mercanton and René Hervil. References are from Boulanger, *Le Cinéma colonial*.

25. Jean Vignaud, *La Maison du Maltais* (Paris: Plon, 1926), 6.

26. Ibid., 27–28.

27. Ibid., 57.

28. Ibid., 79–80.

29. Ibid., 19.

30. Ibid., 38.

31. Ibid.

32. Ibid., 67.

33. Viviane Romance (1912–1991) was a leading female star of the 1930s and 1940s. A onetime Miss Paris, she was typically cast as a vamp or a coquette in such films as *La Bandera* (1935), *La Belle équipe* (1936), *Le Puritain* (1938), *L'étrange Monsieur Victor* (1938), and *Panique* (1946). During the Occupation, she starred in a 1943 version of *Carmen*.

34. Catherine Coquery-Vidrovitch, "Le Cinéma colonial," in *Histoire de la France coloniale, 1914–1990,* ed. Jacques Thobie, Gilbert Meynier, Catherine Coquery-Vidrovitch, and Charles-Robert Ageron (Paris: Armand Colin, 1990), 311.

35. See Ali Behdad, *Belated Travelers: Orientalism in the Age of Colonial Dissolution* (Durham: Duke University Press, 1994), 14–15.

36. Marc Augé, *The Anthropological Circle: Symbol, Function, History,* trans. Martin Thom (New York: Cambridge University Press, 1982), 78. For a more theoretical consideration of issues related to representations of otherness grounded in race and ethnicity, see Robert J. C. Young, *Colonial Desire: Hybridity in Theory, Culture, and Race* (New York: Routledge, 1995).

Whither the Colonial Question?

THREE   *Jean Renoir's* The River[*]

Nandi Bhatia

"Why do we quarrel with things all the time?" asks Melanie of Captain John. To which the captain can offer no reply. The matter is left unresolved: Captain John leaves for America and Melanie apparently reconciles herself to her fate. Melanie's question arises from her inner struggles about her cross-cultural identity. The Eurasian daughter of a British father and an Indian mother, Melanie is the product of the marriage between two opposing cultures, India and Britain—cultures separated by race, class, caste, and religion and marked by colonial struggles that make their partnership unequal. In this partnership, Britain, the colonial master, is superior to India, its colonial subject. Melanie's struggle is located in this union of the master and the subject—a union that gives birth to endless confusion about her racial identity. Melanie's quest to define an identity for herself is, therefore, embedded in a crucial historical moment in a context of power struggles and colonial rule, of British domination and exploitation, and of discrimination against Eurasians.[1] Yet the question regarding Melanie's identity is subsumed in Renoir's movie, in which her identity is accepted as her "manifest destiny."[2]

Melanie's peaceful acceptance and reconciliation epitomize for Renoir qualities that he ascribes to Indians. According to him, such qualities emanate from an intense level of spirituality and communion with nature, attributes that are difficult to find in the West. Hence, instead of seeking answers to her question, Renoir limits his quest for Indian life to what Ronald Bergan calls its "simplicity" and "serenity," "human realities," and "religious spirituality,"[3] interweaving the narrative with the Hindu cycle of birth and death. In so doing, he focuses attention primarily on India's landscapes, its cultural rituals, the festivities of Indian dances, the tranquillity of the river Ganges, the pastoral charm and simplicity exhibited by flowers and picnics in lush gardens amid beautiful trees, soft exotic music in the background, cobras and snake charmers, gods and goddesses, and uncomplaining boat people and factory workers in the jute mills of Calcutta. Consequently, India, in the film, emerges as a repository of peace, calm, and wisdom, possessing a sensual and "timeless" quality, and the Indian subjects are portrayed as nonparticipating, passive, and unchanging, lacking the will to struggle with what the fates have ordained—an essence without a history. Renoir's filmic project to capture the "essence" of Indian life thus reproduces the simplistic dichotomy of the mysterious and spiritual East versus the materialistic West. As Renoir stated:

> It's perfectly possible that Eastern philosophy can help Westerners once again. In India, the people who really lead the philosophical life (really, it's not philosophy, it's just a point of view about life) reach the following result: if they are very poor, they set up housekeeping on the window ledge of a large building, for instance, a bank. In such a spot they store the covering in which they sleep (because sometimes it gets chilly at night, and it also rains during the monsoons), and also whatever utensil they have to cook food, if they find any. There are trams that make a lot of noise, there's a lot of shouting in the street, but they succeed in isolating themselves completely, in thinking about their little concerns with as much intensity as if they were in a country home that was completely isolated and surrounded with greenery. Well, it's a pretty amazing thing! It's a system that's worth learning, and that could be very useful for us.[4]

Renoir's essentialist constructions of the binaries Black/White, East/West, and spiritual/material set up categories that silence differences of class, caste, race, or gender. Producing the film from an authoritarian position of knowledge to present the essential India through dramatizations of life in Bengal, Renoir divests Indian life of its sociohistorical specificities, ignoring in the process the moods and concerns of a colonized nation.[5]

Set in Barrackpore, a town near Calcutta on the banks of the river Ganges, *The River* is the story of a British family in India and is based on the novel by Rumer Godden, an Englishwoman raised in India.[6] The story captures life in India as seen through the eyes of Harriet, a twelve-year-old English girl. Godden collaborated with Renoir on the screenplay, introducing new characters and anecdotes, and incorporated Renoir's perceptions of India in the film. Upon seeing the screenplay, Godden was happy to discover that Renoir had preserved the "essence of her book [which] is a hymn to life incarnated in the ever-present river."[7]

Experimentation with naturalism, color, sets, and "authentic" materials won Renoir the reputation of a master cinematographer and accorded *The River* the status of a "classic" upon its release in 1951. Critics found his portrayal of "authentic" landscapes in Bengal one of the most fascinating aspects of his film. André Bazin, for example, called *The River* "a pure masterpiece" and Renoir "the greatest . . . French director."[8] Such applause over Renoir's aesthetic preoccupation with nature, however, has overshadowed the colonial question. Fetishizing Renoir's film for its representation of nature, critics have ignored or given only marginal attention to the cinematographer's complicitous relationship with orientalist portrayals of India as an "exotic" site. Both Christopher Faulkner and Ronald Bergan have touched upon Renoir's apathy with regard to the colonial question, but no one has yet traced the connections between colonialism and the film, not only as a theme but also as a structuring force that guides the setting, the characters, and the aesthetic principle of naturalism that governs the film.[9] Bazin does point out that Renoir eschews the colonial issue, but instead of taking Renoir to task for glossing over the histories of the people he portrays, Bazin chastises those who might attack Renoir for his oversight: "To reproach him for not using this fleeting love story as a vehicle to describe the misery of India or to attack colonialism is to reproach him for not treating an entirely different subject."[10] Despite Bazin's admission that Renoir's vision of English society in India was "a little superficial, overly optimistic and implicitly imperial,"[11] the film, says Bazin, is "the discovery of love by three adolescents."[12] Such criticism divests the film of discussions regarding the colonial and postcolonial concerns of India.

A rereading of *The River*, therefore, requires us to situate the film against the backdrop of the historical developments in the late 1940s, of the sociopolitical ramifications of the end of British imperial rule and the advent of independence, which began a new chapter in Indian history. The year 1947 brought independence and at the same time heralded the division of the subcontinent into India and Pakistan. The territorial disintegration of the subcontinent manifested itself in a communal holocaust as the most bloody riots broke out between Hindus and Muslims, who moved across the borders to their respective homelands. The situation had barely settled when war broke out in 1948 between India and Pakistan over Kashmir. Following the Indo-Pakistan war, which left the issue of Kashmir unresolved, Hindu-Muslim riots broke out in numerous parts of the country. Renoir himself encountered riots in Calcutta. Moreover, the aftershocks of World War II, which had ended in 1945, could still be felt in the subcontinent. While independence led to the end of territorial colonialism, economic colonialism still continued through capitalist expansion and ownership of numerous businesses by British companies. For example, a large number of jute mills in Bengal remained under British ownership.

Renoir's alignment with the Left in the 1930s and his work in the political avant-garde film movement in France reveal his commitment to issues such as fascism, war, and colonialism. During the shooting of the film in India, he was deeply moved by the plight of the refugees coming into India and the horror of the Hindu-Muslim riots that he witnessed following the subcontinental partition in 1947. Yet it is perplexing that he hardly touches upon the colonial question. In one of the few references to colonialism during discussions of the film, he engages in vast oversimplification, reducing two hundred years of colonial history to this brief account:

> The most important thing I learnt on that first trip [to India] was the reason for the Indians' resentment against the British. It was not because they had conquered them but because they ignored them. They treated them as though they weren't there. But the Indians have a longing for human contacts, a need for living warmth.[13]

If Renoir ignored the colonial question, it was partly because he viewed India primarily as an object of his technical and cinematic experiments: "I saw the colors in India as marvelous motifs with which to test my theories about color films."[14] Hence he set about capturing "la couleur locale, . . . those quintessential elements in the landscape which would be pictorially effective as well as be truly evocative of the atmosphere of the country."[15] Because India became a site for Renoir's experiments with color techniques, he rarely puts these impressions of Indian life in the historical context of the 1940s. Even though the story is about the experiences of a young British girl growing up in India, the landscapes and shots of Calcutta take precedence over the plot.

Renoir's focus on nature and India's aesthetic beauty are in a sense his attempts to recapture elements of impressionist art. Consistent with the aesthetic legacy from his father, Auguste Renoir, he carefully shot the colors and tone that provided the feel of impressionist painting. As Claude Renoir, Jean's nephew who worked with him on the film, records:

For *The River*, Jean Renoir and I did a lot of work together with Renoir, the painter, my grandfather, in the background. All our research on the colors, their rendering, the contrasts between them, were dictated by that. One day, there was a blue vase inside that was not very beautiful (what's more, blue was still a risky color in those days), and I remember Jean telling me. "Listen, Claude, your grandpa would never put a color like that in one of his paintings. . . . Take it away!"[16]

Renoir gave his film, like impressionist art, the quality of pastoral charm, making India an exotic land with the river, the flowers, the trees, and the bouquets—a heavenly abode perfectly suitable for westerners, such as the family of the narrator and the captain. Father, mother, daughters, captain, and little boy live happily in this Indian wonderland in a bungalow with a huge lawn and a variety of India servants. Like painting, however, cinema too serves "a major ideological function."[17] In this case, the cinema reproduces images and essentialist notions about India similar to those that earlier Western orientalist explorations had produced.

One example of misleading orientalist perceptions of India can be seen in the reception, in the nineteenth century, of the ancient Sanskrit drama *Sakuntala*, written by Kalidasa. Translated by William Jones, *Sakuntala* became one of the key texts whereby orientalists, especially Jones, defined the Orient and constructed images of India as a "submissive, indolent nation."[18] While the play was appreciated for its pastoral charm and "lyrical beauty," it presented the Hindus as "degenerate" and "abased."[19] Established as "truths," such perceptions became the basis of such works as James Mill's *History of British India*.[20] Like the nineteenth-century orientalists, Renoir constructed simplistic notions of India: "The Indians have a fondness for white, that ideally simple colour."[21] Similarly, the film features South Indian classical music as a unified "Indian" music, thus homogenizing the multiple strands and schools of Indian music. Such portrayals are both limited and limiting, causing interpretive closure instead of opening up new possibilities for understanding the heterogeneity of Indian life.

Renoir's apparently simplistic view of Indians and his masking of the reality of India's colonial past are manifested in a number of moments in the film, beginning with the visual focus on the strong and beautiful black bodies of the men whose arms synchronize with the waves of the river and with each other as they push the boats. However, Renoir does not attend to the more inchoate forms of political happenings. Nor does he articulate the historical crisis of the boat people's indigence. The boat people's bodies in the film are not the damaged bodies that one encountered on the streets of Calcutta in 1950, bodies that had suffered the mortifying blows of the famine of 1943 and the cholera epidemic of 1946. Not a natural disaster but a result of international political developments, the famine killed an estimated one million people after 1943. The war in Europe had led to inflated prices and shortages of rice and salt. Even though its own economy in England was being run most efficiently, the British government made little or no attempt to check a rampaging black market in the colony. Inflation and food shortages led to profiteering, black-marketing, and hoarding of food, especially as fear spread that the country's food supply was being depleted to feed the Allied troops on the subcontinent.[22] Renoir's portrayal of the boatmen's untarnished and apparently healthy bodies seeks to restore the damage caused by colonialism.

Soon the film introduces other characters: a British couple and their five children, Captain John (an Anglo-American soldier who lost his leg in the war), and Indians, like Nan and Ram Prasad, who occupy the positions of domestic servants, factory workers, or boat people. The world of the film is thus built around hierarchical relationships that place the Whites in positions of power with respect to the natives. Yet, instead of problematizing the roles of the characters in terms of issues of colonialism, gender, race, class conflicts, and caste relations and questioning the existing hierarchical structures, Renoir presents them as "natural." There is, for instance, no historical context provided for the presence of the British family, or of the American soldier, or of an Englishman as the manager of the jute factory. One might, for instance, ask, Why is the American captain there? To what degree was India involved in World War II, why was it involved in the first place, and what were the ramifications of the war for India? Little do we learn of the presence of a large body of Allied troops stationed in India during the war. All we see is a disturbed but friendly soldier landing in India to overcome the loss of a leg in the war. Renoir projects India as a haven of refuge where the wounded soldier can seek solace and comfort, instead of as a station for Allied troops, which it was during the war. Physically wounded and mentally disturbed as a result of the war, John apparently goes back to his country spiritually healed. His journey to India in the hope of recovering from his depression casts India, as opposed to the materially decayed West, in the role of the spiritual healer in the postwar period.[23]

Captain John's amiable and sensitive disposition also serves to hide the reality of the behavior of the Allied troops stationed in India during the war. According to Radha Kumar, "Allied troops stationed in India behaved . . . with a casual brutality towards their hosts. There were innumerable cases of molestation and rapes, against which the Congress repeatedly protested, but with little action by the [British] government."[24]

Another instance of the ways in which hegemonic relations are masked in the film appears in the portrayal of the British jute mill manager as a benevolent employer who loves his "sweat shops," his nickname for the factory: "He loved the never-ending procession of men with the jute piled on their heads," says the narrator. Far from questioning the authority of the Englishman over the natives even after the demise of Empire, Renoir exoticizes the mill workers, in the process obscuring the conditions of workers in the private space of the jute factory. In an article on the jute mill workers, historian Dipesh Chakrabarty explains the complex mechanical processes in a Calcutta jute mill. Workers, he argues, received very little scientific and technical training, and that often resulted in fatal accidents.[25] According to Chakrabarty, who presents a picture contrary to the one painted by Renoir, there was "little value attached to a worker's life."[26] Similarly, Renoir leaves unquestioned the British family's occupation of the position of sahibs and the Indians' of that of servants, presenting it as the norm.

If the film raises the issue of race and caste differences at all, it does so only in the character of Melanie. Acutely aware of her "half-caste" identity, Melanie understands the social limitations imposed by her cross-cultural heritage. Her father's insistence that she marry her Indian fiancé is a clear indication to her that as a Eurasian, she can never share the affections of Captain John in the same way that an Englishwoman could. Melanie's identity, which brings together two worlds polarized on the basis of race, echoes the Kipling-esque refrain that the East and the West can never meet. Cross-fertilization between the two civilizations has serious negative consequences—this is the message that *The River* strongly evokes.

That Renoir paints a picture of India that privileges the British family is hardly a surprise when we consider the sources of his knowledge about India. Even though he shot the film in India to capture the "authenticity" of Indian life, his notions of Indian society were derived from westerners or upper-class Indians. Among them was E. M. Forster, whose *Passage to India*, recalls Renoir, was one the few "excellent" books that he read on the country.[27] As Forster does in his novel, Renoir casts the film into "well-schooled dichotomies," using Hindu and Christian families to represent the East-West struggle, or what he called a "clash of civilizations."[28]

Another informant was Renoir's assistant, Hari Das Gupta, whose family (as described by Renoir), was a model of the Enlightened Indian middle class, and among their numbers were professors, lawyers, doctors, Government officials and members of the liberal professions. Many of the girls had been to Shantiniketan University, a college founded by Tagore which taught the essentials of Western culture while at the same time preserving Indian customs.[29]

As his educational background indicates, Hari Das Gupta belonged to the upper crust of Indian society—a class of Indians that was, as Thomas Babington Macaulay posited in his "Minute on Indian Education," created in the interest of the British Empire:

> It is impossible for us, with our limited means to educate the body of the people. We must at present do our best to form a class who may be interpreted between us and the millions whom we govern; a class of persons, Indian in blood and colour, but English in taste, in opinions, in morals and in intellect.[30]

Renoir's perspective was apparently colored by the perceptions of the prototypes of the Macaulayan interpreters, a class created by British rulers to act as interpreters between the rulers and the ruled. In some ways, this class of Indians preferred to remain oblivious to the problems of the more marginalized sections of Indian society.[31]

Last but not least, Renoir was influenced by Rumer Godden, the author of the novel that provided the main storyline for *The River*. It is not surprising, then, that Renoir expresses his viewpoint through Harriet, whose vision of India, as Bazin says, is colored by her own privileged upbringing in the colony, which "takes for granted the social and economic stabilities." Despite his sympathetic attitude toward India, Renoir's reliance on a Western viewpoint brings a Eurocentric bias to his work.

Midway through the film, Harriet reads the story of Radha and Krishna to Captain John and his lover. Interwoven with Radha's story is the problem of dowry, which, posits Harriet in painting a dreary picture of the lives of little girls born to Indian parents, causes the subordination of women in India. Then Renoir juxtaposes the attitude of Harriet's mother, an Englishwoman who cherishes girls; thus he evokes contrasting images of the "backward" East and the "civilized" West. Even Bogey, the only brother of five sisters, is replaced after his death by a girl, who is a welcome addition to the British family. Despite Renoir's sympathies for India and Indians, the Western value system emerges as more active than that of the inert

East. Moments such as Harriet's story about the plight of Indian females because of dowry and Melanie's quiet resignation to the limitations imposed by her identity project Indian women as meek and passive and mask their attempts to dismantle patriarchal and colonial structures, both during the nationalist movement and after independence.[32]

The question then is, Why did Renoir exclude the colonial question? While it is easy to attribute his choice to his "love for India," issues about audience and viewership may provide some insight. Interviews with Renoir about the film reveal that he clearly intended to make the film for a Hollywood audience. A reading of Rumer Godden's novel, says Renoir, convinced him that the story offered

> the basis of a film of high quality which would nevertheless be acceptable to the Hollywood film magnates—children in a romantic setting, the discovery of love by small girls, the death of a little boy who was too fond of snakes, the rather foolish indignity of an English family living on India like a plum on a peach-tree; above all, India itself with its exotic dances and garments, all this seemed to me to possess a reassuring quality.[33]

Renoir actually told Satyajit Ray, much to the Indian cinematographer's disappointment, that he was making the film exclusively for Hollywood. The film was made for an American audience that, as Renoir learned during his search for a producer, perceived India primarily as a land of "tigers" and "Maharajahs." In his autobiography, Renoir recalls that when he asked his agent to secure an option on the film rights, the agent did his best to dissuade him: "All I can see in India," said the agent, "is elephants and a tiger-hunt. Is there a tiger-hunt in the plot?"[34] It was Renoir's intention, however, to dispel such images by creating an "authentic" portrait of India—a portrait that was to revise notions of India as the land of "snake charmers" and "maharajahs," in ways that were convincing to his audience. And so Renoir set about the task of making the Orientals a subject of his knowledge for a Hollywood audience. In "The Culture Industry: Enlightenment as Mass Deception," Theodor Adorno and Max Horkheimer argue that the "modern culture industry produces safe, standardized products geared to the larger demands of the capitalist economy."[35] Subscribing to a Hollywood audience, Renoir produced *The River* as a "standardized product" for consumption by a Western audience, which, despite its attempts to be different from films about "tiger hunts" and "elephants," in the end reinforces Renoir's obliviousness of the colonial subjects and masks the sociopolitical history of India.

But if Renoir made the film for Hollywood, then Hollywood, in a vicarious way, was certainly responsible for the shaping of the film. The "Red" scare, initiated by Senator Joseph McCarthy's witch-hunt in the 1940s and 1950s, had changed the climate in Hollywood. The House Un-American Activities Committee had begun investigating screenwriters, directors, and producers who were suspected of having opinions favorable to the Soviets. As the threat of communism ran high, numerous directors, producers, and actors with any leftist leanings or subversive tendencies were hunted down and brought before the committee for questioning. Renoir, who "had been mentioned [as a communist] in 1938 in a report to the sadly famous Committee on Anti-American Activities, was as susceptible to scrutiny as any other Hollywood director."[36] A film that overtly attacked colonialism may have been construed as sharing leftist sympathies, and hence its author may have been subjected to the same fate as Bertolt Brecht, who was accused of being a communist, or Clifford Odets, a Left-leaning American playwright and a close friend of Renoir's, who had to explain to the committee the leftist orientations in his plays of earlier decades.[37] According to Celia Bertin, Renoir largely escaped the wretched McCarthy era because he was in India in 1950, the year when McCarthy launched his communist hunt. Among other things, his being in India set him apart from all the rest of Hollywood. "Accordingly," says Bertin, "no one dreamed of adding Jean's name to those of suspected communists."[38]

But McCarthyism had made Renoir wary. He told his son that in the days of McCarthyism it was better to keep one's indignation to oneself.[39] The focus on aesthetic appeal rather than political ideology in *The River* made Renoir safe from censorship attacks. In an interview with Satyajit Ray in Calcutta in 1950, Renoir mentioned that the endless codes of censorship in Hollywood, among other things such as the commodification of films and the "star system," thwarted a director's best intentions.[40] To avoid the censors, Renoir engaged in self-censorship. Perhaps that is what he meant when he made the equivocal statement to Ray: "You don't have to show many things in a film, but you have to be very careful to show only the right things."[41] In 1953, he expressed the same sort of frustrations to Clifford Odets in a letter:

> If we stop to examine our lives in detail, we seem to be in charge of things. Yet we have the feeling that there's something going on that

isn't right. Maybe it has to do with the appearance of the latest silly
trend, 3-D. The few brief contacts I have had with movie people here
have been scary: they really think they can solve their problem with a
technical trick. So it's certainly a fine time to go back to the old stories
and to throw away everything that is a little strange or different. . . .
I have the feeling that it is more impossible than ever to make a good
film in Hollywood.[42]

Renoir's perceptions originated from what he claims was his "love" for India. India's religious and cultural traditions and its lifestyle provided evidence to Renoir of its earthly spirituality and "exotic" patterns. As a liberal
humanist, sympathetic to the country's history of exploitation, Renoir
sought to rupture negative perceptions and notions of what Benita Parry
calls "vestiges of a primordial, dark and instinctual past which [British] . . .
society had left behind in its evolution to mankind."[43] Nonetheless, Renoir's attitude toward India remained one of benevolent paternalism, as he
continued to evoke notions of an exotic and mysterious land, unknown to
and unfathomable by the West:

I loved the steps from the temples leading down to the river; and the
graceful bearing of the women in their saris; and I was fascinated by
what I learned of their music and dancing, and by their touching desire
to make contact. . . . what particularly delighted me as a film-maker
were the Indian colours, which afforded me a marvelous chance of
putting my theories about the use of colour photography into practice.[44]

But Renoir's refusal to engage with the colonial question and his un-
problematized delineation of the British presence in India after independence can at best be seen as a celebration of imperialism. His intention of
bringing to the West what he perceived to be an "authentic" India becomes damaging on two counts: One, it perpetuates orientalist images of
India. Two, its obliteration of the historical narrative obscures the dynamics of gender, race, class, and colonialism as well as the resistances that
marginalized groups forged to existing power structures. Whatever position critics such as Bazin may take, in making a movie on India and ignoring the historical aspects, Renoir fails to force open the more pressing and
significant questions of India's colonial past. This lack of willingness on
Renoir's part to investigate the material conditions of India's fabric can be
comprehended as complicity with those in power.

*I am extremely grateful to Shoba Vasudevan for discussing the film with me and reading the manuscript. Her suggestions have been most useful.

NOTES

1. Melanie is a Eurasian, and because of her mixed birth her position is precarious. Even as early as the eighteenth century, Eurasians faced discrimination from upper-class Indians and the English in India, who considered their social and economic position to be inferior. Regarding their position, Kenneth Ballhatchet in his discussion "On the Margins of Social Distance," cites Charles Trevelyan, a civil servant in India who became the governor of Madras in 1859: "Their situation is unfortunately very equivocal, midway between the Natives and the Europeans— not owned by either—and whatever faults they have, are mainly due owing to the sensitiveness caused by that unhappy situation" (Kenneth Ballhatchet, *Race, Sex, and Class under the Raj: Imperial Attitudes and Policies and Their Critics, 1793–1905* [London: Weidenfeld and Nicolson, 1980], 100). Ballhatchet also points out that it was a common saying among the British that "Eurasians shared the vices of both races" (ibid.). Melanie is obviously suffering from the traces of such biases, which are not fully explored in the film.

2. This concept of "manifest destiny" is also the principle by which Europeans ruled over the colonies, the implication being that it was the destiny of these "backward" people to be ruled by the West. See Edward Said, *Orientalism* (New York: Vintage Books, 1979).

3. Ronald Bergan, *Jean Renoir: Projections of Paradise* (London: Bloomsbury, 1992), 280.

4. Cited in Celia Bertin, *Jean Renoir: A Life in Pictures* (Baltimore: Johns Hopkins University Press, 1986), 248.

5. In *Orientalism*, Said postulates that the Orient was a European invention, homogenized as a single entity, produced and managed from an authoritarian position of knowledge through distinct East/West dichotomies, which deemed the former as exotic yet inferior.
   As part of the Orient, India was conceived of as spiritual and enervated; its people passive, emotional, and sensual; its climate hot with constant threat of danger and disease. As an object of the knowledge of European powers, India became the subject of myths and stereotypes that were disseminated through various cultural productions and acquired the currency of "truths" that became difficult to dislodge.

6. Rumer Godden, *The River* (New York: Viking, 1946).

7. Bertin, *Jean Renoir*, 250.

8. Andre Bazin, *Jean Renoir*, edited and with an introduction by François Truffaut (New York: Simon and Schuster, 1973), 104.

9. See Christopher Faulkner, "An Ideology of Aesthetics: *The River, The Golden Coach, French Cancan*," in *The Social Cinema of Jean Renoir* (Princeton: Princeton University Press, 1986), 162–198; Ronald Bergan, *Jean Renoir*. Also see Leo Braudy, *Jean Renoir: The World of His Films* (New York: Doubleday, 1972); Durgnat Raymond, *Jean Renoir* (Berkeley and Los Angeles: University of California Press,

1974).

10. Bazin, *Jean Renoir*, 112.

11. Ibid., 113.

12. Ibid., 112.

13. Renoir, *My Life and My Films* (New York: Atheneum, 1974), 250.

14. Cited in Bertin, *Jean Renoir*, 249.

15. Bertin, *Jean Renoir*, 255.

16. *Cinématographe* 46 (April 1979): 38; cited in Bertin, *Jean Renoir*, 255.

17. James Spellerberg, "Technology and Ideology in the Cinema," in *Film Theory and Criticism*, ed. Gerald Mast and Marshall Cohen (New York: Oxford University Press, 1985), 762.

18. Tejaswini Niranjana, *Siting Translation: History, Post-Structuralism, and the Colonial Context* (Berkeley: University of California Press, 1992), 14.

19. Ibid., 15.

20. In *Siting Translation*, Tejaswini Niranjana examines William Jones's translation of *Sakuntala* "to show how he contributes to a historicist, teleological model of civilization that, coupled with a notion of translation presupposing transparency of representation, helps construct a powerful version of the 'Hindu' that later writers of different philosophical and political persuasions incorporated into their texts in an almost seamless fashion" (13). She subsequently discusses the influence of Jones's translation of *Sakuntala* on Mill's *A History of British India* (1817; New Delhi: Associated Publishing House, 1972), in which he derives evidence about Indian history and laws from the Sanskrit play.

21. Jean Renoir, *My Life and My Films*, 251.

22. Sumit Sarkar, *Modern India* (Delhi: Macmillan, 1984), 372.

23. Going to India for spiritual rejuvenation after the war was a recurrent theme in war narratives. See, for example, W. Somerset Maugham, *The Razor's Edge* (New York: Doubleday, 1944).

24. Radha Kumar, *The History of Doing: An Illustrated Account of Movements for Women's Rights and Feminism in India, 1800–1950* (London: Verso, 1993), 93.

25. Dipesh Chakrabarty, "Conditions for Knowledge of Working-Class Conditions: Employers, Government, and the Jute Workers of Calcutta, 1890–1940," in *Subaltern Studies II. Writings on South Asian History and Society*, ed. Ranajit Guha (Delhi: Oxford University Press, 1992), 283.

26. Ibid., 285.

27. Renoir, *My Life and My Films*, 252.

28. See E. M. Forster, *A Passage to India* (London: E. Arnold and Company, 1924).

29. Renoir, *My Life and My Films*, 253–254.

30. Thomas Babington Macaulay, "Minute on Indian Education," in *Selected Writings*, ed. John Clive (Chicago: University of Chicago Press, 1972), 249.

31. In her study on British educational policy in India, Gauri Vishwanathan points out that English education in India became a colonial tool for educating a segment of the traditional ruling class of Indians in order to support the British rulers "in maintaining control of the natives under the guise of a liberal education" ("Currying Favor: The Politics of British Educational and Cultural Policy in India, 1813–1854," *Social Texts* 19–20 [1988]: 95).

32. Recent studies on women in India indicate that, far from being passive, women played a crucial role in the nationalist anticolonial insurgency. See Kumar, *History of Doing.*

33. Renoir, *My Life and My Films,* 249.

34. Ibid., 248.

35. Theodor Adorno and Max Horkheimer. "The Culture Industry: Enlightenment as Mass Deception," in *The Cultural Studies Reader,* ed. Simon During (New York: Routledge, 1994), 29.

36. Bertin, *Jean Renoir,* 273.

37. See Michael J. Mendelsohn, *Clifford Odets: Humane Dramatist* (Deland, Fla.: Everette/Edwards, 1969).

38. Bertin, *Jean Renoir,* 273.

39. Ibid., 274.

40. Satyajit Ray, "Renoir in Calcutta," Appendix 1 in *Portrait of a Director: Satyajit Ray,* ed. Marie Seton (Delhi: Vikas Publishing House, 1971, 1976), 322. Renoir does not, however, specify the codes of censorship to which he was referring.

41. Ibid., 321.

42. Letter to Clifford Odets, dated 17 February 1953; cited in Bertin, *Jean Renoir,* 274–275.

43. Benita Parry, *Delusions and Discoveries: Studies on India in the British Imagination, 1880–1930* (London: Allen, 1972).

44. Renoir, *My Life and My Films,* 250.

Regarding Rouch

FOUR *The Recasting of West African Colonial Culture**

Paul Stoller

Recent work in colonial studies has focused on the contested and fragmented nature of (post)colonial discourses. In this emerging body of work, authors attempt to analyze (post)colonialism and the discourses it has produced from a cultural framework that is antiessentialist. As Nicholas Dirks points out: "Colonialism not only has had cultural effects that have too often been either ignored or displaced into inexorable logics of modernization and world capitalism; it was itself a cultural product of control." [1] As Nicholas Thomas puts it in *Colonialism's Culture*, "Colonial cultures are not simple ideologies that mask, mystify, or rationalize forms of oppression that are external to them; they are also expressive and constitutive of colonial relationships in themselves." [2]

Much that has been written about the nature of popular resistance to colonial domination, however, considers colonial discourses in terms of binary distinctions. Colonial historians have long described campaigns of military resistance to the onset of colonial rule. Resistance, of course, has never been limited to military revolt. Historians such as E. P. Thompson and political scientists such as James Scott have written eloquently of the dynamics of cultural resistance in England and Malaysia. Scott has termed the media of cultural resistance "weapons of the weak." From the current critical vantage of colonial studies, there are two major problems associated with the literature on colonial and postcolonial resistance. The first is a lack of ethnographic specificity. Undifferentiated peasants or plebs employ symbolic weapons that "resist" the oppression of colonial rule. [3] Indeed, analysts of resistance movements have sometimes missed the sociocultural nuances embodied in parodic forms of cultural expression. The second problem is brilliantly stated by Achille Mbembe, who writes:

> To account for both the imagery and efficacy of postcolonial relations of power, we must go beyond the binary categories used in standard interpretations of domination (resistance/passivity, subjection/autonomy, state/civil society, hegemony/counterhegemony, totalization/detotalization). These oppositions are not helpful; rather they cloud our understanding of postcolonial relations. In the postcolony the commandment seeks to institutionalize itself in order to achieve legitimation and hegemony, in the form of a fetish.[4]

To construct this symbolic universe, the state—or colonial administration—designs a set of evocative ideas developed from a mix of local cultural repertoires.[5] Using slightly different terms, Mbembe's argument echoes those of Dirks and Thomas. He is writing about the fractures and fissures of (post)colonial discourses from a decidedly cultural vantage.

This essay is not a direct extension of the current debate on contested colonial culture. In what follows I attempt to demonstrate how Jean Rouch's films were an early and unsettling repudiation of the racist and primitivist foundation of colonial culture. I begin with a short exegesis of colonial culture in West Africa and then discuss how Rouch's (post)colonial films are deconstructive. I conclude with a discussion of how and why these films are important.

COLONIAL CULTURE IN WEST AFRICA

The roots of colonial culture in Africa run very deep indeed. From antiquity to the present, writers from the "civilized" West have been fascinated by the "Otherness" of the "primitive." This fascination, however, usually produced textual exoticism, which, in turn, shaped attitudes, practices, and policies concerning Africa and Africans. The exoticism about Africa and Africans begins with Herodotus, who described Africans as "dog-eared men that had eyes in their chests." Early Muslim writers on Africa reinforced this imagery. Ibn Battuta (1307–1377) maintained the distance between savage (African) and civilized (Muslim) through a discussion of cannibalism. "The pagans hadn't eaten him [a Muslim] solely because of his white color. They say eating a White man is unsafe because he isn't ripe."[6] In the sixteenth century Mahmoud Kati, a pious Muslim historian (i.e., civilized) wrote that Sonni Ali Ber, king of the Songhay empire

(r. 1463–1491) was a tyrant out of control. "Sonni Ali Ber was such a tyrannical, hard-hearted king that he would throw an infant into a mortar and force its mother to pound it to death; the flesh was then given to horses."[7] According to Kati, Sonni Ali Ber also tortured pious Muslims by putting their heads into fire until they died. Occasionally he would cut open the swollen stomach of a pregnant woman and pull out the fetus.

Once the "savagery" of African social life was widely known, it became necessary to explain it. Joseph de Gobineau considered race the primary determinant of African savagery:

> The melanin variety is the humblest and lives at the bottom of the
> scale. The animalistic character etched in his loins imposes his destiny
> from the minute of conception. His fate holds him within the most
> limited intellectual scope. However, his is not a pure and simple brute,
> this Negro with a narrow and sloped forehead, who bears in the middle
> section of his brain the signs of grossly powerful energies. If these
> thinking faculties are poor or even nil, he is possessed, by his desire
> and also by his will, of an often terrible intensity.[8]

The imagery of uncontrolled savagery had its impact on a more specific discussion of African (i.e., primitive) religion, which was first known as "idolatry," the absence of belief in a godhead. This absence of belief was thought to imprison the African people in a state of unreasoned and un-controlled madness.[9] In the eighteenth century idolatry is transformed into fetishism, which Charles de Brosses defined as the worship of any given object, dedicated in ritual, that pleased a person or society. In fetishism, then, anything—trees, rivers, mountains, dolls, crocodiles—could be worshiped in a lavish style. The notion of the fetish, the paragon of unreason, became the frame within which the major nineteenth-century writers expressed their ideas about primitive African religions.[10]

In nineteenth-century texts heathenism and cannibalism also become important subjects that categorize the African as unreasoning and un-controlled, a person living in savage circumstances. Describing the bounty of Manyema country, David Livingstone was puzzled by Manyema cannibalism:

> It was puzzling to see why they should be cannibals. New Zealanders,
> we are told, were cannibals because they had killed all their gigantic
> birds, the moa, etc., and they were converted from the man-eating
> persuasion by the introduction of pigs; but the Manyema have plenty

of pigs and other domestic animals, and yet they are cannibals. Into the reason for their cannibalism, they do not enter. They say that human flesh is not equal to that of goats or pigs. It is saltish, and makes them dream of the dead.[11]

Livingstone's explanation for this seemingly irrational choice? The Manyema were pagans who had not yet been converted to Christianity.

Livingstone also complained of the heathenism of Africans. Among the Makololo he was fed well and treated well but "had to endure dancing, roaring, and singing, the jesting, anecdotes, grumbling, quarrelling, and murdering of these children of nature."[12]

Toward the end of the nineteenth century these images of Africans and their "primitive" ways—cannibalism, gluttony, fetishism, and heathenism—are fused into the notion of "darkness," the absence of the light of European values. The ultimate text of darkness is of course Joseph Conrad's remarkable *Heart of Darkness*, first published in 1899. It is a novel in which the European, Kurtz, is stripped of his culture—his senses—and sucked into the void of African darkness, the antithesis of European light. Practitioners of religions lost in time, the savages of *Heart of Darkness* have abandoned distinct human qualities in the shadows of night. Conrad's savages live in a lost world infused with madness that lures the European inexorably in to its barren heart:

> We were cut off from the comprehensions of our surroundings; we glided past like phantoms, wondering and secretly appalled, as sane men would be before an enthusiastic outbreak in a madhouse. We could not understand because we were too far and could not remember because we were travelling in the night of the first ages, of those ages that are gone, leaving hardly a sign—and no memories.[13]

Such textual exoticism, which is very much with us today, is largely responsible for widespread chauvinistic and racist attitudes about Africans.[14] In the French colonies of West Africa the confrontation between the African population and French officials did little to change these long-standing beliefs about Africans, which had been legitimized by Georges Hardy, the chief ideologue of French colonialism. Hardy delimited six characteristics of the Black African: "absence of memory, the absence of a sense of truth, an incapacity for abstraction and judgment, an incapacity for prolonged effort, a sense of respect only for force, and a gregarious instinct."[15] Such beliefs rendered Black Africans silent brutes who lacked history and had no capacity for rational thought. Africans became little more than beasts who respected nothing but brute force. This ideology, then, built the foundation for French colonial practices in Africa: adventuristic and vicious military campaigns; the *indigenat* legal code that stripped Africans of basic rights in the colonies; forced-labor gangs that splintered families and disrupted rural subsistence patterns; *villages de liberté*, where "freed" slaves were enslaved once again to public works for the colonial administration. Although many of the more pernicious French colonial practices had been abandoned by the end of World War II, the ideology that legitimated them remained firmly entrenched.[16]

RECASTING FRENCH COLONIAL CULTURE

One of the first documentary films about West Africa, *Sous les masques noirs* did little to alter the received ideas about Africa and Africans.[17] Made by the pioneering French anthropologist Marcel Griaule, *Sous les masques noirs* was one of the first French documentaries shot entirely in Africa. The film considers Dogon rituals in isolation from the social, historical, and political context of their performance. Griaule appropriates the Dogon voice. In so doing he becomes an omniscient observer who represents the "reality" of Dogon social life as it is lived. Such realistic depiction suggested a certain sense of West African insouciance, and timelessness, as well as an overindulgent sense of the centrality of ritual practices (dancing, music, sacrifice) to African social life.

It is from this intellectual context that Jean Rouch initially comes to documentary filmmaking, though he followed a singularly circuitous route into the domains of cinema and anthropology. Like many of his age mates, Rouch came to anthropological filmmaking from another discipline; in his case it was civil engineering. Trained to build roads and bridges, Rouch found himself assigned in 1942 to Travaux Publics in the colony of Niger, West Africa. Fascination with local customs, including spirit possession, soon compelled him to study anthropology. In 1943 he corresponded with Marcel Griaule, who encouraged the young engineer to study Songhay spirit possession cults. After World War II Rouch returned to Paris and earned a degree in anthropology. In 1946–1947, he realized a dream by sailing a dugout from the headwaters to the mouth of the Niger River. During the trip he took extensive ethnographic notes, and he shot ethnographic footage with an old Bell and Howell camera that he had purchased at a Paris flea market. He returned to France and the Musée de l'Homme and edited his extensive footage. In this way, Rouch made his first film, *Aux pays des mages noirs*.[18]

From the beginning Rouch combined anthropological fieldwork and documentary filmmaking, using the camera as a tool to elicit information. From fieldwork in 1947–1948 Rouch wrote his *doctorat de troisième cycle* thesis, a work on the history of the Songhay, and made three documentary films (*Les Magiciens de Wanzerbe, Initiation à la danse des possédés,* and *La Circoncision.*[19] *La Circoncision* caught the attention of Jean Cocteau, who presented Rouch with a cinematic award in 1949 at the Festival des Films Maudits in Biarritz.

Rouch's early films are by and large the products of his academic training; in them the realist mode is predominant. Collectively, the films focus on such traditional social and ritual practices as hippopotamus hunting, puberty rites, mortuary rituals, sorcery, and spirit possession. Some of the images in these early films are astounding, especially in *Les Magiciens du Wanzerbe.* But the early Rouch, like his ethnographic forebears, did not wade into the turbulent waters of French colonial politics. These films very much reflect the emphasis on documentation promoted by Marcel Griaule in his *Méthode de l'ethnographie.*[20] In that book Griaule suggests how ethnographers should categorize—indeed, dissect—the societies they attempt to represent.

The timeless, apolitical quality of Rouch's early films provoked the criticism of African intellectuals. During a debate, Ousmane Sembene complained to Rouch that he, like other Europeans, "observes us like insects."[21] Here Sembene referred to Rouch's early films—and, of course, to the anthropological tendency to "dissect" societies into social and cosmological structures, consisting of lineages, clans, moieties, exchange networks, as well as "structured" myths of origins reified in the organization of social space.

With *Les Maîtres-fous* Rouch's filmmaking practices change significantly as he backgrounds documentary realism. In the early 1950s Rouch began research among Sahelian migrants to the Gold Coast.[22] Unlike his research in Niger in the 1940s, his work in the Gold Coast confronted head-on the sociology of colonialism in West Africa. *Les Maîtres-fous* is a brilliant filmic articulation of colonial culture, which, like the works of Fanon, is viewed from the vantage of the colonized. The first time that Rouch screened *Les Maîtres-fous* at the Musée de l'Homme in 1954, it provoked angry reactions. Marcel Griaule as well as Paulin Vierya thought the film a travesty; they both agreed that it should be destroyed. Griaule did not like Africans mimicking French colonial culture in the film. Vierya thought that the graphic images of grotesquely possessed Africans slaughtering and eating a dog would reinforce, if not exacerbate, European racist attitudes about Africa. Indeed, the brutal images of *Les Maîtres-fous* overpower the film's more subtle critiques of colonial culture: the oppression of African workers and the pretentiousness of British political and military ritual. After other screenings to selected audiences in France, Rouch decided on a limited distribution—to art theaters and film festivals.[23]

Although *Les Maîtres-fous* won several awards and influenced the likes of Jean Genet and Jean-Luc Godard, its initial reception troubled Rouch. Critics have suggested that the controversy surrounding *Les Maîtres-fous* compelled Rouch to make other films, especially his films of "ethnofiction" that more directly confronted European racism and colonialism.[24] Such a view may well be correct, for after *Les Maîtres-fous* Rouch made a series of films that portrayed the political and cultural perniciousness of European ethnocentrism and colonialism in the 1950s.

Jaguar

Jaguar is infused with what Italo Calvino once called the brilliance of "lightness."[25] I like to call *Jaguar*, "*Tristes Tropiques*, African style" with a very significant twist. Like *Tristes Tropiques* and other works in the picaresque tradition, *Jaguar* is a tale of adventure, a sort of initiation to the wonders of other worlds and other peoples. The protagonists—*un petit bandit* Lam, the Fulani shepherd Damore, and the Niger River fisherman Illo—learn a great deal from their adventures in the Gold Coast. The difference between *Tristes Tropiques* and *Jaguar* is an important one. We expect Claude Lévi-Strauss to be enlightened by his voyage to Brazil. But do we expect the same for three young Nigerians from Ayoru? Can Others embark on philosophical journeys of enlightenment? In *Jaguar*, Rouch reproduces colonial culture in order to undermine some of its presuppositions: that in their "backwardness" all Africans are alike; that in their "backwardness" Africans have no sense of wanderlust; that in their "backwardness" Africans do not extract wisdom from their journeys. With great humor, *Jaguar* shatters our expectations. Along their journey to the Gold Coast, the Others (Damore, Lam, and Illo) confront their own Others; the Gurmantche, who file their teeth into sharp points and drink millet beer; the Somba, who eat dogs and shun clothing. At the Somba market Damore says to Lam:

Mais ils sont complètement nus, mon vieux.

[They are completely naked, man.]

Complètement.

[Completely.] (Says Lam.)

For Lam, Illo, and Damore, such a corporeal display is unthinkable. They have encountered the "primitive's primitive," thus supporting Michel de Montaigne's affirmation that "each man calls barbarism whatever is not his own practice; for indeed, it seems we have no other test of truth and reason than the example and pattern of opinions and customs of the country we live in."[26] Later in *Jaguar*, Damore becomes very "jaguar" with it. Lam becomes a small-time entrepreneur (*nyama izo*, child of disorder), and Illo toils as a laborer in the port of Accra. At all junctures in the film, social, cultural, and regional differences are underscored. Northerners, who are not constructed as homogeneous, are seen wearing long Muslim robes as well as the European garb of their southern hosts. Southerners, whom Rouch depicts heterogeneously, wear European clothing to church but wrap themselves in traditional *kenti* cloth at a political rally.

In *Jaguar*, Africa is no longer a continent of colonial sameness; it is rather a land of finite distinctions, a space for the politics of difference. By highlighting such heterogeneity in urban Africa, Rouch breaks away from the realist/colonialist tradition of his mentors and confronts the social and political complexities of Africa at the end of the colonial epoch. Commenting critically on Kwame Nkrumah and his cronies, Damore says: "Ils sont bien nourris, ceux-là" [These ones are well nourished], a political commentary of visionary proportions, for the leaders of newly independent Africa would become very well nourished indeed—fed by the political systems they created.

And so in *Jaguar*, Africa emerges from the shadows of colonized sameness and is cast into the swift crosscurrents of political fragmentation. Rouch's protagonists, like Susan Sontag's Lévi-Strauss, are heroes—adventurers in a heterogeneous Africa who confront their own primitives and primitivism, as well as the stormy politics of their epoch. As such, these wise and articulate "Others" defy the expectations of colonial culture and make us ponder our own categories of sameness and difference, civilized and primitive. *Jaguar* makes us laugh as it subverts the centuries-old primitivist imagery of Africa; it compels viewers to decolonize their thinking, their "selves."

Moi, un noir

To make *Jaguar*, Rouch employed his friends as actors. Although Damore, Lam, and Illo acted well in the film, they have never been migrants. While he was editing *Jaguar*, Rouch asked Oumarou Ganda to attend a screening. Ganda, who had been a migrant in Abidjan, challenged Rouch to make a film about real migrants, like himself. Rouch took up Ganda's challenge, and the result was *Moi, un noir*, one of the first films, ethnographic or otherwise, that depicted the pathos of life in *fin de colonial* Africa. In the film, we follow Ganda and his compatriots as they work as dockers in Abidjan's port. We see how hard they work, how little they are paid, and how they are belittled as human beings. We see how work and life in colonial West Africa steal from them the last vestiges of their human dignity. In this space of colonial deprivation and demoralization, we are touched by Oumarou Ganda's fantasies. We are saddened by his disappointments. We are outraged by his suffering. We hear his sad voice, for in this film one of the silent ones tells his sad tale. Oumarou Ganda's story enables us to see how the discourse of colonialism and racism disintegrates the human spirit. Are not the dreams of Oumarou Ganda the dreams of the oppressed—the hope against all hope that someday . . . ?

Like *Jaguar*, *Moi un noir* is a film that obliterates the boundaries between fact and fiction, documentary and story, observation and participation, objectivity and subjectivity. Rouch calls the two films works of "ethnofiction," works in which the "fiction" is based upon long-term ethnographic research. In this way both *Jaguar* and *Moi, un noir* are biting critiques of the staid academicism that pervades the university in Europe and North America. Imprisoned by eighteenth-century intellectualist assumptions in a postcolonial epoch, the academy was and is ill-equipped to deal with the complexities and the turbulence of an ever-changing world. These films, which are also indictments of European high modernism that backgrounds human sensibility, remind us that in a world in which expectations are continuously subverted, the sky—to paraphrase Artaud—can suddenly fall down on our heads.[27] The intent of these films is clearly political. Through the subversion of "received" categories, they challenge us to confront our own ugliness.

La Pyramide humaine

Rouch's early critique of European colonial culture does not end with *Moi, un noir*. As he is fond of saying, "One film gives birth to another." *Moi, un noir* prompted Rouch to make another film set in Abidjan—*La Pyramide humaine*.[28] In this film, the title of which is taken from one of Paul Eluard's Surrealist poems, Rouch explores the relations between French and African students at an Abidjan high school. Some of the African students hate the Europeans; some of the European students are unabashedly racist. The students argue about colonialism and racism. The debate intensifies when a new female student from Paris begins to date an African. This social act, which taps the fear of interracial sexuality, unleashes a torrent of emotion and prejudice on both sides. While *Moi, un noir* focused upon the plight of African migrant workers, *La Pyramide humaine* sets its sights on the sexuality of interracial relations in a French colony—a volatile topic in 1959. Not surprisingly, colonial authorities banned the film in most of Francophone Africa. And yet, even today, it speaks eloquently to the issues of the repressed fear of interracial sex and of liberal duplicity and racism in Europe and North America.

La Pyramide humaine is also very conscious of its own construction. Rouch *qua* filmmaker appears in several sequences of the film, using his presence to carefully weave a subplot through the text. The main story involves the confrontation of two worlds, two sets of prejudices; it is about how confrontation can be transformative. The subplot recounts how the making of the film transformed the lives of the actors. The subplot, then, subverts the specious boundary between fact and fiction and shows how film constructs and transforms, how film can be intellectually and emotionally disruptive. Shot in color, this film is disruptive, indeed, for it impels viewers to acknowledge in black and white their culturally conditioned sexual fears and fantasies.

Petit à Petit

"One film gives birth to another." *Moi, un noir* gave birth to *La Pyramide humaine,* which gave birth to Rouch's most famous work, *Chronique d'un été,* a film about Rouch's own "tribe," les Français. In 1960 how did the French deal with difference—with Jews, Arabs, and Africans? The film, which was politically provocative, is considered a landmark in the history of cinema for two reasons: (1) it is among the first works filmed in synchronous sound; and (2) it launched the Nouvelle Vague in French cinema. In the 1960s Rouch continued to film in Africa. He completed *The Lion Hunters* in 1964 and began to film the magnificent Sigui ceremonies of the Dogon of Mali in 1967.[29] But he wanted to make yet another film in France and decided on Jaguar II, which he called *Petit à petit,* after the corporation formed by Damore, Lam, and Illo in the original *Jaguar.*[30]

The scenario of *Petit à petit* focuses on two entrepreneurs, Damore and Lam, who want to build a luxury hotel in Niamey, Niger, that would cater exclusively to Europeans. But Damore and Lam know nothing about Europeans. Like a good anthropologist, Damore decides to travel to Paris to study the lifeways of the French tribe, to observe and measure them. How else would they know how to design the hotel's interiors? How else would they know how to order sofas and beds of the correct dimensions? And so Damore flies to Paris, where he settles sumptuously into a hotel and embarks on his study. But Lam becomes so worried about the cultural impact of France on Damore's being that he decides to join his friend in Paris. With great humor, Rouch tells the story of Damore and Lam's Parisian experience. As in *Jaguar*, Damore and Lam turn the tables on our expectations. Europeans are usually the filmmakers, not the filmed. Europeans are usually the observers, not the observed.

Among the most memorable scenes occurs on the Place Trocadero, between the Musée de l'Homme and the Cinémathèque Française, a space filled with academic significance. It is winter, and Damore, posing as a doctoral student, approaches several French people armed with anthropometric calipers.

"Excuse me, sir," he says to an elderly gentleman, "I am a student from Africa working on my thesis at the university. Would you permit me to measure you?" With the gentleman's willing consent, Damore measures his skull, his neck, his shoulders, his waist. Later on, Damore approaches a young woman and again makes his request. He measures her dimensions and then asks:

Excusez moi, mademoiselle, mais est-ce que je pourrais voir vos dents?

[Excuse me, Miss, could I see your teeth?]

(The woman opens her mouth.)

Ah, oui. Très bien. Merci, mademoiselle.

[Yes, very good. Thank you, Miss.]

There is much, much more to this film, but I describe this scene to underscore Rouch's ongoing contempt of the academy's conservatism—its uneasiness with change; its distaste for innovation—all of which narrows and limits the production of knowledge.

Throughout his films of ethnofiction Rouch casts aspersions on what he sees as one outgrowth of colonial culture: academic imperialism. Rouch used this subversive theme to unsettle scholars who believe in the infallible superiority of reason. More important, Rouch's ethnofiction films cut to the flesh and bone of the ongoing legacy of European colonial culture, jolting us into the discomfort of brutal awareness. These films compel us to reflect on latent racism, our repressed sexuality, the elitist taken-for-granted assumptions of our intellectual heritage. Rouch's films therefore expose the centrality of power relations in the construction of dreams, thoughts, and actions.

THE POET'S PATH

During my research on Rouch's oeuvre I wondered why the philosophical and political aspects of his work—embodied in filmic images—are under-appreciated in Europe and virtually unknown in North America. Why is it that until recently contemporary critics in Europe and North America rarely, if ever, considered the pioneering work of Rouch? The answer, I think, is that most critics, philosophers, and anthropologists are members of the academy that Rouch so skillfully reproaches for its conservatism. Academics are still bound to Reason, to words, to Baconian plain style. Scholars seek the discursive and eschew the figurative. Images are trans-formed into inscriptions that form a coherent discourse. Poetry and what Maurice Merleau-Ponty called "the indirect language" are out-of-academic-bounds.[31]

More than a generation ago Jean Rouch understood how the poetic power of his films might challenge European colonialist assumptions. Many of his films are poetic in the sense recently invoked by Trinh T. Minh-ha:

> For the nature of poetry is to offer meaning in such a way that it can
> never end with what is said or shown, destabilizing thereby the speak-
> ing subject and exposing the fiction of all rationalization. . . . So to
> avoid merely falling into this pervasive world of the stereotyped and the
> clichéd, filmmaking has all to gain when conceived as a performance
> that engages as well as questions (its own) language. . . . However . . .
> poetic practice can be "difficult" to a number of viewers because
> in mainstream films and media our ability to play with meanings other
> than the literal ones that pervade our visual and aural environments
> is rarely solicited.[32]

Although literalness is the curse of the academy, the strong poetic under-currents of a few films and ethnographies somehow survive.

Because of their literalness, academics are often the last people to stum-ble upon innovation. Such is the case in anthropology—visual or other-wise. Such may well be the case in social theory and philosophy. One of my

philosopher friends admitted to me recently that professional philosophers are fifty years behind the times. For inspiration, he advised me, look
to the arts. Indeed, for most of us the epistemology of Baconian plain style
means that photography and film are, to use John Homiak's apt phrase,
"images on the edge of the text." In Rouch's case, this means that his films
are judged in terms of technological innovation.[33] Critics have generally
overlooked their poetic lyricism, their philosophical content, and their political impact.

A generation before the "experimental moment" in anthropology and
the "theoretical moment" in cultural studies, scores of filmmakers, artists,
and poets evoked many of the themes that define the conditions of post-
modernity and postcolonialism: the pathos of social fragmentation; the
recognition of the impact of global economies; the cultural construction of
racism; the banality of state power; the twin legacies of academic imperialism and colonial culture; the quandaries of self-referentiality; the rewards
of implicated participation; the acknowledgment of heteroglossia; the per-
meability of categorical boundaries (fact/fiction, objectivity/subjectivity).
In one of his many interviews Rouch said:

> For me, as an ethnographer and filmmaker, there is almost no bound-
> ary between documentary film and films of fiction. The cinema, the art
> of the double, is already a transition from the real world to the imagi-
> nary world, and ethnography, the science of thought systems, is a
> permanent crossing point from one conceptual universe to another;
> acrobatic gymnastics where losing one's footing is the least of the
> risks.[34]

Rouch's films of the 1950s and 1960s articulated themes—in filmic images—that have been inscribed on the tableau of the anthropology and the
cultural criticism of the 1980s and 1990s. Recent studies of (post)colonial
culture published in "sophisticated" journals express "sophisticated" ideas
in "sophisticated" language. These inscriptions are welcome, but only a
small number of these inscribing authors are willing to confront, as did
Rouch a generation earlier, the sometimes inspiring, sometimes fearsome
world of incertitude.

The sky is lower than we think. Who knows when it will crash down on
our heads?

*Portions of this paper have appeared in early forms in my book *The Cinematic
Griot: The Ethnography of Jean Rouch* (Chicago: University of Chicago Press, 1992)

and in "Artaud, Rouch, and the Cinema of Cruelty," *Visual Anthropology Review* 8 (1992): 50–58. Thanks to Lucien Taylor, who encouraged me to write on this aspect of Rouch's work; to David Napier, who invited me to try out my ideas at Middlebury College; to Dina Sherzer, who graciously asked me to contribute to this volume; and to Rosemary Coombe, whose comments have sharpened my argument.

NOTES

1. Nicholas Dirks, *Colonialism and Culture* (Ann Arbor: University of Michigan Press, 1992), 3.

2. Nicholas Thomas, *Colonialism's Culture: Anthropology, Travel, Government* (Princeton: Princeton University Press, 1994), 3.

3. See James Scott, *Weapons of the Weak* (New Haven: Yale University Press, 1987); and E. P. Thompson, *The Making of the English Working Class* (New York: Vintage, 1966).

4. Mbembe Achille, "The Banality of Power and the Aesthetics of Vulgarity in the Postcolony," *Public Culture* 4 (1992): 3.

5. Ibid., 5.

6. Ibn Battuta, *Textes et documents relatifs de l'histoire de l'Afrique*, trans. R. Mauny (Dakar: Université de Dakar, 1966), 86.

7. Mahmoud Kati, *Tarikh al Fattach*, trans. M. Delafosse (Paris: Maisonneuve, 1911), 8.

8. Joseph de Gobineau, *Essai sur l'inégalité des races humaines* (Paris: Pierre Belfond, 1967), 205–206.

9. See Joseph Bousset, *Oeuvres complètes* (Paris: Lefèvre, 1836).

10. Ibid.

11. David Livingstone, *Livingstone's Africa* (Philadelphia: Hubbard Brothers, 1872), 529.

12. Ibid., 127.

13. Joseph Conrad, *Heart of Darkness* (New York: Norton, 1963), 105.

14. Naipaul's writing is a case in point. In many works he can be seen as the contemporary era's Conrad, especially in "The Crocodiles of Yamassoukrou," originally published in *The New Yorker* and later published in *Finding the Center: Two Narratives* (New York: Knopf, 1984). Vestiges of colonial culture and primitivism are widely reproduced in newspaper reporting, art history, museum displays, travel literature, and advertising; see David Spurr, *Rhetoric of Empire* (Durham: Duke University Press, 1993); Sally Price, *Primitive Art in Civilized Places* (Chicago: University of Chicago Press, 1989); Marianna Torgovnik, *Gone Primitive* (Chicago: University of Chicago Press, 1990); and Mary Louise Pratt, *Under Imperial Eyes* (New York: Routledge, 1992), 15.

15. Spurr, *Rhetoric of Empire*, 105.

16. See Paul Stoller, *Embodying Colonial Memories* (New York: Routledge, 1995); Jean-Pierre Olivier de Sardan, *Les Sociétés Sonay-Zarma* (Paris: Karthala, 1984); and Michael Crowder, *West Africa under Colonial Rule* (Evanston, Ill.: Northwestern University Press, 1968).

17. Marcel Griaule, *Sous les masques noirs* (Paris: CNRS, 1938).

18. Jean Rouch, *Aux pays des mages noirs* (Paris: CNRS, 1946).

19. Jean Rouch, *Les Magicians de Wanzerbe* (Paris: CNRS, 1948); Jean Rouch, *Initiation a la danse des possédés* (Paris, CNRS, 1949); Jean Rouch, *La Circoncision* (Paris, CNRS, 1949).

20. Marcel Griaule, *Méthode de l'ethnographie* (Paris: Presses Universitaires de France, 1956).

21. René Prédal, ed., *Jean Rouch, un griot gallois*. Special issue of *CinémAction* 17 (Paris: Harmattan, 1982), 77.

22. Jean Rouch, *Les Maîtres-fous* (Paris: Films de la Pléiade, 1956).

23. See Nicole Echard and Jean Rouch, "Entretien avec Jean Rouch." *A voix nue. Entretien d'hier à aujourd'hui.* (Ten-hour discussion broadcast in July 1988 on *France Culture*.)

24. See Peter Loizos, *Innovation in Ethnographic Film* (Chicago: University of Chicago Press, 1993).

25. Italo Calvino, *Six Memos for the Millennium* (Cambridge: Harvard University Press, 1989).

26. Michel de Montaigne, *The Complete Essays of Montaigne*, trans. D. Frame (Stanford: Stanford University Press, 1948).

27. Antonin Artaud, *The Theater and Its Double* (New York: Grove Press, 1958). See also Jean Rouch, *Jaguar* (Paris: Films de la Pléiade, 1956–1964), and Jean Rouch, *Moi, un noir* (Paris: Films de la Pléiade, 1957).

28. Jean Rouch, *La Pyramide humaine* (Paris: Films de la Pléiade, 1958–1959).

29. For a detailed analysis of Rouch's Sigui films and their relation to the Dogon origin myth, see Paul Stoller, *The Cinematic Griot* (Chicago: University of Chicago Press, 1992).

30. Jean Rouch, *Petit à petit* (Paris: Films de la Pléaide, 1969).

31. Maurice Merleau-Ponty, *The Prose of the World* (Evanston, Ill.: Northwestern University Press, 1964).

32. Trihn T. Minh-ha and Nancy Chen, "Speaking Nearby: A Conversation with Trihn T. Minh-ha, *Visual Anthropology Review* 8 (1992): 82–91.

33. John Homiak, "Images on the Edge of the Text," *Wide Angle* (forthcoming).

34. Jean Rouch and Enrico Fulchignoni, "Conversation between Jean Rouch and Professor Enrico Fulchignoni," *Visual Anthropology* 2 (1989): 265–301.

Le Colonial Féminin

FIVE   *Women Directors Interrogate French Cinema*

Catherine Portuges

From the beginning of cinema one hundred years ago to the end of the colonial period in 1962, Africa provided an extraordinary range of material for more than 250 fiction films and hundreds of documentaries produced in France alone. Although many other national cinemas, with or without an African colonial presence, produced films whose action takes place on that continent, the most beloved by *cinéphiles* is Michael Curtiz's *Casablanca* (1942). Purveyors of dreams, fantasies, and "exotic" adventures, French *cinéastes* from Jacques Feyder to Jean Renoir at once mirrored and structured France's colonial imaginary.[1] One of the earliest examples is Ferdinand Zecca's 1906 *Le Rêve de Dranem*, a forty-five-second fiction piece, portraying a Black character for the first time—in this case a woman—and accompanied by Pathé's synopsis:

> Dranem seul dans son lit, rêve de tenir une femme dans ses bras. Il l'embrasse, la femme est devenue une négresse, Dranem se détourne. Une femme blanche le réveille, Dranem veut l'ambrasser et se trouve face à face avec la négresse. Dranem frappe l'oreiller.
>
> [Alone in his bed, Dranem dreams of holding a woman in his arms. He embraces her, she becomes a Negress, Dranem turns away. A White woman awakens him, Dranem tries to embrace her and finds himself face to face with the Negress. Dranem strikes the pillow.][2]

For, whatever historical importance the colonial Empire may have had for France, one cannot help but note that the uses to which cinema put this chapter of French national history are at best arguable, most often portraying the French presence in Africa as a *donnée première*.[3]

The past two decades have witnessed striking shifts in the way in which French people—artists, scholars, and ordinary citizens—think about and represent the colonial moments of their nation's history.[4] As part of this reassessment project, French women filmmakers are calling into question France's ambivalent relationship to its colonial past in cinematic projects that focalize first-person, introspective autobiographical narratives. In contrast, for example, to British practice, the fusion of postcolonial with gender-specific topics has in the 1980s and 1990s tended to be represented most consistently in films made by White French women filmmakers.[5] Working primarily within a classical narrative film idiom, they nonetheless confront unequivocally the gender, racial, and ethnic structures of mainstream French cinema.[6]

A number of these texts bear witness to the dynamism of a cinema of memory, a kind of *colonial féminin*, in which border crossings translate into a mise-en-scène that destabilizes hegemonic ideas of nationality, sexuality, and the family. French cinema of the past two decades has consequently been reinvigorated and challenged by this unheralded *deuxième nouvelle vague*. Private experience, fantasy, and desire narrated against the backdrop of historical crisis, these films are also readable as works of unconscious mourning, standing in contrast to films narrated through male protagonists that emphasize reenactments of war, such as Pierre Schoendoerffer's *Dien Bien Phu* and Régis Wargnier's *Indochine*; family portraits of French colonial society, such as Bertrand Tavernier's *Coup de torchon*; or Jean-Jacques Annaud's ferocious satire of French *colons*, *La Victoire en chantant*.[7] As such, they may also be seen as ambivalent interrogations of subjective, spectatorial, and national implication within the enduringly romanticized site of erotic investment that colonial geography remains to this day, more than three decades after the end of *la guerre sans nom*.[8]

Such debates over France's colonial legacy confront the nation just as a rising tide of nationalism is overtaking a European community attempting to reconcile its fractious ethnic and national identities following the collapse of the Soviet system.[9] Yet even within contemporary theoretical perspectives on postcoloniality, gender, and nation, these works offer, it seems to me, more than merely self-promoting exercises in melancholic nostalgia or innocent complicity, for they reinscribe French colonial history within a visual space that—implicitly, if not explicitly—critiques prior erasures of women's subjectivity from the horizon of colonial stories.[10] Represented in films of the 1930s as virgin site of conquest, abounding in sexual metaphor in dialogue as in image, and even viewed as a locus of redemption for those who transgressed against it, the colonial experience of Africa was seen as marking its participants forever. Explains a protagonist in Jean Delannoy's *Paradis de Satan* (1938), "Six mois de colonie expliquent ma dépravation" [Six months in the colonies explain my deprivation]; a character in Jean Dreville's *Maman Colibri* (1937) laments, "Les colonies sont différentes de la Metropole, l'amour y trouve difficilement grâce" [The colonies are different from the metropole, there love is difficult to find]; and Georges Regnier's *Paysans noirs* (1947) notes that "cette vieille Afrique est moins docile qu'une femme mariée" [this old Africa is less docile than a married woman].[11]

Foregrounding the painful question of France's continuing implication in—and repression of—the colonial question, the films of the *colonial féminin* at the same time interrogate aspects of that dynamic, which has been marginalized by, if not altogether excluded from, mainstream cinematic representation—that is to say, the previously unarticulated roles of the dominant culture's female counterparts and their complicity with the colonial Empire away from public political spaces in the introspective, at times dreamlike, sites of the ordinary and extraordinary.[12] By focusing on the wives, daughters, friends, lovers, and sisters, these texts also serve to illuminate generational differences within French women's cinema; in so doing, they restage women's narratives by addressing gendered spectators differently from the ways in which their cinematic foremothers—Agnès Varda and Marguerite Duras, for instance, both of whom directed films that foreground aspects of French colonialism—represented female sexuality and subjectivity. Coproduced in international partnership, they constitute a site of production and reception that instantiates the effects of displacement, absence, and exile within the autobiographical cinematic project.[13]

Three films have contributed significantly to this genre, all first features, two of them directed by former actresses; set apart from mainstream French work, they are linked to the new wave of the late 1950s and early 1960s by an avowedly personal focus. Moreover, the directors—Brigitte Roüan, Claire Denis, and Marie-France Pisier—reject classification as practitioners of a *cinéma des femmes*, having previously collaborated with filmmakers such as François Truffaut, Jean-Luc Godard, and Bertrand Tavernier. Yet despite their makers' explicit refusal of codification within women's cinema, these texts, taken together, may be fruitfully interpreted as visual analogs of *l'écriture féminine*, the feminist literary project of the 1960s and 1970s in which writers wrestled openly in their texts with the complicated project of self-inscription, combining the personal and the social, the corporeal and the intellectual, the lived and the imaginary, the existential present and the remembered past in highly personal language.[14]

Raised in a French colonial family in West Africa, Claire Denis worked with such international filmmakers as Wim Wenders, Jim Jarmusch, Costa Gavras, and Dusan Makavejev before beginning, in 1988, her first feature, *Chocolat*.[15] Set in the late 1950s, the film is narrated from the point of view of France, daughter of a French *commissaire* (district officer) in the French colonial administration. Having decided to revisit the remote region of the Cameroon where she spent much of her childhood, France meets Mungo Park, a Black American who has settled in the country, while hitchhiking to the airport to board a plane into the backcountry. Her mind flashes back to scenes of her youth: she remembers her friendship with the Black servant Protée; the Englishman Boothby arriving for dinner when her father was away and her mother hastily unpacking her evening dress from a trunk; the upheaval caused when a plane crashed nearby and the house was invaded by the crew and passengers, including a White coffee planter and his Black mistress, a young couple on their first trip to Africa who refused to accept treatment from the local doctor, and Luc, an ex-priest who had gone native. Luc detected an attraction between France's mother, Aimée, and Protée, and taunted the mother. When Aimée made a halfhearted attempt to seduce Protée, he turned her down and was banished, at Aimée's request, from the house to the garage, where France visited him secretly. The plane was finally repaired and the guests departed. France's reverie ends as she arrives at the airport. Mungo Park, assuming she is an ordinary tourist, asks if she is disappointed that he is not a real "native."[16]

Chocolat recalls the final years of French West African colonialism through the memory of the young White woman (significantly named "France") and visualizes through languorous camera work the subjective experience of colonialism, both from the perspective of the colonized, embodied by the family's Black servant, and from that of the little girl not yet able to understand the nature of colonial power, who thus treats Protée as both friend and subaltern. The sudden termination of their relationship coincides with the waning of the colonial period; returning to Cameroon much later, in the 1980s, France finds herself incapable of recovering her colonial childhood, resisting the impulse even to visit once again her family home. The physical act of returning to the site of childhood trauma and memory becomes, in these autobiographical narratives, an indispensable element in the process of coming to terms with one's own history.[17]

With regard to her hybridized positionality, Claire Denis observes:

As someone raised in European culture but born outside Europe . . .
I believe you have to live stories before you invent them . . . when you
make a documentary you concentrate on the "other," but when you
make fiction you talk about yourself. Cinema is therefore a very personal medium, and if European cinema is anything it is a reflection of
subjective European experiences. . . . When I was making *Chocolat* I
think that I had a desire to express a certain guilt I felt as a child raised
in a colonial world. When the film was completed, I was asked to write
a piece on it for the press booklet. Unsure of what to write, I found an
introduction to an anthology of Black literature and poetry by Jean-
Paul Sartre which suggested that for three thousand years the official
view of the world had been a white view and he now welcomed an alternative—the view from those who had been watched, what they saw
when they looked at us, the white Europeans. I put this in the booklet
because I thought that there was very little else I could say: knowing I
was white, I tried to be honest in admitting that *Chocolat* is essentially a
white view of the "other." . . . Raising money for the film was difficult
because of the subject matter, but significantly, I did not experience any
problems in actually discussing colonialism—unlike the censorship experienced by filmmakers in France after the Algerian war. I was, however, strongly advised to construct an affair between Protée, the male
Black servant in the film, and the white woman. The producers saw this
outcome as good box office. But this would have totally destroyed what
the film was about for me, so I resisted the pressure to alter the script.
When it came to doing the scene in which Protée resists the possibility
of a sexual encounter with the woman, I shot it quickly in one take, before anyone could even attempt to suggest an alternative. I know this
was a big disappointment for the production company, because they
really wanted me to re-shoot the scene and to change it, but Protée's
refusal was the purpose of the film.[18]

Denis's counterpart and colleague Brigitte Roüan spent her childhood
in Algeria in a strict Catholic family before becoming involved in the 1968
student movement. Her first feature, *Outremer*,[19] set in colonial Algeria,
depicts, with gentle irony and a gift for the quotidian detail, the sheltered
world of an upper-class family of French colonial sisters—Zon (Nicole
Garcia), Gritte (Marianne Basler), and Malène (Brigitte Roüan), longtime
residents of Algeria, against the backdrop of a rapidly intensifying political
revolt, refiguring the "same" events through the triptych of the three sisters' individual points of view. Framed by colonial life in the late 1940s, the

opening sequence of *Outremer* is bathed in sunlight, a seemingly safe Algerian Eden welcoming the lovely young sisters, resplendent in white haute couture dresses, moving toward shore like sea nymphs awaiting the sensual pleasures of an engagement party, seemingly oblivious to the suffering that those of their class have inflicted upon the colonized peoples of North Africa.

Cowriter and costar of this semi-autobiographical film, Roüan uses her personal voice to reveal the sensibility of *le colonial féminin*:

> My father was a naval officer, declared missing in action when I was very young. The Algeria of my childhood was completely explosive. . . . My family's attachment to it was almost physical, and it increased during the war, until when it was time to leave they felt torn from their "lover," the land. Still, after decades in Algeria, they spoke only the least bit of Arabic, just enough to pay the workers and give the servants orders. . . . I wanted to show people hemmed in by inherited property and preconceived notions, occupying prearranged positions, . . . the men of that time were not allowed to cry, they were placed on pedestals, forced to be virile and magnificent statues. . . . The women were addicted to one man. Such an education creates neurotic women, of which I am one. I was brought up to be married, so of course I never married.[20]

Roüan, her two sisters, and her two brothers were raised by their grandmother and a variety of relatives in Algeria and Paris whose anti-Semitic and anti-communist ideas, challenged by the militant student movement, prompted her to become a Trotskyist. Her career as a director began with her pregnancy:

> Although it was impossible to get work as an actress, strange men in cafes and on the street would approach me constantly. So I sat home and wrote a script about a pregnant, out-of-work actress who prostitutes herself for a day's minimum actor's guild wages. . . . There have, of course, been militant films about Algeria (*La Question, La Folle de Toujane*) but that was not my goal . . . if I had wanted to do a film about Algeria, it would have been different.[21]

Roüan's treatment of the "events" prompts the viewer to recall de Gaulle's first state visit to the war-torn region of his country's former Empire, as he stood on a balcony in Algiers, proclaiming: "Je vous ai compris,"

while the Europeans and Algerian natives massively gathered below
wept with joy.[22] But this is a family romance as much about the *colonial
féminin*—that is, the political nation or decolonization itself, seen this time
from the authority of female perspectives—as it is a *prise de conscience* of
complicity and passivity in the Algerian trauma. The title *Outremer* refers
both to France's overseas colonies and to a condition "beyond the mother"
(*outre-mere*), and pregnancy figures prominently in the film. Roüan in fact
dedicates the film to her mother, "qui était si jolie et qui aurait pu être si
belle" [who was nice-looking but could have been beautiful], who died
during her early childhood years in Algeria, and upon whom the character
of the eldest sister is based. Maternal and geographical losses and displacements imbue the film with a sense of broken attachments, the fiercely impossible longing for attachment to one place, a desired homeland. Its narrative construction enables the director to resurrect the dead, so to speak,
and thus keep alive the immortal internal objects of childhood desire.
A similar concern with the effect of war on women's everyday lives and
bodies imparts to *Outremer* its particular ambiance. The women of the
colony—*l'occupant féminin*—are implicated in its conflicts, the film suggests, the front itself being located within the domestic sphere, with its
permeable boundaries that seem to invite revolt from within.

The Algerian struggle is present primarily in off-screen sounds or
sights quickly glimpsed by the camera, whose gaze just as quickly turns
away, as if sensed in the peripheral vision of characters who might otherwise have remained distanced from its insistent presence.[23] Roüan demonstrates the complicity of these husbands and wives in moments such as
Zon's assurance to her daughter that the "Arabs are our brothers—but
only in Jesus." Yet Arab men are denied individual identity throughout the
film, and when they are present it is often in nameless, conspiratorial
groups. Zon dies of cancer, wrapped in her husband's naval officer's jacket,
to the accompaniment of triumphal music as the camera tracks upward
above her body toward the moonlit sky. Malène, the character played by
Roüan, is more involved in the reality of Algeria, working the farm as a
manager; driven by the need to restore her faith in the weak husband she
longs to admire, Malène allows an Arab boy to take the blame for her own
destructive error, and, in that moment, ruptures forever her long-standing
connection to the land and its people. Gritte's moment of truth comes
when, having purposely misguided French soldiers pursuing a fugitive Algerian, she stoops in the doorway of a home in the native quarter, riveted
by the face of the Algerian rebel standing above her. This moment of fear
fused with forbidden—and unspoken—eroticism is echoed by an earlier

one when as a young girl, Gritte is seen sitting in the mud, watching her outlaw Arab lover asleep with his head in her lap, the interracial sexual liaison suggested as a profoundly transgressive act against the codes of her class.

Perhaps precisely on account of their focus on interiority, the representation of history, memory, and family that emerges from these films has been termed by some French critics as "soft" (i.e., feminine or subaltern, colonized) in comparison with that of their presumably "harder" (i.e., White male, nonimmigrant, "truly" French) counterparts. I propose instead that they offer a collective portrait that invites spectatorial reconsideration of precisely that which has been excluded from the visual space of the genre of exile memoirs. Roüan's film suggests some of the ways in which the intrusion of violent force into the pre-Oedipal bliss of a paradise peopled primarily by sisters, mothers, daughters, and women friends is handled visually. Yet it should be noted that the gaze in these texts is historical only to the extent that it refers to a personal narrative, and especially to a childhood that was spent not in France but elsewhere, in exile. Driven inexorably by sexuality and politics into tragic outcomes, the sisters' narratives, retold from the point of view of each, moves from marital or colonial rule to an illusory liberation whose site of struggle is women's bodies and female subjectivity.

Barbed-wire barriers are a frequent reminder of the state of siege in which they live, a sign of confinement, of the carceral universe representing the realities of the Arabs of Algeria. They recall, too, films such as Theo Angelopoulos's *Le Pas suspendu de la cigogne* (Greece/France/Italy, 1989), a powerful document of contemporary European cultural migrations; they mark the interrogation of neocoloniality by other indigenous, aboriginal, and oppositional filmmakers, as well as those working within and against mainstream cinema; and they evoke other claustrophobic spaces where expatriates, exiles, and émigrés exist in conditions of self-narratized liminality.

Like the "screen memories" of Freudian origin, this cinema of memory is as intimate as writing, yet without literariness, a kind of "cinécriture" (in Agnès Varda's formulation) that draws from new wave theorist Alexandre Astruc's concept of personal filmmaking as a "camera-stylo," extending the experiments with feminine temporality initiated by Varda four decades ago with *La Pointe Courte* (1954). By means of its expressive experiential vitality, this cinema seizes the shifting signifiers of the past, entering into the repressed mise-en-scène beneath and beyond the surface appearance of the family photograph album.

The representation of childhood, female friendship, and sisterhood; the confrontation with exoticism and the gaze of the "Other"; the persistence of the autobiographical as a restructuring strategy—these, then, are subjects deepened by a generation of women directors bearing witness to the dynamism of a cinema of memory, the *colonial féminin* in which border crossings translate into a mise-en-scène that destabilizes traditional assumptions of ethnicity, nationality, sexuality, and the family. This exilic cinema transgresses boundaries through a self-narrativization informed by the deterritorialization of distance and loss.[24] The desire to imagine another, archaic place of remembrance in the first person creates a bond of solidarity with the viewer, in contrast to the omniscient or effaced narrator of colonial films whose project tends to unfold on a more epic scale. This form of visual enactment at once creates and illustrates a self-reflexive presence concerned not only with the self but also with the larger dis/ affiliated group, in this instance the fragmented, multiauthorial community of *le colonial féminin*. Like the texts of *l'écriture féminine*, they arise from a perceived prohibition against "writing" the self—amorous, political, familial, social. Childhood links, intimate references, and spatial enclosures further mark this richly ambiguous universe, coexisting as it does alongside the carceral universe of the Arab community, so liminally present in *Outremer*.[25] Rereading these texts as a collective portrait solicits reconsideration of that which has been repressed from the visual space of remembrance. By suturing the spectator into what appears on the surface to be a classical commercial film, these directors end up implicating themselves, the viewer, and the occupying forces in the violence that remains present but unseen beyond the confines of claustrophobic domestic enclosures. In so doing, they destabilize traditional binarisms of inside/outside in the *terra incognita* of the former territories.

Considered in conjunction with *Outremer* and *Chocolat*, Marie-France Pisier's *Le Bal du gouverneur* (1984)[26] may be inserted among other historically oriented films on the margins of more-commercial feature work on the contemporary French cultural landscape. Its colonialist context recalls that of Jean-Jacques Annaud's controversial treatment of Marguerite Duras's novel, *L'Amant;*[27] Régis Wargnier's *Indochine*, the seventh-largest box office success in France for 1992; and Pierre Schoendoerffer's fictionalized cinematic reenactment, *Dien Bien Phu*. Framed throughout from the point of view of Thea Forestier, the film's opening overhead shot of books strewn about her bedroom sets the stage for the childhood stories and romantic novels that nurture the character's internal world, while the film's closing shot reprises this same sequence. Enclosed within that filmic space, the viewer is drawn into intimate encounters with the daily dramas of childhood—jealousy between friends, first love, a spirit of adventure, the disappointing behavior of adults—against a background of the early stages of decolonization in New Caledonia in the mid-1950s. Evoked indirectly rather than portrayed overtly is an adulterous affair between Thea's mother, Marie Forestier, and an attractive doctor from the island, observed by the child, who watches through venetian blinds as her mother goes off to ride her horse on the beach. The drama erupts as Marie returns late for breakfast with a wounded leg after being thrown off her horse. Like Thea, the viewer has seen nothing but has understood all, whereas the "Others"—the island's indigenous inhabitants, the parents of Thea's classmates—have seen everything, letting the knowledge be known by way of the children in a classroom scene in which Thea is humiliated.

Le Bal du gouverneur, like *Chocolat* and *Outremer*, thus foregrounds questions of difference—racial, religious, ethnic, sexual—that are the story of the colonies. Yet each film remains relentlessly and unapologetically personal, resisting efforts to impose meaning by direct confrontation or articulation, preferring instead an allusive richness of scenes dispersed among multiple sites, as if to insist upon the plurivocality of the subjects they address. According to Pisier,

> Dans cette spécificité il y a ma féminité mais cela ne me paraît pas spécifiquement féminin. Cela me paraît spécifiquement personnel . . . le roman familial [a lieu] là ou les souvenirs du passé découvrent le chemin de leur expression, surgissant avec évidence, empruntant les détours de la méthode ou de l'imaginaire, les images de la mémoire s'imposent comme un désir de cinéma.

> [My femininity is a part of this specificity, but to me it isn't explicitly female, but instead specifically personal. . . . The family romance takes place in the space where memories of the past discover the path of their own expression, revealing themselves, taking on the shape of method or imagination; these images impose themselves like the desire for cinema itself.][28]

The first version of Marie-France Pisier's scenario was written from the point of view of the children, that of the parents coming into focus only later. In the final version, beginning with recollections from her own childhood, the director invokes an image reminiscent of that of Duras in *L'Amant* (and that constituted, according to Duras, the original title she

imagined for *L'Amant:* "La photographie absolue"—the departure of a
boat on which she found herself, the first profound grief of a misunder-
stood child:

> Je suis partie de souvenirs de ma propre enfance mais rien d'autre
> n'aurait pu débrider autant mon imagination et m'entrainer aussi loin.
> Un fait réel est un appel de fiction bien plus considérable que tout ce
> qu'on peut imaginer d'extravagant au départ. Il y a trois ou quatre an-
> crages extrêmement précis qui sont, la plupart du temps, des images
> autour desquelles le romanesque s'est mis en place. Dans mon souvenir,
> Noumea restait liée à ma première grande douleur d'enfant incomprise:
> le départ d'un bateau sur lequel je me trouvais. La topographie même—
> la ville blanche et la ville des usines, le sémaphore sur la colline, était
> inscrite en moi de manière très violente, sans que je comprenne bien
> pourquoi c'était si fort.

> [I began with memories of my own childhood . . . nothing else could
> have unleashed my imagination as much, nor taken me as far. A fact can
> offer an even stronger call for fictional form than even the most extrav-
> agant things one might at first imagine. There are three or four ex-
> tremely precise moments that are, most of the time, images around
> which fiction was eventually developed. In my memory, Noumea re-
> mained linked to my first great suffering as a misunderstood child: the
> departure of a boat on which I found myself. Even the topography—
> the bleached-out city and the city of factories, the semaphore on the
> hill, were inscribed within me very violently, without my being able to
> understand why it was so.][29]

Organizing the logic of its mise-en-scène, memory intervenes as a particular image of the colony: what is autobiographical, according to Pisier,
is not a morality or an ethics but the "I" of the camera eye—in other
words, autobiography itself that creates the point of view of the colonial
universe. The original scenario for *Le Bal du gouverneur* was conceived
strictly according to the point of view of the children, with the parents'
story attenuated. Marie, the maternal figure, carries the film's thematic
heft by embodying the colony itself, the colonized person pointing the
way toward decolonization:

> J'ai essayé de décrire cette femme avec toutes ses contradictions, sans
> me rendre compte que je disais très precisement ce que je pensais de la

colonisation française à cette époque-là . . . la colonisation, pour moi,
ce n'est pas la schlague que je n'ai pas connue, mais cette douceur ram-
pante et abominable du "chacun à sa place." Les Blancs et les Noirs ne
vivaient pas ensemble mais il y avait dans leur façon de vivre côte à côte
une espèce de sensualité et le film dit qu'entre eux quelque chose était
encore possible sans en arriver à la violence. Ce qui a pu gêner les gens
c'est que je ne mette pas davantage en scène les dominés. Il me semble
que je ne parle que de ça, d'une part, et que le principe du film reposait
vraiment sur ce non regard, ce voile, cette impossibilité de voir les
colonisés, sauf dans cette tentative de grève qui tourne court.

[I tried to describe this woman with all her contradictions, without re-
alizing that I was saying very clearly what I thought about French colonization at that time. . . . For me, colonization was not about the flog-
gings I didn't know about, but that craven and abominable sweetness
that comes from "knowing one's place." The Whites and the Blacks did
not live together, but there was a kind of sensuality in their way of living side by side, and the film suggests that something could still be possible between them that didn't lead to violence. What might have both-
ered some people is that I didn't concentrate more on the dominated
peoples. It seems to me that that's all I do talk about, and that the principle of the film rests truly on that nongaze, that veil, that impossibility
of seeing the colonized, except in the aborted attempt at a strike.][30]

As in all three films, here, too, dialogue escapes from the conventional
play of question-answer to take an elliptical and nuanced form; it is a way
of not saying everything, inscribed cinematically to reflect a defining feature of the indisputability of colonial law and custom.

Dans la scène où la petite fille en classe récite un poème, beaucoup de
choses sont dites sans être exprimées, les élèves qui font "tagada" sur
leur chaises disent des choses monstrueuses, sa copine qui ne dit rien en
dit aussi. Je préfère que les choses soient un peu trop plurielles, un peu
trop contradictoires que l'inverse. . . . Il y a aussi l'idée qu'on ne peut
même pas se fier aux mots puisque, à cette époque, les mots changent:
colonie devient Territoire d'outremer, le gouverneur devient le Haut
Commissaire. C'est pourquoi j'aimais beaucoup l'image du tonneau sur
lequel est inscrit T.O.M., et qui une fois renversé fait M.O.T.

[In the scene where the little girl recites a poem in class, a lot is said
without being expressed; the kids doing "tagada" with their chairs say

monstrous things, her little girlfriend says a great deal by not uttering a word. I prefer that things be rather too multifaceted, too contradictory rather than the contrary. . . . There is also the idea that one cannot even trust words since, at that time, words were changed: colony became "overseas territory," governor became "high commissioner." That's why I loved the image of the cask with the initials T.O.M., which, inverted, reads M.O.T.][31]

Meaning articulated obliquely through gesture and mise-en-scène characterize a fourth film, tangential, though inescapably related to this group: *L'Odeur de la papaye verte*,[32] a visually ravishing, nearly mystical recreation of Vietnam before the war and the first feature of a filmmaker born in Vietnam in 1962 who moved to Paris in 1975, where he made his first short film, *The Married Woman of Nam Xuong*. *L'Odeur de la papaye verte* is one of the few films on the recent French cultural landscape made by a colonial "insider," and it is one whose own identity is also hyphenated. Shot entirely in Vietnamese, the film re-creates the Vietnam that existed before the director, Tran Anh Hung was born but that he claims to have sensed through his parents—the everyday world of a bourgeois merchant household in Saigon in 1951 and 1961 into which a ten-year-old girl, Mui, comes to begin work as a servant. Although it was his intention to shoot his first feature film in Ho Chi Minh City, for technical reasons Tran ended up re-creating the world of his childhood on a soundstage near Paris with a nonprofessional cast:

> What was important for me was to create a specific rhythm, to find the very movement of the Vietnamese soul. Perhaps it sounds pretentious, but that is what I wanted to do. . . . What I think I have understood of the Vietnamese people is that they don't have to talk to one another in a rational way in order to communicate. Rather there is this notion that they . . . understand things without being precise, without using words.[33]

As in the other films considered here, in this one also the French occupation of Vietnam at the time is alluded to only by refraction. Here, too, the domestic world of women is the heart of the film: both the servant Mui and the mistress of the household are expected to serve with grace and absolute submission. Tran achieves a luminous portrait of life in an enclosed family community, where women's work, primarily cooking, ritualizes relationships on many levels. The aggregate of precise gestures—peeling, chopping, mopping, frying—that constitute its visual space become a kind of homage to traditional women's culture.

> Ever since I was a little child I would watch my mother working alone in the kitchen. When I visit my mother now, I am often struck by the calm freshness of her gestures, the way that she arranges food . . . her entire life has been nothing but servitude, and when I look at other women of my mother's age, it's the same. I wanted to render homage to those women who live that way.[34]

The Bressonian intensity of Tran's use of silence and understatement brings each scene into hyperreal focus, creating a striking intimacy between spectator and image.

At the film's conclusion, Mui is reading *Oreiller d'herbe* (Grass Pillow) by Soseki, a Japanese prose writer, a text that Tran says "speaks to the permanence of things, something very deeply embedded in Asian philosophy . . . ultimately, things remain the same. In a sense, that is the pessimistic side of this ending." Symbolic of that permanence, green papaya is picked, washed, peeled, and prepared by women and served to men, evoking in the director the timelessness of maternal gestures. Thanks to this Proustian strategy, the filmmaker unveils the emotions, desires, and deceptions that lie beneath the surface of a bourgeois Vietnamese household similar to that of his childhood. It is 1951 Saigon, far from the sounds of war ravaging the northern portion of the French protectorate. The hushed, tranquil atmosphere that permeates the large, rambling house is enhanced by music from the father's guitar and a profusion of exotic flora that softens the light filtering through the windows. The grandmother lights incense on the altar of her dead ancestors; the mother, while caring for her husband and three sons, measures and cuts clothes for customers in her fabric shop. None of these ritualistically performed actions, however, can mask the undercurrents of unhappiness that pervade the household. The father has left with his wife's savings; the two youngest sons aggressively vent their anger on Mui, recalling that other French Indochinese family configuration so hauntingly portrayed by Marguerite Duras in her semi-autobiographical novels, *Un Barrage contre le Pacifique* and *L'Amant.*[35]

The film's emphasis on childhood, however, recalls the idealizing tendency of fiction by colonized peoples solicited by French publishers in the 1950s, interpreted by some as an attempt to neutralize the anticolonial threat and the "Otherness" of indigenous cultures. Within such a perspective, films such as *Chocolat, Outremer,* and *L'Odeur de la papaye verte* may be seen as serving secondarily to alleviate or reassure the *mauvaise conscience* of the dominant culture by linking colonization itself with childhood innocence, even with an essentialized femininity that is uncritically—albeit perhaps unconsciously—equated with subaltern and colonized groups. Yet it should be remembered that, as autobiographical texts, they are primarily concerned with scrutinizing and exploring a private past in the interest of knowing the self in the present, and with the dialectic interplay between reality and fantasy, between remembering and forgetting.

A cinema of private memory in search of the past, of a nation's collective memory of its repressed colonial history, of an individual artist's family romance: this is not so much nostalgia as a recovery, in the psychoanalytic sense, of images, less souvenir than rememorialization, or what Nathalie Sarraute has referred to as *la sensation* of the past retrieved in the present, incorporated within a fictionalized narrative, that marks the director's interrogation of personal and national identity, of what was repressed, silenced, or distorted.[36] Yet the autobiographical perspective also affirms a point of view, and it is not that of male authority or of official history, nor that of commercial cinema, nor even that of the subaltern, colonized people whose voice is not heard; but rather a certain gaze upon the idea of the colony, a distancing of the paternal law whose violence recurs in intimate, daily, secretly painful echoes.[37] For the subject of these films is in the end perhaps neither the political nation of the colony nor decolonization itself, but rather an anticolonial consciousness or conscience. It is the pernicious eruption of force in a lost paradise upon a childhood lived not in France but elsewhere, in exile.

Claire Denis claims in fact to have abandoned this link with Africa in a more recent film, *S'en fout la mort* (No Fear No Die) (1990):

Cette trace autobiographique s'est inscrite un peu à mon insu. Avant *Chocolat*, j'avais eu un projet de film qui se passait en France, un documentaire que je voulais tourner sous forme de fiction. J'ai fait un voyage en Afrique et je me suis trouvée confrontée à un nouveau projet purement documentaire: une communauté de Noirs américains, anciens du Vietnam, qui vivait au Sénégal. C'était un très beau sujet et je me suis dit que cette fois il ne fallait plus se raconter qu'on allait faire de la fiction. . . . Après *Chocolat*, je me suis rendu compte que les films qui parlent de la colonisation le font souvent à travers des enfants. . . . Si je voulais refaire un film sur la colonisation, le point de vue intéressant serait celui du boy. D'une certaine facon, il est traité comme un enfant et la littérature africaine a fait du domestique noir un personnage vraiment important.

[This autobiographical trace inserted itself more or less unconsciously. Before *Chocolat*, I had a film project that was to take place in France, a documentary that I wanted to shoot using a fictional form. I took a trip to Africa and found myself confronted with a new, entirely documentary project: a community of Black Americans, Vietnam veterans, living in Senegal. It was a beautiful subject and I told myself that, this time, I mustn't delude myself into thinking I was going to make a fiction film. . . . After *Chocolat*, I realized that films that speak of colonization often do so through the point of view of children. . . . If I wanted to make another film on colonization, the interesting point of view would be that of the "boy." In a certain way, he is treated like a child, and African literature has made Black domestic servants into very important characters.] [38]

Thus does the film problematize the impossible desire for reconciliation between colonizer and colonized, suggesting that the latter has inevitably been transformed, no longer defining the self in silent desire, as did the faithful Protée, nor in terms of marginalized dependency. The aptly named France must, then, ultimately come to terms with her own irrelevance in a postcolonial Africa, and she is framed as a marginalized, invisible bystander without subjectivity. Even the African American seeking his roots discovers that he is finally not African but American: "They've no use of my being here. Here I am nothing, a fantasy," he realizes. In that sense, *Chocolat* is readable as a mournful testament of reproach to French—and, for that matter, also European—inability to come to terms with its own colonialist presence.[39]

Denis's most recent film, *J'ai pas sommeil* (France, 1994) considers the colonial legacy of racist hatred from the perspective of Paulin of Guadeloupe, who is tried and convicted of murdering old women and condemned to prison, where he dies of AIDS. A monstrous person, he evinces no apparent hatred beneath a cool exterior; without identity, of indeterminate sexuality and indistinct race, he foreshadows a society that has become racially miscegenated—*métissée*.[40] His murderous tasks are carried out bloodlessly; he is courteous, calm, even thoughtful, recounting these acts with detachment and indifference. Denis's portrayal of this disturbing yet fascinating character leads the viewer to suspect that, behind the facade of apparent indifference, there might well be a structure of radical hatred seething in a character too stylized and cultivated to express it violently.

Pierre Schoendoerffer has argued that "avec *L'amant*, *Indochine* et *Dien Bien Phu*, la perle de notre empire colonial est revenue . . . au premier plan de l'actualité culturelle. Un vrai roman policier politico-historique raconte le piège ou tomba la France." [With *L'amant, Indochine,* and *Dien Bien Phu,* the pearl of our colonial Empire has returned . . . to the foreground of the cultural landscape. A real politico-historical thriller tells of the trap into which France fell.][41] Current preoccupations with postcoloniality and postnationality recall earlier debates such as the notion articulated in 1931, according to Dudley Andrew, of a French "native hunger for its native tongue,"[42] echoes of still earlier exhortations: "Aidez la France . . . colonisée par le cinéma américain" [Help France, colonized by American cinema].[43] These discursive and visual strategies for voicing the contested dislocations of difference—of race, gender, and ethnicity—negotiate the conflictual relationship between colonial "selves" and colonized "Others," seeking to complicate, problematize, and interrogate deeply internalized images produced by French cinema over the past century.[44] In their censored (1953) documentary film, *Les Statues meurent aussi,* Alain Resnais and Chris Marker observed:

> Il n'y a pas de rupture entre la civilisation africaine et la nôtre. Les visages de l'art sont tombés du même visage humain, comme la peau du serpent. Au-delà de leurs formes mortes, nous reconnaissons cette promesse, commune à toutes les grandes cultures, d'un homme victorieux du monde. Et Blancs et Noirs, notre avenir est fait de cette promesse.
>
> [There is no break between African civilization and our own. The faces of art have come out of the same human face, like a snake shedding its skin. Beyond their dead forms, we recognize this promise, common to all great cultures, of a man victorious over the world. And, White and Black, our future is made of this promise.][45]

Forty years later, cinematic works of the *colonial féminin* gesture toward redressing the geographical amnesia, cinematographic orientalism, and exoticizing distortions of a chapter of colonial history that may well mask unconscious French attachments and material interests in its former Empire. As childhood screen memories and family romances of the colonial moment, they re-produce the shock of recognition, at once intimate and violent, of France's repressed elsewhere: imperialism and its taboo image, the colonies.

NOTES

1. See *Images et colonies: Iconographie et propagande coloniale sur l'Afrique française de 1880 à 1962* (ouvrage sous la direction de N. Bancel, P. Blanchard [ACHAC] &

L. Gervereau [MHC-BDIC], UNESCO-Paris, 1993), 170–173. Feyder's adaptation of Pierre Benoît's *L'Atlantide* (1921), France's first true overseas cinematic adventure and a runaway hit, was shot on location in the deserts of Djilelli and Bab el Oued in improvised studios, Renoir's *Le Bled* (1929), originally titled *La Prise d'Alger*, was commissioned by the government and celebrated the centenary of the landing of French troops in Algeria. Other early examples of the genre include Jacques de Baroncelli's *SOS Sahara* (1936); Jean Gabin in legionnaire's uniform in Julien Duvivier's 1935 *La Bandera* and, in 1937, his classic *Pépé le Moko*, set in the Kasbah of Algiers; and Dimitri Kirsanoff's *Sables* (1927), a somber family melodrama situated in the thenceforth mythic setting of the Sahara desert. Perhaps best known among the films of the period is Léon Poirier's *L'Appel du silence* (1936), a monument of colonialist cinema financed by more than 100,000 French citizens; winner of the Grand Prix du Cinéma français, it portrayed the martyrdom of Viscount Charles de Foucauld, an officer who becomes a Trappist monk, a holy man among the Touaregs.

2. My translation. Cited in "L'image de l'Afrique dans le cinéma," in *Images et colonies*, 246.

3. See Marcel Oms, "L'Imaginaire colonial au cinéma," in *Images et colonies: Regards sur l'Afrique* (Paris: SYROS/ACHAC, Actes du colloque de janvier, 1993), 103. This volume considers the nature, discourse, and influence of colonial iconography in relation to colonial propaganda and the representation of Africans and of Africa in France, from 1920 to independence.

4. See Aimé Césaire, *Discours sur le colonialisme* (1955; Paris: Présence africaine, 1989); Jean-Claude Charles, *Le Corps noir* (Paris: Hachette, 1980); François Chavaldonne, *Le Cinéma colonial en Afrique du Nord: Naissance et fonctionnement d'un code* (Paris, 1982); Yves Courrière, *La Guerre d'Algérie en images*, 4 vols. (Paris: Le Club français du livre, 1972); Jean-Louis Fischer, *Races imagées et imaginaires* (Paris: Maspero, 1983); François Gère, "Imaginaire raciste, la mesure de l'homme," *Cahiers du cinéma*, no. 315, Paris 1980; Abdelghani Megherbi, *Les Algériens au miroir du cinéma colonial* (Alger: Ed SNED, 1982); Albert Memmi, *Portrait du colonisé* (Paris: Correa, 1957).

5. It is worth noting that British cinema took on far earlier than did the French the serious problems of colonization, beginning in 1900 at the time of the Boxer wars when the pioneers Robert William Paul and James Williamson invented the rudiments of film language by reconstructing in Brighton a brief version of *Attack of the Mission in China* (1901). During this same period, the Lumière Society was sending its cameramen to North Africa to film picturesque scenes for documentaries on themes such as the muezzin's prayers, an Arab market, the port of Algiers, the streets of Tlemcen, and the bay of Tunis *(Images et colonies*, 170).

6. Ginette Vincendeau, "Deconstructing Masculinity: Fathers and Daughters in French Cinema from the 20s to La Belle Noiseuse," in *Women and Film: A Sight and Sound Reader*, ed. Pam Cook and Philip Dodd (Philadelphia: Temple University Press), 156–163. There are, of course, important films made by second-generation North African emigrants: 1980s "Beur" (slang for "Arab") films include Mehdi Charef's *Le Thé au harem d'Archimède* and Abdelkrim Bahloul's *Le Thé à la menthe*, which bear witness to the racism experienced by first-generation emigrants, films in which the mother figure is central "both in the social world and in the imaginary one which links the Arab motherland and the French *patrie*," in con-

trast to male Beur films and literature, which typically display little if any gender awareness. For his perceptive analyses of Beur literature, I wish also to acknowledge Jean-François Llorens's unpublished doctoral dissertation, "La Voix des 'Beurs' dans la littérature française des années 1980: Une quête d'identité multiculturelle" (February 1995, University of Massachusetts, Amherst).

7. *Indochine* (France, 1992), directed by Régis Wargnier; screenplay by Wargnier and Catherine Cohen, Louis Gardel, and Erik Orsenna; lead actors: Catherine Deneuve, Vincent Perez, Linh Dan Pham, Jean Yanne; produced by Eric Heumann; a coproduction of Paradis Films, La Générale d'Images, Bac Films, Orly Films, TF1. Filmed in Vietnam, Malaysia, Switzerland, and France. 155 minutes. Wargnier suggests that, at the twilight of their rule in Indochina, the French saw themselves not as the region's colonizers—ravaging its natural and human resources—but as its foster parents, nourishing its "children" with the civilizing bounty of French culture.

A fictional reenactment, *Dien Bien Phu* (yet to be released in the United States) meticulously restages the climactic French defeat as if it were about only artillery and not national destinies. The film was shot with high production values, extensive location shooting, and cinematic techniques that elicit spectatorial identification (such as use of hand-held camera, zoom lenses, and personal testimonies and documents). It was supported by French government grants.

8. See John Talbott, *The War without a Name: France in Algeria, 1954–62* (London: Faber and Faber, 1981).

9. See Catherine Portuges, "Border Crossings: Recent Trends in Central and East European Cinema," *Slavic Review* 51, no. 3 (Fall 1992): 531–535.

10. See also Françoise Lionnet, *Autobiographical Voices: Race, Gender, Self-Portraiture* (Ithaca: Cornell University Press, 1989).

11. My translation. Quoted in *Images et colonies*, 247.

12. Benjamin Stora's *La Gangrène et l'oubli: La Mémoire de la guerre d'Algérie* (Paris: La Découverte, 1992) is one of the most important analyses of French collective memory of the war; his project is to seek reasons for the perceived absence of filmic texts that take up the Franco-Algerian conflict.

13. See, for example, J.-P. Jeancolas, "Le Cinéma des guerres coloniales," in his *Le Cinéma des Français: La Ve République (1958–1978)* (Paris: Stock, 1979), 156–162, in which the author discusses the "strange silence of the French cinema regarding decolonization."

14. For a compendium of women's cinema in French, see Paule Lejeune, *Le Cinéma des femmes* (Paris: Editions Atlas, 1987).

15. Denis's other films include *Man No Run* (documentary), *S'en fout la mort* (1990), and *J'ai pas sommeil* (1993). *Chocolat*: 1988, France/Germany/Cameroon; producer: Alain Belmondo; cinematographer: Robert Alazraki; screenplay: Claire Denis, Jean-Pol Fargeau; lead actors: Isaach de Bankolé, Giulia Boschi, François Cluzet, Jean-Claude Adelin. Cinéannuel/MK2 Productions/Cerito Films/SEPT/Caroline Productions/TFI Films, in cooperation with FODIC, Wim Wenders Production, with the participation of the Centre National de la Cinématographie, SOFICA SOFIMA.

16. See Duncan Petrie, ed., *Screening Europe* (London: BFI Publishing, 1992), 117–118, based on a conference in which Claire Denis participated and screened her film.

17. The disdain with which such treatments are viewed by some critics is well captured in *The Tradition of Women's Autobiography: From Antiquity to Present* (Boston: Twayne, 1986), in which Estelle Jelinek states: "Thirty years ago Richard Lillard listed ten techniques *not* to use when writing an autobiography: flashbacks, anecdotes, reconstructed scenes and dialogue, slabs of undigested diary or journal notes, set pieces on ancestors or parents, details of trips, random memories of youth, name dropping, racing too fast, and covering up—all characteristics of women's autobiographies" (188).

18. Petrie, *Screening Europe*, 66–67.

19. *Outremer* (Overseas) (France, 1990). Directed by Brigitte Roüan; screenplay (based on a story by Roüan) by Roüan, Phlippe Le Guay, Christian Rullier, Cedric Kahn; cinematography: Dominique Chapuis; sound: Dominique Hennequin; lead actors: Brigitte Roüan, Nicole Garcia, Marianne Basler, Philippe Galland, Yann Dedet, Bruno Todeschini; production: Daniel Champagon, with C.N.C. and the Ministère de la Culture et de la Communication.

20. Press notes, *Overseas*: interviews with Brigitte Roüan, (Aries film release), Dennis Davidson Associates, New York City, 1991, 3.

21. Press notes, *Overseas*, 3

22. A powerfully charged *mot d'ordre*, "Algérie Française" originated with the European settler community, linguistically suggested an inseparable connection between the territories in question, a term that de Gaulle scrupulously avoided in public pronouncements after his return to office in 1958.

23. The film's packaging for the American video market is typically misleading: "Three women with man trouble," proclaims the jacket cover, in what is surely one of the most egregious misrepresentations in recent memory, lending further credence to the French film industry's protective concern for its cultural patrimony.

24. See Hamid Naficy and Teshome Gabriel, eds., *Otherness and the Media: The Ethnography of the Imaged and the Imaged* (New York: Harwood, 1993).

25. I wish to thank Hamid Naficy for his illuminating presentation "Epistolarity and Transnationality" as a contribution to the panel "Imagining Nation: Film and the Construction of (Trans)national Identity," Society for Cinema Studies, New York City, 5 March 1995.

26. *Le Bal du gouverneur* (France, 1990, 1 hour, 38 minutes), directed by Marie-France Pisier; scenario: Pisier, from her novel (Grasset); cinematography: Denis Lenoir; music: Khalil Chahine; editing: Claudine Merlin; sound design: Pierre Lenoir; costumes: Christian Gasc; leading actors: Kristin Scott-Thomas, Didier Flamand, Laurent Grevill, Jacques Seyres, Vanessa Wagner; production: Philippe Carcassonne (Cinea) and FR3 Films Production, with Sofinergie, Investimage, CNC, and the participation of the Territory of New Caledonia.

27. *L'Amant* (*The Lover*, 1992, France/U.K., in English), from the novel by Marguerite Duras; screenplay by Annaud and Gerard Brach; director of photography: Robert Fraisse; production design: Thanh At Hoang; costume design: Yvonne Sassinot de Nesle; music: Gabriel Yared; historian: Son Nam; lead actors: Jane March, Tony Leung, Frederique Meininger, Arnaud Giovaninetti, Jeanne Moreau (narrator); Xiem Mang. Claude Berri presentation, Renn/Burrill/Films A2 Co-Production. The film was shot primarily on location in Vietnam. The French colonized Indochina, which encompassed Vietnam, Cambodia, and Laos, in 1897, during which time some 40,000 French colonials presided over the 19 million

inhabitants of Vietnam. Marguerite Duras's novel *L'Amant* was released in Europe in 1984.

In what appears to be a paradoxical gesture in the last decade, the French government, in conjunction with European institutions, has pursued a film policy that encourages the making of high-budget productions and coproductions in English not unlike the Hollywood model. The purpose of this policy, it would seem, is to capture a larger share of the global market and to increase French film exports, especially to the United States. In place of a culturally specific paradigm linked to national traditions and aspirations, the new globally oriented French films would attempt to eliminate the mark of national difference or transform culturally bound elements into mere folkloric visualizations. A well-known case in point: Jean-Jacques Annaud's *L'Amant* exploits a media-popular theme—interracial sexuality; a box office success in France and abroad (9 million viewers), the film has only moments of French language.

28. My translation. Marie-France Pisier, *Cahiers du cinéma*, no. 434 (July–August 1990): 30.

29. My translation. Ibid.

30. My translation. Ibid., 31–33.

31. My translation. Ibid.

32. *Mui Du Du Xanh/The Scent of the Green Papaya*, directed by Tran Anh Hung (France, 1993); written by Tran, in Vietnamese with English subtitles, 104 minutes); winner of the prestigious Camera d'Or (Best First Film) at the Cannes Film Festival and the first film submitted by Vietnam for consideration for the Academy Awards competition for Best Foreign Film.

33. Cited in Alice Cross, "Portraying the Rhythm of the Vietnamese Soul: An Interview with Tran Anh Hung," *Cinéaste* 20, no. 3 (1994): 35–37.

34. Tran professes understanding and respect for the sacrifices of women: "I don't believe it is for us to say to such women, 'Everything that you have lived up to now is an error'" (ibid.).

35. Duras wrote a sequel to *L'Amant*, *L'Amant de la Chine du nord*, also a bestseller, presumably as a comment on Jean-Jacques Annaud's appropriation of her novel for his film *L'Amant*.

36. See Catherine Portuges, "Seeing Subjects: Women Directors and Cinematic Autobiography," in *Life/Lines: Theorizing Women's Autobiography*, ed. B. Brodzki and C. Schenck (Ithaca: Cornell University Press, 1988), 338–350.

37. When asked about his feelings about other recent French films about Vietnam, such as *L'Amant* and *Indochine*, Tran responds: "These are films that worked commercially, which means they have a certain number of good qualities. What they said about Vietnam, however, is uninteresting to me. The stories could have taken place in Kenya. The humanity of the Vietnamese people is not visible through those films; all they have is a setting" (cited in Cross, "Portraying the Rhythm of the Vietnamese Soul," 36).

38. My translation. *Cahiers du Cinéma*, no. 434 (July–August 1990): 30.

39. With regard to film production in Africa, according to African film scholar Manthia Diawara, "African cinema does not exist because film distribution is not in Africa's hands . . . nor would I put all the blame on foreign distributors, as French scholars and administrators often do. Rather, I propose to analyze the structures of

film production since colonialism and the different stances toward film production promoted by governments and individuals in the colonialist countries and then later in the African nations" (Manthia Diawara, *African Cinema: Politics and Culture* [Bloomington: Indiana University Press, 1992], viii–ix). Diawara emphasizes the role played by the Federation Panafricaine des Cinéastes as well as "new measures taken collectively or by individual countries to liberate African cinema from its colonial trappings."

40. For a related work, see Kim Lefèvre's autobiographical *récit, Métisse blanche* (Paris: Editions Barrault, 1989), which traces the childhood and adolescence—the exclusion and humiliation—of a Eurasian child born in colonial Vietnam. The author has lived in Paris since leaving Saigon in 1960, returning for the first time in thirty years in 1990, an experience recorded in her second book, *Retour à la saison des pluies* (Paris: Editions Barrault, 1990). In the first text, the first-person narrator places at its center the presence of her Eurasian *corps métis:* "Je suis née, paraît-il, à Hanoi un jour de printemps, peu avant la Seconde Guerre mondiale, de l'union éphémère entre une jeune Annamite et un Français" [I was born, it seems, in Hanoi on a spring day just before the second world war, of the ephemeral union of a young Annamite and a Frenchman] (17).

41. "With *L'Amant, Indochine,* and *Dien Bien Phu,* the pearl of our colonial empire has returned . . . to the foreground of the cultural landscape. A real politico-historical thriller tells of the trap into which France fell" (quoted in *Le Match de Paris,* June 1993, 16). Characterizing the battle of Dien Bien Phu, Schoendoerffer cites Jean-Pierre Dannaud in his book *Guerre morte,* dedicated to those of all races who fell for France in Indochina: "Commencée dans l'ignorance, menée d'abord clandestinement, continuée dans l'équivoque, perpétuée par inertie autant que pour l'honneur, sans vraie volonté de vaincre en France et sans moyens véritables de vaincre sur place, la guerre d'Indochine s'est terminée à Dien Bien Phu dans l'écroulement du crépuscule des dieux" [Begun in ignorance, fought at first in clandestine form, continued in uncertainty, perpetuated by inertia as much as for honor, lacking the will to conquer in France, and without real means of conquering in the region, the Indochinese war ended in Dien Bien Phu in the collapse of the twilight of the gods]. My translation.

42. Dudley Andrew, presentation for "National Cinemas Revisited," conference at Ohio University, Athens, Ohio, October 1993.

43. I wish to thank Jens Ulff-Melle of Brandeis University for bringing to my attention the existence of French manifestos from the 1920s on this subject. Yet in a postnational view, the contested terrain of film is demonstrably no longer a national but rather a global cultural product; just as France's GATT stance speaks to a resistance to Hollywood by insisting upon the right not to be destroyed by the flood of Hollywood's images, so, too, does it mask a still unresolved postcolonial tension between a renascent hegemonic desire in the realm of the moving image, attested by France's growing financial involvements in international coproductions in Eastern Europe and Africa.

44. Dislocated and decentered identity is a prevalent theme of these directors, considered here to include such colonial-era thematized films as *La Bataille d'Alger* (Gillo Pontecorvo, Italy and Algeria, 1962), *Rue Cases-Nègres* (Sugar Cane Alley, Euzhan Palcy, Martinique), and *Muriel* (Alain Resnais, France and Algeria, 1962),

among the most important works on memory and the only one of its time to address the issue of torture during the Algerian war. It is also possible to read Resnais's 1955 documentary *Nuit et brouillard* (Night and Fog) as an allegory of the French army's activities in Algeria, for when questioned about its politics, the director responded that "the whole point was Algeria" (Alan Williams, *Republic of Images: A History of French Filmmaking* [Cambridge: Harvard University Press, 1992], 369). For his part, Jeancolas lists nearly a hundred filmmakers whose work was released between 1958 and 1962, thereby qualifying as part of an *oeuvre* pronouncing itself on the Algerian question, including Jean-Luc Godard (*Le Petit Soldat*), Chris Marker, whose *Le Joli mai* (1962) was the only film at the time to give a voice to Algerians living in Paris, and Alain Cavalier (*Le Combat dans l'île* [1962]).

45. My translation.

Empire as Myth and Memory

SIX   Naomi Greene

One of the most striking phenomena in recent French cinema is, certainly, the number and range of works devoted to France's colonial past. In this essay, I would like to concentrate on two films that deal less with the actual history of that past than with memories of it—in particular, with memories of the traumatic era of decolonization in Algeria. I am speaking now of Pierre Schoendoerffer's *Le Crabe-tambour* (The Drummer Crab, 1977) and Brigitte Roüan's *Outremer* (Overseas, 1991). Although seemingly very different from one another, both films filter the era that marked the end of French rule in Algeria (although *Le Crabe-tambour* also deals with Indochina) through the memories of two social groups who were deeply affected by these events: that is, the military (*Le Crabe-tambour*) and the Pieds-Noirs, or French settlers, in Algeria (*Outremer*).

In embracing a perspective that is clearly partial and subjective, these films raise several vital issues. Most obviously, perhaps, they suggest some of the ways in which the memories of individuals are shaped, transformed—indeed, created—by a shared vision of the past, driven by its own logic and desire. At the same time, the opaque and private shapes assumed by memories in these films indicate some of the difficulties involved in remembering, or mourning, one of the most divisive wars in French history. And these issues, in turn, lead into broader considerations concerning the very nature of memory—especially the memories of social groups such as those represented here—in the contemporary world.

In looking at the intensely private and coded nature of the memories evoked in *Le Crabe-tambour* and *Outremer*, it is important to keep in mind just how difficult it has been to remember, or discuss, France's long struggle to retain Algeria. In fact, the difficulties of "remembering" the Algerian war constitute the subject of a series of essays found in an important historical work, *La Guerre d'Algérie et les Français*, published in 1990. In one of these essays, Robert Frank notes that "although the wars of Indochina and Algeria were the longest and the most recent of the four wars France has fought in the twentieth-century, they appear the most forgotten. Despite the fact that the Algerian war has left burning traces in our memory, or perhaps because of this, the process of commemoration has taken place in the most difficult manner."[1] If France's humiliating defeat is one reason commemoration has been difficult, the unpopularity of the Algerian war is certainly another. It was an unpopular war for a variety of reasons. While only a minority of French people actively sympathized with the Algerians' struggle for independence, many more saw the army's routine use of torture as a chilling reminder of Nazi atrocities. Moreover, while Algeria was technically French, to most French people on the mainland the fields of battle seemed distant and unknown, devoid of emotional resonance. Deemed a "phantom" war or a "war without a name" because of de Gaulle's refusal to admit that France could be at war with one of its own *départements*, it was, above all, a struggle without a clear and compelling message. And to come back to the question of memory, how could one mourn or commemorate a struggle without such a message? "The survivors," to cite Robert Frank once again, "could celebrate the fact that they did not die for nothing. But by honoring the memory of their fallen comrades, they would implicitly be asking the terrible and, by definition, the most taboo of questions: why did they die? . . . It is because this question is basically unbearable that this war is uncommemorable."[2]

Given the divisiveness of the war, the fact that it has still to find a place in national memory, it is hardly surprising that only those directly involved—like the army or the Pieds-Noirs—should retain vivid memories of it. Memories all the more vivid, perhaps, since the vast majority of their countrymen and women wanted so clearly to forget. But it is also true that these groups do, indeed, have much to remember. After years of anguish and struggle, the Pieds-Noirs—many of whom were small farmers or businessmen—were forced to flee to France, to a "mother country" many had never seen. Not only did these refugees lose home and country but they often found little sympathy or understanding awaiting them when they arrived in France. Blamed for an unpopular war, they were frequently cast in the role of the "Other," a role that they had always assigned to Arabs. Small wonder that the rage many continue to feel has helped fuel the extreme Right in France or that, as *New York Times* commentator Marlise Simons phrased it in 1992, many still "ached for Algeria thirty years after the war."[3]

In the case of the army, feelings of bitterness and betrayal went, perhaps, deeper still. Enlisted men and professional soldiers may have viewed the war differently—a "dirty war" for the former, for the latter it was a defeat that could have been avoided—but both, as historian Isabelle Lambert notes, felt "abandoned and rejected" by their country.[4] Moreover, the professional army—which often included men who had served in Indochina as well as Algeria—may well have been the sector of the French population, as historian Pierre Nora suggests, most deeply attached to the idea of a national empire. "In the end," observes Nora, "the overseas army is the only sector of the national community to have lived the colonial problem as a national problem."[5] And the resentment of the professional military was exacerbated by the conviction that Algeria was but a terrible replay of Indochina. Professional soldiers felt that they had been twice betrayed by the government's vacillations and lack of resolve. "It was in fact during the conflict in Indochina," says historian Alain Ruscio, "that the 'army's malaise' began, an army betrayed by the civilian population, by politics, by defeatists."[6] When de Gaulle finally signed the treaties ending the Algerian war, this "malaise" erupted into violence: disaffected veterans attempted an aborted coup d'état, or putsch, against the Republic and rallied to the OAS (Organisation de l'armée secrète), a "secret army" that resorted to terrorist tactics in Algeria and on the mainland in its continuing efforts to bring down the civilian government, which, the veterans felt, had abandoned them and betrayed the best interests of France.

In light of these events, it is not difficult to see why many Pieds-Noirs as well as many veterans should have been haunted by what happened in Algeria long after the war itself had ended, long after most of the settlers, in particular, had established new lives for themselves in France. Events that barely touched many of their compatriots determined the course that lives would take, the shapes that identities would assume. But if memories remained vivid, so, too, did they remain difficult to express. Denied entry into a shared past, imbued with the guilt and unease surrounding the war, they became even "guiltier" as the social and cultural climate changed. As the very project of colonialism became imbued with opprobrium, memories of the colonial past—and, especially, memories infused with nostalgia for a colonial order now recognized as unjust—became less "admissible" than ever before.

It is precisely this dilemma—that is, both the need, and the difficulty, of remembering and representing a past imbued with guilt—that seems to have inspired the particular shapes and impulses assumed by memory in *Le Crabe-tambour* and *Outremer*. Neither film leaves any doubt that the past remains vivid and alive: permeated by a sense of intense melancholy and nostalgia, these films depict survivors for whom time has stopped, men and women who continue to live in the past. But at the same time this past with all its weight of guilt and unease has been transformed by memory. That is, while the precise historical context that gave rise to the melancholy that is felt here is not hidden, its exact outlines remained blurred. Assuming an intensely private and subjective cast, memory leads us away from the continuities of history and into an atemporal zone marked by the absolute cast of dreams at once collective and individual. Drawn away from the clearings and explanations of history, we enter an ambiguous world of private symbols and allusions, a mysterious world marked by the displacements and repetitions of dreams. It is a world where the most troubling and "guilty" aspects of the colonial past—particularly the scandal at its heart, that is, the relationship between oppressed and oppressor are consistently obscured or erased. Drawn into the undertow of memory, we enter a world dominated by a melancholy nostalgia that, unable to represent the true object of its desire, takes the form of existential longings for a dreamlike moment of youth and innocence, for a world before the fall from grace. Historical trauma is veiled and disguised even as forgetting is no longer a passive process but instead, to borrow a phrase from Michel de Certeau, an "action directed against the past."[7] Here, as critic Alain-Gérard Slama has written in regard to several novels dealing with Algeria, nostalgia impels memory not to "confront" but rather to "reject" history.[8]

While both *Le Crabe-tambour* and *Outremer* "reject" history, they do so in different ways. In contrast with *Le Crabe-tambour*, which takes us into the realm of collective dreams and myth, *Outremer* pulls us into the narrow tunnel of the individual psyche, into the subjective and intensely private landscape of haunted dreams. This essential difference, in turn, may well be linked to what is the most obvious point of contrast between the two films: that is, while the world of *Outremer* is dominated by women, that of *Le Crabe-tambour* is almost exclusively masculine. Reflecting Schoendoerffer's own experience in the military in Indochina (where he was made a prisoner of war at the time of the decisive French defeat at Dien Bien Phu), *Le Crabe-tambour* focuses on the career officers who fought in France's last colonial wars.

The three principal protagonists of *Le Crabe-tambour* are, in fact, present or former naval officers. As the film opens, two of them are crossing the Atlantic aboard a vessel of the French merchant marine. One, who narrates much of the film, is the ship's doctor; the other, a man whose mortal illness ensures that this will be his last journey, is her captain. Slowly, they become friends as they reminisce about their experiences; as they do so, remembered flashbacks disrupt the present and transport us to the past that so obsesses them. It was a past, we gradually learn, dominated by a former comrade of theirs, Wilsdorf. Presently captain of a fishing boat, Wilsdorf served with the doctor in Indochina and with the captain in Algeria. As fragments of the past are brought to life, we learn of the bleak and traumatic moment that dramatically altered the captain's life, as well as that of Wilsdorf. This critical moment—which, significantly, is never seen—was that of the aborted putsch in Algeria. At that time, the paths of the captain and Wilsdorf diverged radically: unlike the captain, Wilsdorf chose to join those comrades who rebelled against the civilian government, an act that led to imprisonment and expulsion from the navy. While the captain refused to join the rebels' ranks, the sympathy he obviously felt for Wilsdorf and his cause prompted him to promise the latter that whatever the outcome of the putsch, he would resign from the navy. His subsequent failure to keep this promise—a failure that he sees as a kind of betrayal—has troubled him ever since. On this, his last voyage, he wants nothing more than to bid his former comrade-in-arms a final adieu. In what is probably the film's climactic moment, the captain's wish is granted when, for a brief instant, his ship passes Wilsdorf's fishing vessel on the high seas and the two men speak, from afar, one last time.

Even this brief summary suggests, surely, some of the deep-seated emotional currents—of honor and betrayal, of melancholy and decline—associated with the memories of former military men. The protagonists embody those veterans who became known as *les soldats perdus* (lost soldiers), whose lives were shattered by their experiences in Indochina, and especially Algeria. Prisoners of a traumatic past, they suffer from a sense of lost hopes and futile sacrifices. As if in limbo, these eternal nomads now spend their days in endless journeys from one end of the globe to another. Reading from his cherished Bible, the captain repeats the question that haunts them all. "What have you done with your gifts?" he sadly intones. Still guided by the codes of honor and stoicism, of bravery and solidarity, that held sway in the military, they do battle against that most elemental of foes: the sea. A long and beautiful sequence of the ship's prow breaking up ice floes embodies the harshness of their struggle against freezing temperatures, gales, and high seas. At the helm of his ship, the captain is in his element, for he is a master of waves and tides, a lover of the sea who will return to land only to die.

Like the captain, few of these restless adventurers would exchange their lonely and harsh existence for the ease of life on land. This is a sentiment that Schoendoerffer appears to share, for the single view of Paris afforded by *Le Crabe-tambour* depicts a desolate city peopled by prostitutes and marked by ugly posters and seedy bars. And the sense of decline implicit in this sequence—a decline associated by the military with the end of Empire—reverberates throughout the film. It is no accident that the men are bringing mail and medical assistance to the rocky promontory of St. Pierre off the Canadian coast: one of France's last colonies, this snow-clad coast is a barren reminder of a lost empire that once extended throughout North America.[9] Neither is it mere happenstance that the broadcasts that issue forth from their radio describe the last spasms of another doomed colonial struggle—that of the war in Vietnam.

But the bleaker the present, the more the past seems to assume the glowing intensity of a lost paradise. Significantly, perhaps, of all the films dealing with this period, it is *Le Crabe-tambour*—which springs from what historian Claude Liazu calls the most "impossible" of memories or discourses concerning the war—that does most to transform the past. (For Liazu, the military discourse is so "impossible" precisely because it contracts the nation's "conscience and its historical imaginary.")[10] In no other film is the contrast between past and present so stark, the loss of youth and hope, of grace and innocence, so absolute. We are reminded of it each time a flashback takes us from the harsh gray seas of the North Atlantic to the lush greens and oneiric mists of Asia, from the ice and cold of the present to the warmth and beauty of the past. Seen through the lens of an all-powerful and transforming memory, Asia is not a war zone of enemy ambushes, of mud and grenades, but a dreamlike land of soft mists and hazy rivers. "All these wars," writes director Schoendoerffer revealingly in a 1969 novel, "are sadly always the same: we slogged through the mud, we waited forever, we shot, they died. That is what war is. . . . But the wind has blown away the odor of the corpses and all that remains in our memory is the blaze of youth."[11]

But the ugly realities of war—as well as the terrible moment of the putsch—are not, of course, the only ones that vanish in the "blaze of youth" conferred by memory. Telling omissions and ambiguities work to erase the most troubling recollections of the past. Some of the most subtle of these involve the film's depiction of native peoples. For, like the "odor of corpses," these people too—people whose very presence serves as a reminder of the historical scandal at the heart of colonialism—have also disappeared from a remembered past. They appear in fact in only two scenes—scenes that say far more about Schoendoerffer's taste for myth and legend (including the racial stereotypes they often contain) than about his taste for historical realities. In one of these scenes, Wilsdorf is captured by a Black tribe after a shipwreck off the coast of Africa. At first he is their helpless prisoner, exhibited in a cage like a prized and rare specimen. But at a critical moment he becomes their talismanic leader when he teaches them how to aim their guns and kill their enemies. If this scene hints at the myth of White supremacy (Wilsdorf is a far better warrior than the natives), the other encounter raises the specter of Asian barbarism. Here, Wilsdorf visits a native village, only to suddenly discover that some of the faces he sees around the fire belong to decapitated heads, which are leering at him from spikes.

A reminder of Asian "Otherness," this last scene also seems a deliberate echo of a similar episode in Joseph Conrad's *Heart of Darkness*. (Interestingly, this sequence from *The Heart of Darkness* also inspired similar scenes in Malraux's 1930 novel *La Voie royale* and in another film that does much to turn a divisive war—that of Vietnam—into myth: that is, Francis Ford Coppola's *Apocalypse Now*.) And, indeed, *Le Crabe-tambour* says far more about Schoendoerffer's love for the mythic adventures told by writers of the last century—by Conrad and Melville, and by Jules Verne—than about the recent historical past. Wilsdorf himself is hardly an ordinary mortal. Instantly set apart from the others by dress and demeanor—in the first scene he is seen in gleaming white holding a black cat—his character was, in fact, based on a legendary French soldier who was imprisoned at the time of the putsch. A kind of romantic adventurer, a latter-day T. E. Lawrence who has put home and country far behind him, he cries out, "Old Europe, to hell with you," as he prepares to sail a Chinese junk halfway around the world. Endowed with as many lives as his mysterious cat, he has performed deeds admired by seamen all over the globe. Indeed, whenever his name is mentioned, someone has yet another exploit to recount, another tale to add to his legend. In fact, if this way of describing his life—that is, through flashbacks remembered by different people—forces us to decipher and reconstruct the past as we would a dream, so too, as French critic François de la Bretèque has astutely observed, does it create the sense that we are watching a legend unfold. Since each character recalls a different moment in Wilsdorf's past, notes de la Bretèque, we learn about his life "in a fragmented and indirect way rather than in a strict chronological order. This remarkable *procédé* gives him a mythic aura and transforms the search for him into a symbolic quest. He incarnates the past of each of the protagonists and, beyond that, of colonial France herself."[12]

While the daring figure of Wilsdorf dominates *Le Crabe-tambour*, other aspects of the film clearly reinforce its epic cast, the way in which memory transforms history into myth. Shot in beautiful color by master camera-man Raoul Coutard, the film has the temporal and spatial sweep of an epic as it takes us from youth to old age and from one end of the globe to the other. As de la Bretèque goes on to note, the very fact that the same few characters repeatedly meet one another in totally different parts of the world creates the sense of a ritualistic drama that takes the entire globe for its stage. In this sense, the current journey portrayed in the film—a jour-ney that takes the men from the Old World to the New even as it leads to the final act in the captain's life, that is, the meeting with Wilsdorf—takes on symbolic resonance. As compelling as the search for the great white whale in *Moby Dick* or the terrifying trek into the heart of darkness taken by Conrad's protagonist, this voyage takes place not in the zone of history but in that of myth. When the captain finally meets Wilsdorf, the leg-endary being who has haunted him for so many years, everything in the scene—the movement of the waves, the distance that still separates the two ships—heightens the epic cast of their encounter. Even Wilsdorf's ship, which bears two painted eyes upon its prow in the Asian manner, ap-pears to be a fabulous sea creature as it slowly comes into the captain's line of vision. Although their final adieu cannot help but recall the political events that drove a wedge between former comrades, those events are sub-merged by the haunting mood of the scene. Imbued with all the melan-choly of approaching separation and death, their meeting speaks, above all, of failed hopes and brave sacrifices, of exile and memory, of life and death. Here, human life, seen against the boundless and eternal landscape of the sea, is as brief as the greetings exchanged by passing ships.

Like *Le Crabe-tambour*, *Outremer* was also inspired, in part, by memo-ries drawn from the life of its director.[13] And, no less than Schoendoerf-fer's film—in which remembered flashbacks constantly eclipse the pres-ent—the very structure of *Outremer* bears witness to the power of such memories and the spell they cast upon the present. In *Outremer*, three sep-arate narratives draw us into the past obsessively and insistently, for each successive narrative returns to moments and events evoked by the preced-ing one. Each time, these moments are seen from a different perspective, since each narrative is focused on one of three Pied-Noir sisters living in Algeria at the time of *les événements* (as the Algerian struggle for indepen-dence was euphemistically called). Almost invariably, the moments and events depicted involve deep-seated currents of passion and longing, of love and desire. Even as this intensely subjective focus, as well as the repetitions inherent in the tripartite structure, confer a dreamlike sense upon the moments depicted, the elliptical and partial nature of each narrative gives rise to mysterious ambiguities and omissions. Once again, the past we encounter resembles a dream that must be painfully deciphered and reconstructed. Only gradually, with difficulty and uncertainty, do we begin to understand the complex psychological mechanisms that govern the sisters' inner lives.

The first narrative reflects the perspective of the oldest sister, Zon, who has married a naval officer. Devoted to husband, home, and children, she seems to lead the most conventional life of the three. But soon it is clear that disturbing emotional currents lie below the surface. Consumed by longing for her husband—who is absent much of the time—she is unable to accept his death when he is declared missing in action. (She makes a melodramatic and disturbing bargain with God: she will give up her children, she declares, if only he will return her husband to her.) Before long, she herself is taken ill with cancer and, in a very strange and troubling deathbed scene, she dons her husband's uniform and writhes in spasms of agony (which have a strange sexual cast) on the bed they have shared before falling, lifeless, to the ground.

After Zon's death, the film's focus shifts to the second sister, Malène. Once again, on the surface all is well: Malène has made a "good" marriage with a wealthy man who adores her. But he is an ineffectual dreamer and so, despite herself, she must play the "man": that is, make all the decisions and do all the work on the beloved farm they own. Ultimately, her refusal to leave this farm leads to her death: while doing an errand in the car she is killed by an Arab bullet that was probably intended for her husband.

Only the third and youngest of the sisters, Gritte, refuses to follow the conventional path taken by her sisters. Spurning eligible and attractive suitors, she takes an Arab rebel as a lover. But she is not immune to violence and death: she loses not only her sisters but also her lover, who is shot by French soldiers when he is on his way to see her one night. The psychic toll of all the horror she has endured is made very clear in the final scene of the film. In a dramatic temporal ellipse, a shot of Gritte about to leave Algeria is followed by one of her standing, years later, in a Parisian church, where she is about to be married. As the camera explores the vast hall, the past comes to life: the whispering voices of her dead sisters are heard and, soon, their ghostly faces are seen superimposed on the stone walls. In this haunted atmosphere, all the death and violence Gritte has experienced seem to reach out into the present and smother it. For when she is asked to take the marriage vows she hesitates, unable—it seems—to begin life anew, to put down new roots to replace those so brutally severed in the past. She remains mute, paralyzed, as the camera backs away; the credits appear on the screen while the voices of little girls are heard singing the ditties of childhood.

The film ends, then, on the same note of terrible nostalgia and melancholy that permeates *Le Crabe-tambour*. Like Wilsdorf and his comrades, Gritte is a survivor, condemned to spend what remains of her life in limbo. While Schoendoerffer's film is haunted by the "blaze of youth," *Outremer* looks still further back in time—to the innocence and joy of a paradisaical childhood. Once again, we enter a world where time loses its precise chronology and gives way, instead, to the wrenching contrast between past and present, between a luminous "before" and a dark and somber "after." If the children's songs that are heard at the end of *Outremer* recall the innocence and joy of a world before the fall, the final scene embodies the powerful charge of loss and exile at the heart of Pied-Noir memory.

In an attempt to discover the general shapes taken by this memory, more than a quarter of a century after the end of the Algerian war a French historian, Anne Roche, conducted a series of interviews with former Pieds-Noirs. The responses of those with whom she spoke leave little doubt that the terrible contrast between past and present—the contrast that is so dramatically embodied in *Outremer*—continues to haunt the vast majority of Pieds-Noirs. "The interviews as a whole," observes Roche, "clearly bring to light the creation of a 'before' and an 'after' which . . . always function in the same way. . . .'Before' is strongly valorized and the subject of nostalgia; 'after' is seen pejoratively."[14] Nor, according to Roche, was this the only dimension of Pied-Noir memory that finds a powerful echo in *Outremer*. Compelling resemblances link the memories voiced by Roche's subjects to those embodied in the film in two other vital domains. One concerns the ways in which the history of the war itself has been remembered; the other bears upon the all-important relationship between Arabs and Pieds-Noirs.

In the course of her interviews, Roche was struck by the ambiguities and omissions that seemed to cloud the memories of her subjects (most of whom were women) whenever it came to these domains. She notes, for example, that her subjects appeared to repress the precise outlines of the convulsions that had overtaken Algeria. While most of them displayed a "myopic concentration" on the details of daily life in Algeria, their recollections of historical and political events were hazy and confused. Most notably, she observes, they lacked a sense of the "different phases of the way [and] a synthesizing view of the forces at work." [15] Along with this refusal to confront what had happened went a continuing need to repress the memory of social injustice, the enormous social gap that existed between them and the Arabs. Hence they remembered Algeria as a "paradise without colonial sin," a land where everyone, Arabs and Europeans, lived in harmony and plenty. When confronted, however, with the obvious discrepancy between these happy memories of an "idyllic world" and the brutal facts of rebellion and war, they tended to establish a dichotomy between a few individual "good" Arabs (who bore witness that French rule was a benevolent one) and Arabs seen as an "undifferentiated, confusing, and probably manipulated mass." [16]

It is, precisely, in these two critical areas that *Outremer* reveals the same complicated mechanisms of repression and denial as those displayed by Roche's interviewees. Indeed, virtually every aspect of this film works to draw us away from the shared realm of history—a realm marked by temporal markers and clear outlines—into the subjective realm of memory and dream. As suggested earlier, the obsessive repetitions inherent in the tripartite narrative structure as well as the elliptical and mysterious nature of each narrative all suggest a world composed of primal moments of longing and desire. Shifting perspectives and temporal gaps, mysteries that are not always elucidated by a subsequent narrative, all conspire to disorient us, to keep us off balance, to deny us the sense of ordered chronology necessary to a historical overview. The convulsions of history may be felt in the violence that invades the sisters' very bodies, but the historical context for this private violence never comes into focus. Instead, we are led into psychic crevices where desires and feelings condition perception itself. Even time is subject to the play of emotions, the pull of fear or desire. "Sometimes," writes critic Jacques Siclier, "time is suspended in illusions, sometimes it stretches out due to the effect of precise dangers and changes in the relationship of French and Arabs." [17]

This intensely subjective realm is one in which vivid and fragmented images assume the private codes, the symbolic resonances, of those in dreams. All of this is dramatically announced in the film's disorienting and mysterious opening sequence, which, repeated at critical junctures throughout the film, becomes a kind of leitmotiv. A shot of barbed wire seen through the credits is followed by one of three young women in a small boat waving to someone. Abruptly, this gives way to the close-up of a man in a white uniform. But, contrary to all expectations, as the next shot reveals, he is not the person to whom they were waving. Instead of establishing us in space and time, this opening has left us with a series of questions. Who and where are these women? To whom are they waving and why? Although we must wait before these questions are answered, from the first it is clear that the dreamlike images of the opening embody the deeply felt emotions that run throughout the film: a sense of limbo (the open sea); of claustrophobia (the barbed wire); of lost innocence (the three young girls in the boat); of exile and separation (the sea).

Marked, as this sequence suggests, by the logic of dreams, *Outremer* is, significantly, at its most mysterious, its most ambiguous and elliptical, when it comes to the darkest areas of memory: that is, in those scenes that reflect the vital relationship between Arabs and Pieds-Noirs. It is here—where the director's vision appears to merge with that of her protagonists—that we enter the most troubling zones of the film, the underlying strata of ambivalence and denial. Not surprisingly, it is also here that the gap between the different layers of the film—between attitudes that are voiced and overt and those embodied at a deeper, formal level—is most intense.

On the surface, of course, the film appears to criticize Pied-Noir attitudes toward Arabs. Not only does it appear to mock the sisters' racist remarks but it also depicts a love affair—between a European woman and an Arab—that breaks one of the most fundamental taboos of the colonial system. Still, when it comes to what we see rather than what we hear or are told, disturbing ambiguities and omissions begin to make themselves felt. The sisters' view of Arabs may appear ludicrous; but when Arabs themselves are seen they invariably correspond to Pied-Noir stereotypes: shadowy and menacing, they suddenly materialize from nowhere and mutter among themselves in a conspiratorial fashion. It might be argued, of course, that we are seeing them from a Pied-Noir perspective: that is, they *appear* menacing to the sisters and other Europeans. But the film gives no indications that the view we are seeing of the Arabs is the view through the sisters' eyes—above all, through their fears. Without such indications, the power of film is such that we tend to believe in the reality of what is shown. In this case, this means that we too see the Arabs as faceless members of a conspiratorial and frightening group or (as Roche has it) an "undifferentiated mass."

The suspicion that this portrayal of Arabs reflects the director's own ambivalence(s)—be they conscious or unconscious—is confirmed, moreover, by several critical scenes. In one such scene, the Arab laborers on the farm owned by the middle sister and her husband—a farm to which she is passionately attached—begin to mutiny as one after another expresses discontent when handed his meager wages. Faced with their anger, the sister expresses great surprise; she can do nothing, she says, because it is her husband who determines their wages. Our first reaction is to believe her and to sympathize with her plight: she is the main character, with whom we tend to identify. But with reflection come disturbing questions. After all, the film has clearly established that she, and not her husband, runs the farm. Why, then, does she immediately blame him? Since she appears to be genuinely shocked and distressed, it is difficult to take her response as a calculated and self-protective lie. But that leaves only one conclusion: she believes in her professed innocence precisely because she desperately wants to ignore, to repress, the terrible truths of social injustice. Like those interviewed by Roche, she too wants to believe that everyone in Algeria, including the Arabs on her farm, lived in harmony and plenty. And doesn't the profoundly ambiguous nature of this scene—which somehow invites us to believe that she is telling the truth—suggest that the director herself shares this thirst for innocence?

In this respect, it is telling that the scenes depicting the forbidden love affair between the youngest sister, Gritte, and the Arab rebel are the most ambiguous and elliptical of the entire film. True, all the men in *Outremer* are vague figures. But each of the other men—be he a suitor or a husband—has a clearly marked identity, a psychological profile. Not so the Arab. Mute and spectral, he is but an icon of passion, the embodiment of European desires as well as, perhaps, fears. Silent, rough, and grimy, in what appears to be their second encounter (although even this is not made clear), he suddenly appears on the road next to Gritte and wordlessly pulls her toward him as if he meant her bodily harm. After this episode, they are seen together for the briefest of sequences. Since Gritte's sisters have been depicted with their husbands in intimate moments, this omission is disquieting. Does it mean that even the director cannot imagine how an Arab and a Frenchwoman would behave together? Or what they would talk about? Or does the silence of the film reflect the taboos that cling to the affair? Furthermore, it is odd that in a film which dissects the slightest tremor of the psyche, the motives for their affair remain opaque: Is her passion for him mixed with rebellion? With guilt? And his love for her is even more mysterious. Is it motivated by revenge? By the color of her skin? Such questions must remain unanswered because they never interact as a couple and because the Arab is deprived of those traits that would bring him to life not only as a lover but as a human being.

The mysteries and ambiguities that envelop this affair provide a vivid illustration of the denials and repressions at work in Pied-Noir memory.

The way these scenes are depicted suggest that, perhaps despite herself, the director cannot confront the darkest zones of the past, the most inadmissible of historical truths. In this sense, the silence that shrouds Gritte's doomed and passionate affair corresponds to the absence of the putsch in *Le Crabe-tambour.* In both instances, the most troubling and guilty zones of the past—those involving rebellion (if not treason) and racism—are those that cannot be represented. In their refusal to confront these zones, both films point to the extent of the divide between the brutal facts of history and the transformations wrought by memory.

There is no doubt, as suggested at the beginning of this essay, that this divide is particularly acute in *Le Crabe-tambour* and *Outremer* because both portray memories of a "taboo" war, memories that have been rendered even more "inadmissible" with the passage of time. But an important and influential essay by historian Pierre Nora suggests that the divide between history and memory that is felt here may well reflect broader social impulses. Titled, significantly, "Entre Mémoire et histoire" (Between Memory and History) Nora's essay serves as the introduction to *Les Lieux de mémoire,* a highly influential collection of essays devoted to the ways in which the memories invested in *les lieux*—whether these "places" be physical (as in the case of archives and museums) or symbolic (as are, for example, holidays and emblems)—both reflect and influence changing perceptions of history.

   At the heart of Nora's essay is his conviction that the decline of traditional, largely rural societies has entailed a radical transformation in the form and function of memory and, especially, in its relationship to history and to the individual. In the past, he asserts, memory was largely a collective phenomenon—linked, especially, to the nation-state and to its history. Transmitted from one generation to the next, memory provided a powerful existential link with the past—a link connecting people to their ancestors and, beyond them, to the "undifferentiated time of heroes, origins, and myth."[18] But, continues Nora, the "acceleration" of history, the dislocations of the modern world, have hastened the demise of traditional societies and radically altered the role and nature of memory. Just as the collective (and frequently religious) idea of a unified "nation" has given way to that of "society" (with, one supposes, its connotations of diversity and secularism), so too has collective memory largely been replaced by the more "private" memories (*la mémoire particulière*) of different social groups. Like the two social groups represented in *Le Crabe-tambour* and

Outremer, such groups share common loyalties by virtue of a shared heritage, or culture, or religion. "The end of history-memory," observes Nora, "has multiplied individual memories (*'les mémoires particulières'*) which demand their own history."[19] More limited in scope than collective memory, these "private" memories are also, asserts Nora, different in kind. And it is here, where Nora elaborates upon these critical differences, that one begins to sense the affinities between *la mémoire particulière* as described by Nora and the social memories represented in *Le Crabe-tambour* and *Outremer*. For what he sees as the defining characteristics of *la mémoire particulière*—that is, its deeply psychological and private nature and the distance it establishes between past and present—are precisely those traits that give these films their special cast.

It is Nora's contention that these traits started to make themselves felt, and to alter the very nature of memory, toward the end of the last century—during the era, significantly, of Proust and Bergson. As the rural world began to collapse, and memory was displaced from the central role it had played in the life of the nation-state, it also underwent a dramatic shift from the "historical to the psychological, from the social to the individual, from transmissive to subjective, from repetition to commemoration. . . . The total psychologization of contemporary memory has led to a conspicuously new economy in the identity of the self, in the mechanisms of memory, and the relationship to the past."[20] This "new economy," continues Nora, manifests itself in several distinctive ways. Whereas collective memory was a spontaneous phenomenon, private social memories must be consciously cultivated and protected by individuals if they are to preserve their very identity. The "obligation to remember" thus assumes "an intense power of internal coercion. The psychologization of memory gives everyone the feeling that salvation ultimately depends upon repaying this impossible debt."[21] Spurred on by the force of this "obligation to remember," groups and individuals seek to preserve every shred or fragment of the past, to establish archives and museums to keep memories alive. But now a paradox arises. For these very efforts to entomb and preserve the past create a distance between past and present. The lived and spontaneous link with the past that characterized traditional societies—where memory was passed down from one generation to the next and the past was relived in the present (as in the rituals of earlier peoples)—has vanished. Discontinuity, not continuity, reigns. "The past," writes Nora, "is seen as radically other; it is the world from which we are forever cut off. And it is by showing the extent of this separation that memory reveals its essence."[22] Hence, not only is modern memory lived as a "duty" (or "obligation") and embodied in the "archive" but—paradoxically—it is "distanced" from the very past it strains to embrace. Historical memory (*mémoire-histoire*) has thus become, declares Nora, archival (*mémoire-archive*), obligatory (*mémoire-devoir*), and distanced (*mémoire-distance*).

"Distance"; "archive"; "obligation." It would be difficult, I think, to find terms better suited to describe the memories represented in *Le Crabe-tambour* and *Outremer*. The protagonists of these works cling to memory with a determination that bespeaks, certainly, a kind of inner "coercion." They desperately need to remember the past because it offers them not only the warmth and life lacking in the present but a sense of their very identity as well. At the same time, however, in re-creating a world forever lost, such memories emphasize not the link between past and present but, instead, the absolute discontinuity. Marked by its "distance" from history, in these films memory seeks less to recapture the past than to re-create it; it wants not to confront the ghosts of history but rather to establish a place where they may flourish forever. If the private and coded memories of these films suggest the difficulties of remembering a "taboo" war, the force of desire embedded in them, the rupture they establish between past and present, as well as the distance that separates them from history, all point to impulses that transcend any particular war, any single experience.

Which leaves "archive"—a word central not only to Nora's essay but, indeed, to the entire project of *Les Lieux de mémoire*. And it may well be a word that goes to the heart of these films. For like an archive, don't these works preserve the memories of distinct social groups? If, as Nora observes, an archive or (more generally) a "place of memory" is designed to "stop time and block the work of memory," don't the images of these films accomplish precisely that by creating a changeless and compelling past? Distinguishing between history (or historical memory) and memory, Nora tells us that "places of memory do not have referents in reality. Or, rather, they are their own referent: pure, self-referential signs. This is not to say that they are without content, physical presence, or history: quite the contrary. But what makes them places of memory is that, precisely, by which they escape from history."[23] It is, I think, precisely this "escape" that is effected in these films. Pulling us into the timeless world of myth and dream, they create "places of memory" for those whose "impossible" memories have been excluded from history—that is, from a shared national past. Muted and silenced, history gives way to a remembered world in which time has stopped and the past has absorbed the present.

NOTES

1. Robert Frank, "Les Troubles de la mémoire française," in *La Guerre d'Algérie et les Français*, ed. Jean-Pierre Rioux (Paris: Fayard, 1990), 603.

2. Ibid., 607.

3. Marlise Simons, "Still Aching for Algeria, Thirty Years after the Rage," *New York Times*, 20 July 1992.

4. Isabelle Lambert, "Vingt ans après," in Rioux, *La Guerre d'Algérie et les Français*, 557.

5. Pierre Nora, *Les Français d'Algérie* (Paris: Julliard, 1961), 71.

6. Alain Ruscio, "French Public Opinion and the War in Indochina: 1945–1954," in *War and Society in Twentieth-Century France*, ed. Michael Scriven and Peter Wagstaff (New York and Oxford: Berg, 1991), 119.

7. Michel de Certeau, "Psychanalyse," in *La Nouvelle Histoire*, ed. Jacques LeGoff, Roger Chartier, and Jacques Revel (Paris: Retz, 1978), 477.

8. Alain-Gérard Slama, "La Guerre d'Algérie en littérature ou la comédie des masques," in Rioux, *La Guerre d'Algérie et les Français*, 597.

9. I am grateful to Jim Harmon for this telling observation.

10. See Claude Liazu, "Le Contingent entre silence et discours ancien combattant," in Rioux, *La Guerre d'Algérie et les Français*, 513.

11. Pierre Schoendoerffer, *L'Adieu au roi* (Paris: Grasset, 1969), 21.

12. François de la Bretèque, "L'Indochine au coeur d'une oeuvre: L'Illiade et l'Odyssée de Pierre Schoendoerffer," *Cahiers de la cinémathèque*, no. 57 (October 1992): 76.

13. Some of the autobiographical elements in *Outremer* are discussed by director Brigitte Roüan in an interview with *France Magazine* (Winter 1991): 43.

14. Anne Roche, "La Perte et la parole: Témoignages oraux de Pieds-Noirs," in Rioux, *La Guerre d'Algérie et les Français*, 527.

15. Ibid., 531.

16. Ibid., 532.

17. Jacques Siclier, *Le Cinéma français*, (Paris: Ramsay, 1991), 2:205.

18. Pierre Nora, "Entre Mémoire et histoire," in *Les Lieux de mémoire*, ed. Pierre Nora (Paris: Gallimard, 1984), xviii.

19. Ibid., xxix.

20. Ibid., xxx.

21. Ibid., xxx–xxxi.

22. Ibid., xxxi–xxxii.

23. Ibid., xli.

Filmic Memorial and Colonial Blues

SEVEN   *Indochina in Contemporary French Cinema*

Panivong Norindr

> *La nostalgie de l'Indochine, ceux qui ne l'ont pas éprouvée,
> ne peuvent pas en savoir l'envoûtement.*
>
> *[Nostalgia for Indochina, those who have not felt it cannot
> understand what it means to be under its spell.]*
>
> —JEAN HOUGRON

In 1984, Salman Rushdie deplored the fact that the vogue for the British
Raj had made a comeback in Great Britain. Among the numerous films,
television shows, and novels that forlornly hark back to the British Empire, Rushdie is particularly critical of the revisionist enterprise of English
filmmakers such as Richard Attenborough and David Lean, whose works
he sees as an unfortunate attempt at "refurbish[ing] the Empire's tarnished
image."[1] Rushdie examines the complex relationships among history, politics, and fiction, focusing his attention more specifically on the discursive
context that enabled this type of cultural production to emerge. He concludes that the critical success and commercial appeal of these colonial
fictions can be ascribed, in part, to a nostalgia for a "defunct empire" and
"the rise of conservative ideologies in modern Britain" (92), at a moment
when the influence of Great Britain on the world stage has declined
considerably.

Rushdie's penetrating observations find resonance in the French context. A similar trend can be perceived in France today. *L'Empire colonial
français* has aroused the interest of French artists, scholars, and experts in

all fields. Films and documentaries on the colonies have been produced, novels written, "*enquêtes*" conducted, and colloquia organized around this problematic issue.[2] Thirty years after the end of the Algerian war or "*Guerre sans nom*," as Bertrand Tavernier and Patrick Rotman called it so provocatively,[3] the French are confronting the question of the colonies in an attempt to reevaluate *l'idée coloniale* and come to terms with their role as a colonial power.

Indochina has recently achieved prominence as the privileged subject of a great many French writers and filmmakers. The publishing and cinematic industries have further contributed to the creation of an aura surrounding Indochina, commodifying it through the re-edition of novels and the publication of new travel narratives on Indochina. The story of Pigneau de Béhaine, the French missionary responsible for the "opening" of Cochinchina in the eighteenth century, even inspired Christophe Bataille's novella *Annam*, which, significantly, won the Prix du premier roman.[4] Whereas creative and critical works that dealt with the French colonial subjugation of the Maghreb and Africa have fostered new lines of inquiry, it is my contention that our understanding of the imperial domination of Indochina by France continues to be reassessed nostalgically, in rather problematic terms. The privileged and most pervasively used metaphor for describing the conquest, colonization, and subsequent loss of the eastern part of the Indochinese peninsula remains, to this very day, that of a passionate romance or a stormy love affair. One revealing example should suffice to convey the tenor of this problem: Bruno Masur, the most widely watched French television news anchor, described the historical ties that bound France and Indochina for almost a century thus: "La France et l'Indochine . . . c'est une vieille histoire d'amour" [France and Indochina . . . it's a old love-story] (France 2, 9 February 1993). The bloody history of French colonial rule is entirely evacuated from this romantic fantasy.

French contemporary cinema resorts to similar analogies, translating and displaying what I will call the erotic and libidinal dimensions of the French "romance for Indochina" in readily recognizable cinematic figures. In fact, the elaborate mise-en-scène of Indochina in recent French films may be largely responsible for reconfiguring and accommodating many of the phantasms that have sustained the myths of the legitimacy of the French colonial presence in Indochina—founding myths of this "geographical romance" first elaborated by writers such as Claude Farrère, Myriam Harry, and André Malraux in the interwar period. One of the aims of this essay is to show how the desire for Indochina is signified in

French cinema. The modalities of a libidinal economy—the affective investment or romance for the country, its people, its landscape—appear to
be the primary modes by which French directors re-present Indochina and
perpetuate received ideas about the country and its people. Three recent
films operate within that "romantic" nostalgic framework and merit our
critical attention: Régis Wargnier's *Indochine* (1992) triumphed as Best
Foreign Film only a decade after Attenborough's *Gandhi* (1982) won the
Oscar for Best Film; Jean-Jacques Annaud's filmic adaptation of Marguerite Duras's novel, *L'Amant* (1984), shot in English for wider commercial distribution and aptly called, *The Lover* (1992); and Pierre Schoendoerffer's "docudrama" war movie, *Dien Bien Phu* (1992), a fictional
reenactment of the battle that ended French colonial hegemony in Indochina. Incidentally, these three feature films, all shot on location in Vietnam at the same time, are among the most expensive films ever produced
in French cinematic history: *The Lover* reached $30 million, *Indochine*
required the same amount, and *Dien Bien Phu* cost $25 million.

In his classic study *What Is Cinema?* André Bazin described cinema as
"the creation of an ideal world in the likeness of the real, with its own temporal destiny."[5] The French directors discussed here seem to have taken
heed of Bazin's 1945 formulation. In their films, they have created "an
ideal world in the likeness of the real," what I would call a phantasmatic
world. This mimetic conception of cinema is problematized by Teresa de
Lauretis, who sees cinema as "an apparatus of social representation," involved in "the production of signs."[6] To analyze these movies as "signifying practice" in a given sociohistorical situation, one must therefore consider both the material conditions that have allowed their productions and
their implications "in the production and reproduction of meanings, values, and ideology."[7] In other words, a politically consequent materialism
in film demands that we examine the mediation that intervenes between
"reality" and "representation," re-presentation as a process of translation,
as the central mode of production of strategies of containment, an issue of
particular importance to postcolonial studies. Translation creates "coherent and transparent texts and subjects," and "participates—across a range
of discourses—in the *fixing* of colonized cultures, making them static and
unchanging rather than historically constructed."[8] This essay also attempts
to determine to what extent these filmic texts "fix" and mediate historical
memory, and participate in the construction and re-configuration of a collective memory of Indochina.

Régis Wargnier's movie is engaged in re-creating a coherent vision
of Indochina by relying on a melancholic (hi)story and "geographic ro-

mance." Naming his film "Indochine" signals, in a most lapidary fashion, Wargnier's faith in the evocative power of the name. The title puts in place and condenses in its more reductive and phantasmagorical form a certain "imaginary" of Indochina. The filmic strategies deployed by Wargnier in *Indochine* "construct images or visions of social reality," inscribe "the spectator's place in it," and "produce effects of meaning and perception, self-images and subject-positions for all those involved, makers and viewers." De Lauretis describes this predicament as "a semiotic process in which the subject is continually engaged, represented, and inscribed in ideology."[9] Thus, particular attention must be paid to the film's vision/filmic construction of space and the address of the film, as well as the ideology of vision, the way it constructs narrative space, and the implication of space and spectator in the narrative.

The film's initial sequence foregrounds many of the issues to which we have just alluded. The opening shot strikes the viewer in its blank whiteness. The first image of what appears to be white clouds has the ephemeral and insubstantial quality of a dream. The sound track features a chanting chorus of unaccompanied voices. The spectator seems to have been transported into a phantasmatic world. The effect is broken when numerous boats filled with Asian officiants dressed in white, mauve, and black, emerge from the mist, partially resolving the unintelligibility of the shot. At the same time, the credits begin to roll. The first credit, in white letters, records the movie's star, Catherine Deneuve. The sounds and sight of a lone drummer seem to guide this exotic procession of boats. The mystery of this sequence is not fully penetrated until the two cenotaphs that have been laid side by side come into view. The viewer's suspicion that the "exotic" and enigmatic ritual pertains to a funeral is confirmed by the medium close-up of Catherine Deneuve, veiled and dressed in black. The voice-over—in the actress's voice—begins the narration and informs us that we are the witnesses to the funeral of Prince N'Guyen and his wife, lost at sea in a plane accident off Saint-Jacques Cape. Eliane, the narrator, goes on to furnish more details, about the identity and legal status of the little orphan girl, Camille, dressed all in white and standing beside her. Eliane has lost her best friends but gained a daughter when she adopted Camille, the little princess from Annam.

The opening sequence of expository scenes situates the characters in space and time. The viewer quickly realizes that the preceding shots were seen from Eliane's vantage point and organized from her point of view as well. As both protagonist and narrator, she exerts complete control over the filmic narration, its development, its resolution. In fact, *Indochine* adopts and emulates every cinematic convention of classical Hollywood cinema, including plot linearity, the reliance upon an axis of action and upon the love story, the use of the protagonist as the principal causal agent and chief object of audience identification,[10] and so on, to produce and anchor its images of Indochina.

Mary Ann Doane remarked that "rather than activating history as mise-en-scène, a space, the . . . love story inscribes it as individual subjectivity closed in on itself. History is an accumulation of memories of the loved one."[11] In *Indochine*, French colonial history becomes visible as Eliane's memories of events in her colonial past and of individuals she has loved. These "memories" are recorded as a unified or preconstituted visual space. One mediation specific to cinema is spectator positioning. *Indochine* exploits the identificatory mechanism of cinema on behalf of the colonizer: the spectator is sutured into a colonialist perspective. Through a mechanism of cinematic identification such as "suture," Eliane becomes the embodiment of the French colony in symbol and image, the "colonial Marianne"; simply put, she personifies Indochina.[12]

Eliane's relation to the "geographical" narrative is made unambiguous when the narrator/protagonist describes herself as "une Asiate." Here the term "Asiate" does not have its common pejorative signification such as the one popularized by Jean Hougron, the novelist who wrote an entire novel on the subject, *Les Asiates* (1954). It does not mean "céder au milieu, devenir des 'Asiates,' perdre [son] identité en somme" [to give in to the milieu, to become "Asiate," in sum, to lose one's identity] (xii); here, it describes more simply a French woman who was born in Indochina and has never left it. The term also suggests, however, that the "Français d'Asie" also considered themselves to be the legitimate heirs of the great and powerful civilizations that once dominated the Indochinese peninsula.

A "découpage" of the film into analytic scenes would reveal that all of the scenes where Eliane appears are merely clichéd images, postcardlike cinematic portrayals of colonial life in Indochina. She administers the land and the people, gathers with friends on the terrace of the Continental Hotel, entertains at her colonial estate, smokes opium in an opium den. All of these scenes of colonial everyday life are designed to reinforce her love and attachment to her native land, and they implicitly legitimate her presence there.

It can be argued that, rather than "activating history as a mise-en-scène, a space," as Doane noted, these images construct a feminized space that allows the erotic overinvestment of the White female "colonizer." The viewer identifies Eliane as the substitute mother, the embodiment of "l'Indochine des années trente, un paradis colonial" [Indochina in the 1930s, a colonial paradise]. As I suggested earlier, the opening scene constructs Eliane as a caring mother who protects the natives. The irony of the name "protectorate," which designates a juridical regime that grants control over a subjugated country for a colonial power, can hardly be lost on the film's audience.

In contrast, the native protagonist, Camille, is divested of her "femininity" as the film unfolds. In this manner, she can be re-presented as the masculine *"princesse rouge,"* who, after killing a naval officer, escapes in the company of another naval officer (of course, Eliane's ex-lover). She bears his child, is tracked down, captured, and condemned to spend the rest of her life in the Poulo-Condore penal colony. Then, amnestied by the representative of the newly elected Front Populaire government, Camille chooses to commit herself exclusively to the national liberation struggle, effectively abandoning her child to Eliane's care. By the end, she has become literally invisible to the viewer, completely elided from the filmic text. In the last sequence of the film, her son, while expressing a desire to see his "birth mother," who is part of the Vietnamese delegation at the 1954 Geneva Peace Conference, simply gives up on the idea of seeking her out and mutters that Eliane is his "mother." Camille is denied not simply the status of "mother" but more problematically the status of subject on the screen, erasing at the same time "ethnic" female sexuality.

One of the projects of colonialism, as Gayatri Spivak reminds us, seeks to constitute the colonial subject as Other. By exploiting the figure of the "monstrous" native mother, Wargnier deflects our attention from the colonialist projects of appropriating and exploiting the land, and of dominating its people economically, culturally, and politically. In Wargnier's film, French colonialism in Indochina as an oppressive economic, social, and political apparatus is merely used as a backdrop, diffused and "screened" into the background to bring the "mother-daughter plot" and the parallel love stories to the fore. And although the filmic text evokes certain aspects of French colonialism—in particular, the carceral universe of enslaved peasants, and the repression, torture, and killings of suspected nationalists performed by the French Sûreté—these "events" are staged to underscore the fact that *l'Indochine française,* or "L'Indochine avant l'ouragan" [Indochina before the hurricane], as one writer put it,[13] needs to be saved and protected from a barbaric (native) society whose population can only act out irrationally and violently. The raging anger of a nationalist/communist mob and its ensuing reign of terror are dramatized in a scene where the nationalists torture a local mandarin whose ostensible support for French colonialism led to his summary execution: death by fire on a makeshift pyre erected from his worldly possessions. Similar tragedies may have indeed occurred in the history of the Vietnamese fight for their independence from France. The inclusion of a well-known French historian as a consultant to the film ought to deter anyone from contesting the film's historical accuracy. What is disturbing, however, is the manner in which "historical events" are used and framed simply to advance the plot, and to play up and render more harrowing the predicament of our "heroines," rather than to question French colonialist practices. The most revealing example that comes immediately to mind concerns the way the Sûreté chief confronts Thanh, Camille's intended husband, who has been expelled from France for supporting the Yen-Bay rebellion. Furthermore, he participates in the Vietnamese student demonstration against French colonialism in front of the Elysée Palace, an episode that received much attention in daily papers in France and Indochina in the 1930s.

A more comprehensive analysis of the movie would attend to its blindness and omission, particularly in its use of female protagonists. Feminist film theory can be invoked to show that the "representation of woman as image (spectacle, object to be looked at, vision of beauty),"[14] women as the privileged site of desire (Laura Mulvey), the locus of filmic position of woman as "narrative image" (de Lauretis), and as a construct for ethnic female spectator (Rey Chow) determine the centrality of female subjectivity in the construction of cinematic representation.[15] These theories can help us better assess cinematic signification and representation and the ideological subtext of the movie. *Indochine* offers a particularly striking example of how a different (Other) culture can be "produced" as a feminized spectacle. This idea is confirmed by the film's reception in the French press. Jacques Siclier, the film critic for the French daily *Le Monde*, symptomatically titled his review "Indochine, ton nom est femme" [Indochina, your name is woman]. He goes on to explain in the following terms the reasons that *Indochine* struck a responsive chord among so many spectators: "C'est splendide parce que les clichés romanesques sont avoués, évidents, et transcendés par le lyrisme d'une mise en scène qui lie étroitement les éclairages, les décors, les costumes, les sons, la musique." [It's splendid because the novelistic clichés are acknowledged and evident, and transcended by the lyricism of a mise-en-scène that links closely the lighting, the decor, the costumes, the sound, and the music.] For Siclier, romantic excess is a deliberate strategy, a cinematic convention designed to frame and narrate a love story. But as others have remarked, Siclier is also a "film critic who dislikes being anything but positive,"[16] and who consequently does not have any misgivings about Hollywood cinema. The director of

Indochine can therefore feminize the other culture with impunity by relying on a cinematic representational practice that privileges visual pleasure. The spectator is "penetrated" by the image of the Other. The blue-green hue cast by the Bay of Halong, the blue-gray of the bleeding of the rubber trees, and the smoky-blue squalor of an opium den arouse strong visual responses because these "postcard" images of colonial life in French Indochina are an always-already part of the French collective memory and have been assimilated by the public at large. Hence, Eliane remains the paradigmatic figure of the *bâtisseur d'empire*, the female epitome of French colonialism who is clothed in elegant costumes designed especially for Catherine Deneuve by the Oscar-winning Italian designer Gabriella Pescucci.

The movie's opulence and lavishness overwhelm its manifest content, displacing its ostensible subject (Indochina) onto the woman at its center, Catherine Deneuve. *Indochine* is not about French colonialism in Indochina at all; it is about Wargnier's fantasies of colonial Indochina. Critical and popular acclaim notwithstanding, Wargnier's re-presentation of Indochina exerts a dangerous fascination precisely because it brings visual pleasure without questioning or subverting any preconceived ideas about French colonial rule in Southeast Asia. *Indochine* merely displays beautiful images and should only be remembered as a symptom of the current French fad for things exotic.

RESTAGING INDOCHINA: ANNAUD'S PHANTASMIC LOVE AFFAIR WITH INDOCHINA

Jean-Jacques Annaud's filmic vision of Indochina is entirely mediated by Duras's novel, *L'Amant*.[17] Annaud is unabashedly candid about the effect that Duras's novel had on him and his attempt to locate it in space and translate it into the filmic image:

I was on a quest for the emotions I had felt when reading *The Lover*. Marguerite Duras had plunged me into Asia. The pages smelled of jasmine, charcoal fire, and incense. With her I crossed the breathtaking immensity of the Mekong, I wandered the flatness of the delta's rice paddies that run as far as the eyes can see. I followed the rosewood-hatted young girl that she had been along the wide, tree-shaded avenues of the colonial city. I ambled beside the gardens overflowing with flowers, caught glimpses of the villas with their verandas in the white part of town. I accompanied her up to the haughty French High School building. Then I lost her in the red-and-gold exuberance of the

Chinese part of town. And at dusk, in the silent solitude of the dorm, with her I heard, carried over on the wind from the laguna, the faraway singing of a beggar-woman.[18]

Like many readers, Annaud is seduced by Duras's lyrical evocation of Indochina. Duras's imaginative geography, however, has assumed the status of the "real" for Annaud. Distinct urban and rural markers circumscribe his mediated Indochina: the Mekong River, the rice paddies, the colonial city with its white villas and gardens, the lycée, the boardinghouse, and Cholon. Rumor has it that Duras herself wandered these wide streets on her way to the Lycée Chasseloup-Laubat or to the Pension Lyautey when she was not meeting her Chinese lover in Cholon.

To remain faithful to the spirit of her work and make his film more "real," Annaud believed he had no alternative but to shoot it on location.[19] He scouted Vietnam in the hope of finding appropriate sites, that is to say, those evoked by or resembling the ones described by Duras in her novel. But the "spectacle" unfolding before him only disillusioned him:

> But, lo, the airplane's door opened not on the mythical Indochina of the '30s but, rather, on the tragic reality of contemporary Vietnam, with its Third World pauperization and overpopulation made worse by 30 years of war followed by 30 years of Stalinism.
>
> Duras' flowered streets are cemented over by the Bulgarians. The fancy white villas are replaced with gray prefab council housing. The broken streets are swamped by the compact swarm of backfiring scooters. The Soviet trucks honk themselves a difficult path, leaving a thick billow of black smoke behind. As the billboard reads when you enter Da Nang, beneath the screeching of MIGs taking off for the Chinese border: WELCOME, TOURIST FRIENDS?
>
> The countryside will be different, I think to myself. Untouched, still "Asian." No. It, too, is Socialist. Looking for green, we find gray. The rice paddies hide behind the walls of the endless shantytown that stretches along the motorway. The Mekong, laden with motorboats with corrugated-iron roofs, looks more like a freeway outside Mexico City than the legendary river flowing all the way down from China.[20]

Contemporary Vietnam no longer resembles "the mythical Indochina of the '30s" portrayed in Duras's novel. The quaint French colonial city has been transformed into an overpopulated Third World Socialist city with its unattractive billboards, shantytown, and prefab council houses. Erstwhile elegant boulevards have disappeared under the concrete poured by

Bulgarians. The congested city is now filled with undesirable natives (or signs of their presence—the scooters, trucks, and MiG's left by the Soviets, the last among many unsuccessful waves of would-be conquerors). Even the countryside appears to have been contaminated by Socialist "filth." Annaud refuses to see in these new "signs" the contemporary "reality" of Vietnam. An abyss seems to separate Ho Chi Minh City from Annaud's idealized vision of an alluring French colonial city. For him, Ho Chi Minh City makes manifest the ill effects of unplanned urban development and the deleterious impact of Socialist progress and modernity on numerous Third World countries that have not successfully negotiated their passage to a postindustrial economy. Disappointed, he leaves the country for Thailand, Malaysia, and the Philippines, more appropriate parts of Asia, "where it [Vietnam] is normally filmed." And yet something he cannot describe or articulate compels him to return:

> So we [Annaud and his production manager] . . . went back to Vietnam. Strangely enough, that country we had rejected cast a delayed spell. Our memories sifted away the dirt, the pollution, the everyday troubles. What remained was what my lens had spontaneously isolated, separated from its background during my first scouting: the "Flemish" beauty of the endless plains, the bustling of life on the canals and on the river, the continuous presence of water. Captured also: the smiling seriousness of this ascetic population, so integrated, blended into the background, eternal. Its extraordinary dignity in the face of misery. And then, the unique relics of French presence, with its caricature Napoleonic order of avenues and monuments, the quaint charm of the Parisian "Belle Epoque" architecture, that feeling of resort towns, or an end-of-the-century "Riviera," moved to the equator. Jewels in the midst of ruins. The "good" side of poverty: The administrations were not able to move to new locations, so they remained in the most beautiful buildings from the colonial days. The façades have been kept up. That is where they hang banners "to the glory of the Socialist successes."
>
> Thus, triumphant Ho Chi Minh City, the tropical clone of Moscow's suburbia, has saved decadent Saigon, the 19th-century French town. Despite it, because of it, all of Vietnam, too, is a museum. Set in the new Asia of skyscrapers and material success. A tired museum, weary and unique.
>
> We shot the whole film in Vietnam.[21]

Annaud believes that he can now recover the mythic Indochina of his dreams and phantasms through the act of remembering and by abstracting vision: "Our memories sifted away the dirt, the pollution, the everyday troubles. What remained was what my lens had spontaneously isolated, separated from its background." Paul Virilio compares "the field of vision . . . to the ground of an archeological excavation."[22] This analogy describes perfectly the process by which Annaud comes to terms with contemporary Vietnam. The camera lens has become a more probing extension of his eye, capable of zeroing in, isolating, separating the essential from the inconsequential, the Socialist filth covering the surviving French monuments, "jewels in the midst of ruins."

Nonetheless, Annaud's newly envisioned Indochina resembles only in a remote fashion the one that Duras described in her novel. Gone are the *compartiment indigène* that appeared in Duras's urban landscape, the gray prefab council housing that made land speculators like the Chinese lover's father very rich. Willed away also are the smiling (if "dignified") natives "so integrated, blended into the background, eternal." Indochina, for Annaud, is not inhabited by the indigenous people of Southeast Asia. This "ascetic population" is simply viewed in cinematic terms for its potential use as decor, extras, or props. The motion picture technique of the fade-out as an allegory of Annaud's directorial mise-en-scène of his Indochina suggests how contemporary Vietnam can be made to disappear and rendered invisible, when it is not completely assimilated into the background.

Contemporary Vietnam strikes a discordant note among its rich, developed neighbors that constitute "the new Asia of skyscrapers and material success," Annaud seems to scorn. Annaud privileges the "Vietnam in ruin" precisely because it preserved, paradoxically, the infrastructures of the French presence in Southeast Asia, what he vulgarly calls "the 'good' side of poverty." Thus, no mention is made of the material and political conditions that brought destitution and hardship on Vietnam, nor of the economic embargo that was imposed by Western countries after Vietnam won the war against the United States and only recently has been lifted. Annaud can therefore regard Vietnam nostalgically as a vast museum where the cinematographer as archaeologist/curator can excavate in order to recover surviving French artifacts. The silence on the economic and political determinants and the flippant declaration that Vietnam is a museum illustrate perfectly what Tejaswini Niranjana described as "the fixing of colonized culture," of "making them static and unchanging rather than historically constructed."[23]

Oblivious to these questions, Annaud sets out to find French administration buildings still standing or, as he called them himself, "the unique relics of French presence." He does so not simply to resurrect "the 19th century French town" but to set the stage for his story. By refashioning the old colonial city onto the surviving "façade" of French monuments, Annaud demonstrates the efficacy and power of cinematic capital to recover French colonial Saigon from the Socialist ruins of Ho Chi Minh City, using contemporary Vietnam simply as yet another, if a more elaborate, prop:

> L'équipe du film investit le Vietnam, obtient la confiance des autorités et la liberté qui en découle, restaure les bâtiments, refait les routes, répare les moteurs, replante les arbres, dessine et fabrique sur place les 2000 costumes, les décors, les vélos, les bateaux du film, fait venir de Seattle la limousine du Chinois, la seule Morris Léon Bollée 1929 détectable; traque dans tous les ports le vieux paquebot d'époque et le découvre à Chypre; repeint des quartiers de Saigon aux fraîches couleurs de la colonie française.

> [The film crew invades Vietnam, earns the authorities' trust and the freedom dependent on such trust; it restores buildings, rebuilds roads and motors, and replants trees; it also designs and makes on location two thousand costumes, the decor, the bicycles, the boats used in the film; the Chinese man's limousine—the only traceable 1929 Morris Léon Bollé—is located in Seattle and sent to Vietnam; it tracks down the old period-liner in every port and locates it in Cyprus; it repaints entire areas of Saigon in the fresh colors of the French colony.][24]

Beyond the immediate benefit of injecting much-needed capital into an assailed economy, the exorbitant cost and the all-pervasive nature of the production leave its mark and filmic trace on a "Vietnam in ruin."[25]

The reasons Annaud wanted to adapt Duras's novel for the screen deserve attention for this analysis. First, the filmmaker found *L'Amant* to be inspiring, "a very beautiful novel, a good subject for a film." Second, he claims to have been seduced by Duras's portrayal of feminine sensuality, an aspect of sexuality he had never filmed before in his previous, immensely successful commercial films. Moreover, as we see in his following comments, the French colonial past holds him in the sway of nostalgic fascination: "Je portais comme une sorte de culpabilité le fait de n'avoir traité au cinéma qu'une moitié du monde: la partie mâle, et j'étais particulièrement attiré par l'évocation de la sensualité féminine." [I carried around a type of guilt for having dealt in cinema with only half of the world: the male part, and I was particularly attracted by the evocation of feminine sensuality.] He acknowledges one final motive:

Il y a dans ce livre un autre élément qui me fascine: l'empire colonial français. J'ai gardé cette nostalgie de cette époque de présence et de grandeur françaises, bien que je ne l'aie pas vécu, moi, c'est l'époque de l'indépendance. J'ai vécu au Cameroun en 1967, et passé sept ans à sillonner, à apprendre l'Afrique, pour tourner mon premier film, "La Victoire en chantant": cette expérience, ces climats, ces cultures, ce rapport à l'autre m'avaient préparé aux dimensions exotiques, coloniales, interraciales de "L'Amant."

[There is in this novel another element that fascinates me: the French colonial empire. I have kept a nostalgia of this era of French presence and grandeur, even though I had not experienced it personally, it is the era of independence. I lived in Cameroon in 1967, and spent seven years crisscrossing and learning about Africa, to shoot my first movie, *Black and White in Color:* this experience, these climates, these cultures, this rapport with the Other had prepared me for the exotic, colonial and interracial dimensions of *The Lover.*][26]

Annaud is both "fascinated by French colonial empire" and nostalgic for the "[grande] époque de présence et de grandeur françaises." *L'Amant* seems to be an appropriate choice for his filmic adaptation, since Duras's novel takes place in Indochina during the golden age of French colonialism. It is worth noting that in his first feature film, *La Victoire en chantant* (1976), Annaud evoked a biting satire of French and German colonialism in Africa. This film, for which he won the Academy Award for Best Foreign Film, was shot for a mere half million dollars. More important, linking his latest production to the first one serves the purpose of situating his most recent movie in an ideologically uncontested terrain, while providing at the same time the genealogy for his interest and understanding of the "exotic, colonial and interracial dimensions of *L'Amant.*"

In *La Victoire en chantant,* Annaud succeeds in questioning the absurdity of the colonialist powers' presence in Africa and in debunking colonial myths of the White man's burden, a belief zealously enforced by benevolent civil servants, evangelical missionaries, and military troops who did not hesitate to resort to physical and spiritual violence and torture to subjugate the African people in order to promote and enforce the civilizing mission. *The Lover,* unfortunately, does not raise the same kind of questions. The Indochinese colony is merely reconstructed as an elaborate stage where a love affair can be filmed. Not that an interracial love affair cannot be an adequate vehicle for raising serious questions—Alain Resnais's *Hiroshima mon amour* (1959), with a screenplay written by Marguerite Duras, remains to this day one of the most thought-provoking examples of an interracial love story. In Annaud's film, what is central is the illicit love affair between the fifteen-year-old girl and the Chinese man.[27]

It has been reported that "the film's huge commercial appeal is mainly due to its five sequences—a total of 20 minutes—of frank if tasteful erotica." Annaud wants to repoliticize his movie by placing emphasis on the importance of the "interracial love affair." The race of the Chinese lover does play an important role in the doomed love affair. "Her family willingly compromise moral and racist objections for the sake of the financial benefit the liaison brings,"[28] writes Robinson. Because of the liaison, the young girl is also ostracized by her classmates, denounced and vilified by the entire White colonial society (except the teaching corps) for having transgressed sexual and racial taboos. But in the end, the issue of class difference seems to play an equally important role.

Annaud acknowledges that his greatest challenge as a film director was the five love scenes of the movie: "to show physical love in its natural beauty . . . the beauty of carnal passion," declared the director. He went to great lengths to show difference in mood, selecting various lightings to convey passion, gloom, romance, and violence, even resorting to the use of what he calls scientific cinema, that is to say, macro-photography and endoscopy in order to place the camera between the bodies of the lovers. He acknowledges: "J'étais dans les corps, dans les parties les plus secrètes, mais ça ne se voit pas." [I was in the bodies, in their most secret parts, but it does not show.] What needs to be stressed, however, is the fact that these scenes were shot not on location but in a Parisian studio.[29]

What, then, is gained (or lost) in filming *The Lover* on location? The answer may lie in French cinematic history. The argument for shooting on location is indeed an old one. In 1921, Jacques Feyder adapted Pierre Benoît's *L'Atlantide* to the screen, shooting all of the desert scenes in the Sahara rather than in studio sandboxes. The distance from the studio and the difficulty in transporting and protecting all of the technical equipment from the heat and the sand did not deter Feyder from shooting his story of empire building in the putative site of the action. In fact, his film benefited at the box office from having being filmed in the desert, making it appear "more real" to viewers in search of exotic sensations. *The Lover* enjoyed the same advance publicity. The public's knowledge that it was filmed in Indochina made it all the more seductive and appealing.

Annaud insists that one of the reasons for his adaptation of Duras's novel is the "fact that this story took place in a French colony. Put differently, it was not simply a love-story: there was also the encounter (*le contact*) between two races, two cultures."[30] Adapting *L'Amant* to the screen can be regarded as a phantasmatic mise-en-scène of Annaud's love affair with Indochina.

DIEN BIEN PHU: PIERRE SCHOENDOERFFER'S FILMIC MEMORIAL TO INDOCHINA

"Docu-drama," *film-vérité* (Jean-Luc Macia), or even *fresque historique* (Jacques Siclier) have been used to describe Schoendoerffer's *Dien Bien Phu*.[31] Did the subject of the film, the filmic reenactment of the decisive battle that ended the Franco-Indochinese War and effectively put an end to French colonial domination in Southeast Asia, make these critics attach such labels to this film? Were they caught up in the filmic images of war and overwhelmed emotionally by the sight of French and Vietnamese extras drawn from the battalion of legionnaires and Vietnamese troops who actually fought the battle in 1954, the use of period tanks, artillery pieces, and planes as props, the shooting on location at a site that resembled the historical battlefield? So caught up that they forgot that these elements merely constituted the "reality effect" of the movie and may not have deserved the name of "document," "truth," or "history," unless of course one speaks of "filmic truth" or problematizes what each of these terms means?

Schoendoerffer himself seems reluctant to place his movie in a precise filmic category. Although he admits to have filmed "a fiction," when asked if his movie is "a historical evocation," he answers: "Yes. And no! It is a fresco, a saga."[32] His ultimate aim is to render "the essence of Dien Bien Phu" and to reveal a forgotten (and shameful) chapter of French colonial history to the viewers. In an illuminating essay titled "From the Battle to the Movie," Schoendoerffer elaborates on what he has tried to achieve in his film: "My movie, *Dien Bien Phu*, wants to be like [*se veut semblable à*] a symphony . . . a visual and auditory symphony" (118, 128). The musical simile is indeed an appropriate, if clichéd, analogy. It should come as no surprise to learn that the sound track was recorded first, even before actual filming began:

> Georges Delerue composed a concerto, the "Concerto de l'adieu," magnificent, premonitory of what was to be the soul of the film. A concerto is a dialogue between an instrument and an orchestra. In the movie, the instrument, a first violin, a woman, is the voice of France; the orchestra of Hanoï is Viêt-nam. Delerue's music, noble, rigorous, charged with restrained emotion, participates in a larger concerto; it dialogues with the terrible percussion music composed of the sounds and furors of war. (128)

Unfortunately, Schoendoerffer, like the music, succeeds in evoking a sentimental war story only by drawing a parallel between "les derniers feux d'une époque coloniale" [the disappearing colonial world of Indochina] [33] and that of the bloody battle. Thus, at the very moment the battle of Dien Bien Phu begins, Schoendoerffer is following the wanderings of Howard Simpson, an American journalist stationed in Hanoi in search of a scoop, a character reminiscent of the scheming and manipulative Fowler in Graham Green's *The Quiet American* (1955). Simpson will attend the last "soirée of the empire" at the Hanoi opera house, as will the French governor-general and the entire French colony. Although this last concert is also meant to signify the end of an era, it fails completely to establish a semblance of a dialogue between France and Vietnam as Schoendoerffer would have it. This is due, in part, to the director's own totalizing ambition. Schoendoerffer wrote the screenplay, the dialogue, and the commentary. He also narrates the voice-over. The spectator is merely subjected to endure the "vision" of a female violin soloist and the maudlin sound of a "musical interlude" before the onslaught.

This singular sight contrasts markedly with scenes that depict the horrors of war. Images of life in the fortified camp are interrupted by the pounding of mortar shells, which kill and maim indiscriminately. Unlike the "air cavalry sequence" in Francis Ford Coppola's *Apocalypse Now*, in which helicopters attack invisible enemy targets, accompanied by the sound of Wagnerian music, these scenes fail to convey the absurdity of war. They merely present and reinforce the image of the heroic soldier who fought courageously against an enemy superior in number—the Vietminh outnumbered the French four to one—and in "firepower." One of the movie's last sequences, picturing antlike Vietminh soldiers overrunning the French "entrenched camp," the doomed fortified camp deep in enemy territory, is symptomatic of this impulse.

To be fair, Schoendoerffer does portray the anxieties and fears of the soldiers. He also cuts to scenes that focus on the actions of the cowards—or the "rats," as they are called—who come out only during the night to look for food that has been parachuted in. But ultimately, his movie pays tribute, in the "memorializing mode" of the official public commemoration, to the heretofore unsung heroes of the Indochinese war—the anonymous and forgotten French soldiers who, with their comrades from North and Central Africa, and the Tonkin, have fought and died for France. *Dien Bien Phu* is a movie that honors the men who never question authority, soldiers who "hate to be wasted." The only indictment is aimed at the incompetence of the military high command and its shortsighted war strategies. [34]

The monologic perspective of Schoendoerffer's filmic vision can be better circumscribed if we compare it to the way Patrick Jeudy, a French independent director/producer, constructs his own documentary film on Dien Bien Phu. Although feature films and documentaries belong to two distinct genres, each with its own protocol and its own distinct conventions and styles, the differences may not be as great as one may expect. Schoendoerffer's attempt to erase the fiction/documentary divide enables this type of linkage. There are definite points of convergence between the documentary and the feature film, which transcend the subject they treat (their thematic content) or their status as part of an apparatus of representation, of a signifying practice. They both elaborate a certain vision of Indochina through filmic narration and construct an identity by inscribing desire on a space marked by different narrative strategies by engaging "the spectator in the process of that reproduction as articulation of coherence."[35]

Titled *Récits d'Indochine: Chronique des journées de la bataille de Dien Bien Phu*, Jeudy's film complements the fiction of Dien Bien Phu. Jeudy's ambitions are much more modest. He does not want his film to be either a "history film" or "a commentary on the war" but simply *"une plongée à l'émotion"* [a high-angle shot into the emotions] of the days and nights of combat. Borrowing techniques of mass media, reportage, hand-held cameras, frequent zooms to express a variety of points of view—strategies that would find their narrative equivalent in Michael Herr's *Dispatches* (1968)— the director weaves a narrative using information gleaned from a number of archival sources. These include the writings of war correspondents, sequences drawn from amateur films, excerpts from letters written by soldiers and members of their families, American and French newsreels, testimonies of soldiers, doctors, nurses, and journalists. This documentary chronicles the suffering, anguish, and hope of the legionnaires and depicts different types of war scenes—images of the burial of the dead during combat, of the vertiginous fall of the (parachuting) paratroopers—and jumps to the celebration of Christmas Eve and Easter Mass at the scene of battle. The director quite successfully conveys and highlights the bitterness and suffering of the soldiers in the war zone, and their coming to knowledge of the imminent defeat, with its impending humiliation and suffering. War footages are placed in radical juxtaposition with scenes shot in France during the New Year's Eve celebration, presenting the fear of family members and the reaction of the French press to the cease-fire negotiations.[36] This montage, this mix of different media, works not because it presents a coherent view of the battle but precisely because of its refusal to reconstitute a homogeneous space, to accept a monologic perspective, to position the spectator as the unified and unifying subject of its filmic vision. These images produce contradictions in both subjective and social processes.

Schoendoerffer's *Dien Bien Phu*, on the other hand, fails to engage viewers, to move or convince them, because of its filmic unself-consciousness, its inability to question its structuring vision, its will to contain the heterogeneous and bind the subject. It simply memorializes without addressing larger political issues. It never questions, for instance, the logic behind the presence of the French in Southeast Asia. What were the French fighting for? Why did the French underestimate the strength and determination of the Vietnamese (a trace of their arrogance)? Was war the only remaining alternative to resolve political disputes? What does "Indochine française" mean in the 1950s? These questions were not asked because they would have undermined the whole project of the "memorialization" of Indochina, a mode that also pervades Régis Wargnier's *Indochine* and, to a lesser extent, Jean-Jacques Annaud's *The Lover*.

The critical reception of Schoendoerffer's film has been lukewarm, though it should have been criticized severely. It is as if French movie critics believed that panning the film amounted to being disrespectful to the memory of the war dead and, more important, to the vision of an eyewitness account that survived the battle, the death march, and the imprisonment. *Dien Bien Phu* continues today to be understood emotionally rather than assessed critically for its filmic quality. And yet it has found attentive support from an unlikely source: the French government. Schoendoerffer's film could not have been produced without the active intervention and patronage of the French government. The French Ministries of Foreign Affairs and Defense, using their diplomatic prerogatives, persuaded the Socialist Republic of Vietnam to allow *Dien Bien Phu* to be shot on location. In addition to that political and diplomatic assistance, *Dien Bien Phu* also enjoyed the sanction of the Ministry of Culture. Although the French film industry always had the support of Jack Lang, the scope and manner of government patronage in the case of *Dien Bien Phu* is perhaps unprecedented.[37]

Why did the French government take such a strong interest in Schoendoerffer's filmic project at this particular historical juncture? What was at stake? I will begin to answer these questions in a somewhat oblique fashion. I would argue that the French government's "investment" in Schoendoerffer's project transcends the realm of financial considerations, the economics of filmic production, and extends itself into the realm of affect, a hypothesis confirmed and made evident in Vietnam.

On the second day of François Mitterrand's official visit to Vietnam
(10–12 February 1993), the first one by a Western head of state, the
French president visited the battlefield of Dien Bien Phu, a visit described
in the press as a *"recueillement."* Mitterrand's pilgrimage to the site of "one
of the worst defeats inflicted on the French army" was a means to "exorcise
a painful past" (France 2, 10 February 1993). Mitterrand was accompanied
not only by General Maurice Schmidt, the former chief of staff of the
French army, who as a young enlisted man fought at Dien Bien Phu.
Schoendoerffer also made the visit, giving his own personal account of
the battle, which he survived and chronicled as a cinematographer and
photographer for the French armed forces. The significance of Schoendoerffer's presence, next to Mitterrand, should not be lost on the public. It
conferred a certain moral authority upon Schoendoerffer's movie. Furthermore, the invitation to join the presidential party at the site of the
battle bestows an official stamp of authenticity, sanctioning the movie's
legitimacy. *Dien Bien Phu,* then, appears to be a fitting tribute, a "filmic
memorial" to a traumatic historical past.

I provide the political "context" to the filmic text to draw attention to
questions that bear directly on the production, distribution, and reception
of the movie, because films are indeed "cultural events." My contention is
that the notions of "memory," "commemoration," and "memorial" constitute the modalities by which *Dien Bien Phu* (and, to a lesser extent, *Indochine* and *The Lover*) operate; they "memorialize" or address the spectator
by constructing a memorial. They form as well the bases on which France's
desires to pay homage to the memory of the war dead are inscribed and
projected, what we could call the processes (both conscious and unconscious) through which Indochina is reconstructed as an important chapter
in the French historical past, its collective memory, and its *imaginaire
national-républicain.*

The commemorative "text" takes a full range of different forms: the
decorative façade, the war memorial, the funeral inscription, the historical
fresco, and as I have argued, the filmic text. The only requirement is that it
leaves a historiographic, monumental, ceremonial, or visual trace. Cha-
grined by the absence of any "commemorative" marker in Dien Bien Phu,
Mitterrand expressed the hope that "a monument, to the memory of the
French dead" would be raised there in the near future.

This wish has been realized in an unlikely site, in the city of Fréjus. A
memorial had been planned by its mayor, François Léotard, the honorary
president of the Parti Républicain and the defense minister in Edouard
Balladur's government. Jacques Chirac, the president of the RPR, set the

first stone of the memorial in 1988. And upon his return from Vietnam, François Mitterrand, the Socialist president, inaugurated the Mémorial des Guerres en Indochine on 16 February 1993. We see that the political use of "national" memories, what Eric Hobsbawm and Terence Ranger call the "invention of tradition"—a "process of formalization and ritualization, characterized by reference to the past, if only by imposing repetition"[38]—transcends party affiliations. Léotard was proud of this "continuity" and couched it in these terms:

> Il y a des morts, il y a maintenant presque quarante ans, qui sont tombés sous les couleurs du drapeau de la République, et c'était bien que l'on soit ensemble, de droite et de gauche, au delà des philosophies, au delà des religions, au delà des opinions, pour célébrer leur sacrifice. Et c'est ça le message d'aujourd'hui. Et c'est celui de la République, au fond.

> [The dead fell, almost forty years ago, under the colors of the flag of the Republic, and it was appropriate that we gather together, from the Right and the Left, beyond our philosophical differences, beyond religion, beyond our convictions, to celebrate their sacrifice. And that is today's message. And it is also that of the Republic.] (France 2, February 10, 1993)

Here, historical memory is manipulated rhetorically. The summation of the Republic and its idealized precepts—the notion of sacrifice—and the conscious manipulation of its symbols—the flag—serve to contain history and justify the homogenizing and violent impulse deployed in the edification of a national memory of Indochina, which relies on an authoritarian, unitary, universalist, and intensely *passéiste* construct.[39] This *rassemblement* included not only French political figures from different parties, but also the veterans (*anciens*), the legionnaires and paratroopers, as well as indigenous troops, Vietnamese and North African soldiers who fought for France alongside the French. The presence and incorporation of "native troops" at the ribbon-cutting ceremony, which fulfilled the official desire to be inclusive, served the egalitarian or democratic intent of representation and lent, at the same time, a semblance of authenticity and truth. Everyone, regardless of spiritual, ideological, religious, or racial differences, paid homage to the men who fell "under the colors of the flag of the Republic." What we have before us is nothing less than the construction of new political allegories.

This "official ceremony," for some people, makes up for the nation's political amnesia. But it must also be underscored that it took the French (not unlike the Americans), almost forty years to pay tribute to those who died for the continued colonial domination of France in Southeast Asia. The Mémorial des Guerres en Indochine would now stand as a monument to the war dead, dedicated, as its name suggests, to the wars in Indochina (my emphasis). The attempt to establish a continuity with a suitable historical past is reinforced by the commemorative words inscribed on the marble: "Ici reposent les corps de 3152 militaires morts pour la France en Indochine 1939–1954." [Here lie the bodies of 3,152 soldiers who died for France in Indochina 1939–1954.] These dates are indeed important because they rewrite France's colonial history as a benign chapter of a larger world conflict: World War II, then, becomes its new historical point of reference. The soldiers who are being honored include those who fought the "invading Japanese" as well as those who perished in that infamous battle.

These official displays and public commemorations, carefully staged to include ("*rassembler*") the forgotten "Other"—Vietnamese and North African members of the *troupe coloniale*, who fought alongside the French and awaited official recognition of their actions[40]—do not end the political amnesia and silence surrounding the "Indochinese question." Rather, they displace or erase a not-so-heroic vision of France's historical involvement in Southeast Asia from the collective memory. The Fréjus memorial, while honoring the men who sacrificed their lives for France in Indochina, refuses to name Dien Bien Phu, submerging the memory of the military defeat in the plural "*guerres en Indochine*" [Indochinese wars]. Moreover, by presenting themselves at their most "heroic" and "commemorative," the French are determined to create a new official "*paysage mémoriel*" [memorial landscape]. Who, or what, then, is really being mourned here? Admittedly the war dead, but there are also other "subjects" of loss that remain unacknowledged: the loss of an era, of a colonial empire, of a utopian world; the loss of France's influence and prestige.

Current French cinematic production on Indochina is part of a complex "cultural memorial," a means for the French to "work through" and mourn the loss of Indochina, the jewel in the former French colonial empire. Because the relation between Indochine and France has always been—and still is—compared to a love affair, the process of remembrance of its loss resembles that of mourning. The "work of mourning," as Jean Laplanche and J.-B. Pontalis remind us, is an "intrapsychic process, occurring after the loss of a love object, whereby the subject gradually manages to detach himself from this object."[41] Schoendoerffer's entire filmic and novelistic career—he is one of the few to have evoked the Indochinese war throughout his career, with *La 317ème Section* (1965), *Le Crabe-tambour* (1977), and *Dien Bien Phu*—does not tend toward liberation of affect and discharge (abreaction)[42] as in catharsis, but "works through" certain issues in the commemorative remembrance of the war. Pierre Schoendoerffer asked himself "why the French are prepared to spend $25 million on a film of our most terrible defeat. . . . The answer, he believes, lies in romanticism: 'Indochina was a long love story for France, beginning with the missionaries. *Dien Bien Phu* is my adieu to that story.'"[43] Hence, Schoendoerffer could write in all seriousness that "the shooting of this movie was a matter of love (*"une affaire d'amour"*). I think that the battle, in a strange way, was also a matter of love (*"une affaire d'amour"*).[44] Like *Dien Bien Phu*, *Indochine* and *The Lover* are part of that filmic memorial that has been "erected" to remember the French colonization of Indochina as an extraordinary and memorable relation that linked "men and women, mountains and plains, humans and gods, Indochina and France" (*Indochine*). These movies sustain and reinforce the founding myths of the French colonial presence in the Indochinese peninsula.

The place of Indochina in the French imaginary is far from resolved. It will continue to arouse interest and provide an ideal topos for writers and filmmakers. What we desperately need, however, is to go beyond the romantic love story to address crucial questions that remain to be raised and answered. The problematic filmic *engouement* that I have called "colonial blues" moves us even further away from a serious historical interrogation of the colonial situation. Colonial blues refers not simply to a nostalgic sentiment for a bygone era—life in French Indochina in the 1930s—a willful ignorance of the history of the region, or a feeling of benevolence toward the natives. More important, it calls attention to the strategies and modes of representation used by French film directors to stage and "memorialize" French Indochina as a collective fantasy of French colonial history in Southeast Asia.

NOTES

1. Salman Rushdie, "Outside the Whale," in *Imaginary Homelands* (London: Penguin Books, 1991), 91.
2. French television was a very effective vehicle for disseminating information on the subject. Schoendoerffer presented *Dien Bien Phu* (1992, 140 minutes) *en avant première* in the *journal regional de Franche-Comté*. TF1 presented *Récits d'Indochine* (60 minutes), a 1992 documentary made by Patrick Jeudy, on Friday, 6 March 1992, at 23.50. Bernard Pivot devoted a special "Bouillon de culture" to the subject

of Dien Bien Phu on Sunday, 1 March 1992. FR3 returned to this subject on Thursday, 19 March 1992, with an evening program titled "Hommes de caractères." After screening Pierre Schoendoerffer's *Le Crabe-tambour*, a documentary on Dien Bien Phu titled *La Mémoire et l'oubli* (1992) (60 minutes), directed by Yves and Ada Rémy, was presented. For a more detailed view of the programming, see Colette Bouillon, "L'Offensive télévisuelle," *La Croix L'Événement* (Friday, 6 March 1992), 3.

3. "Entre 1954 and 1962, officiellement ils participaient à des opérations de maintien de l'ordre, puisque cette guerre n'a jamais voulu dire son nom. Patrick Rotman et Bertrand Tavernier la nomment pourtant cette guerre: en demandant à ceux qui ont été les acteurs de la raconter et en laissant la caméra "écouter" ces quarante témoins, tous originaires de la région de Grenoble. Quatre heures d'immersion dans l'Histoire, par le seul truchement de la narration. Pas d'artifice, pas de mise en scène, mais un simple montage qui ordonne le propos. La caméra film en plan serré. Rotman pose des questions simples. Ils se souviennent."

[Between 1954 and 1962, they participated, officially, in operations for the maintenance of law and order, since this war was never given a name. Patrick Rotman and Bertrand Tavernier, however, name this war by asking the actors of this war to tell it and by letting the camera "listen" to these forty witnesses, all of them natives of the Grenoble region. Four hours of immersion in history through the sole mediation of narration. No artifice, no staging, but a simple montage that organizes the words. The camera shoots in close-ups. Rotman asks simple questions. They remember] (Alain Bouzi, "La Guerre sans nom," *Première* [March 1992], n.p.).

4. It is worth mentioning that all three movies on Indochina were accompanied by either a photographic album of the shooting (see Jean-Jacques Annaud, *"L'Amant": Illustré par les photos de Benoît Barbier* [Paris: Grasset, 1992], and Pierre Schoendoerffer, *Dien-Bien-Phu: De la Bataille au film* [Paris: Fixot/Lincoln, 1992]) or an outright novel (see Christian de Montella, *Indochine* [Paris: Fayard, 1992]). Following the success of the movies/books, Jean-Luc Coatalem published his *Suite Indochinoise* (Paris: La Table Ronde, 1993), and Christophe Bataille published *Annam* (Paris: Arlea, 1993). The collected works of Jean Hougron had appeared in two volumes under the title *Nuit indochinoise*. Military accounts of the war were also re-edited (see in particular the work of Erwan Bergot and Pierre Schoendoerffer).

As far as cinema is concerned, only a few films on Indochina were ever shot. Very little attention has been paid to French feature films on Indochina, in part because of their scarcity—Pierre Sorlin finds only one film that takes place in Indochina in the thirties (Pierre Sorlin, "The Fanciful Empire: French Feature Films and the Colonies in the 1930s," *French Cultural Studies* 2 [1991]: 135–151). Pierre Boulanger, in his study of colonial cinema, *Le Cinéma colonial: De l'Atlantide à Lawrence d'Arabie* (Paris: Sehers/Cinema 2000, 1975), concentrates on the Maghreb and Central Africa and does not deal in detail with any other parts of the French Empire. The cinematic love affair with Indochina is a recent phenomenon. Why, one may ask, such an interest, an *engouement, un coup de foudre, un coup de coeur* (Jacques Siclier, "Indochine, ton nom est femme," *Le Monde* [Friday, 17 April 1992]: 14) for the Indochine of the interwar period? Such a filmic passion for colonial movies was not always a prevailing trend. Of the 1,305 adventure films shot in the 1930s, only 21 were made in Asia, and not a single one featured Indochina, making it remarkable in its absence (see Jacques Thobie et al., *Histoire de la France coloniale 1914–1990* [Paris: Armand Colin, 1990], 305).

5. André Bazin, *What Is Cinema?*, trans. Hugh Gray (Berkeley: University of California Press, 1967), 1:10.

6. Teresa de Lauretis, *Alice Doesn't: Feminism, Semiotics, Cinema* (Bloomington: Indiana University Press, 1984), 15, 4.

7. Ibid., 37.

8. Tejaswini Niranjana, *Siting Translation: History, Post-Structuralism, and the Colonial Context* (Berkeley: University of California Press, 1992), 3.

9. de Lauretis, *Alice Doesn't*, 37.

10. David Bordwell, "Classical Hollywood Cinema: Narrational Principles and Procedures," in *Narrative, Apparatus, Ideology*, ed. Philip Rosen (New York: Columbia University Press, 1986), 18.

11. Mary Ann Doane, *The Desire to Desire: The Woman's Film of the 1940's* (Bloomington: Indiana University Press, 1987), 96.

12. Régis Wargnier wrote the screenplay with Deneuve in mind. The role of Eliane was created especially for her: "Il m'avait parlé d'un projet tournant autour d'un personnage de femme ayant des responsabilités d'homme mais gardant les avantages d'être femme. Il est parti de cette idée simple, de l'Indochine et d'une petite princesse orpheline. Je lui ai donné un accord de principe. Puis l'histoire s'agrandit." [He had told me of a project about a woman character whose responsibilities were those of a man but who retains the prerogatives of being a woman. He began with this simple idea, of Indochina and a young orphaned princess. I agreed in principle. From there, the story developed] (*Paris-Match 69*).

13. Jean Noury narrates the history of French presence in Indochina through postcards in *L'Indochine avant l'ouragan* (Chartres: Imprimerie Charon, 1984).

14. de Lauretis, *Alice Doesn't*, 37.

15. See Teresa de Lauretis, *The Technologies of Gender: Essays on Theory, Film, and Fiction* (Bloomington: Indiana University Press, 1987); Laura Mulvey, *Visual and Other Pleasures* (Bloomington: Indiana University Press, 1989); Rey Chow, *Woman and Chinese Modernity* (Minneapolis: University of Minnesota Press, 1991) and Primitive Passions (New York: Columbia University Press, 1995).

16. Jill Forbes, "Review article: Jacques Sicler, *Le Cinéma français*, 2 vols. Paris: Ramsay, 1990, 1991," *Screen* 34, no. 4 (Winter 1993): 408.

17. Marguerite Duras, *L'Amant* (Paris: Les Editions de Minuit, 1984).

18. Jean-Jacques Annaud, "Impressions of Vietnam," *Harper's Bazaar*, September 1992, 174.

19. Annaud also provides the following reasons for adapting Duras's novel: "Parmi les raisons qui m'y ont poussé, il y avait le fait que cette histoire se déroulait dans une colonie française. Autrement dit il ne s'agissait pas que d'une histoire d'amour: il y avait aussi le contact de deux races, de deux cultures, phénomène qui me fascine depuis le jour où, frais émoulu de l'Idhec, on m'avait envoyé comme coopérant au Service des arts et du commerce de l'industrie cinématographique de la république fédérale du Cameroun. J'avais alors été bouleversé par l'Afrique."

[Among the reasons that led me to adapt it to the screen was the fact that this story took place in a French colony. In other words, it wasn't simply a love story: it also involved the encounter of two races, two cultures, a phenomenon that fascinated me ever since the day, when, having just graduated from the IDHEC, I was sent as a delegate to the "service des arts et du commerce de l'industrie cinématographique" of the Federal Republic of Cameroon. Africa had overwhelmed me] (*L'Amant: Illustré par les photos de Benoît Barbier* [Paris: Grasset, 1992], 12).

20. Jean-Jacques Annaud, "Impressions of Vietnam," *Harper's Bazaar*, September 1992, 176.

21. Ibid.

22. Quoted by Jonathan Crary, *Techniques of the Observer: On Vision and Modernity in the Nineteenth Century* (Cambridge: MIT Press, 1990), 1.

23. Niranjana, *Siting Translation*, 3.

24. Jean-Jacques Annaud, "L'Amant," *Le Point*, 1992, no. 192: 62.

25. The following passage exemplifies the working conditions in "ce pays totalement démuni" (this completely impoverished nation): "Des assistants, des régisseurs étaient depuis plusieurs mois installés au Viêt-nam. Ils défrichaient la Cochinchine, ouvraient des comptes en banque, demandaient les autorisations de tournage, remettaient le scénario aux censeurs, contactaient la milice, la police fluviale, s'entouraient de conseillers historiques, faisaient accepter pour les douanes l'importation du matériel. L'équipe chargée des décors avait construit un immense hangar qui abritait des pousse-pousse, des tilburys, des vélos, un car de brousse, des voitures anciennes, des chars à boeufs, des charrettes, de vieux châssis, qu'au fil des semaines les derniers artisans locaux apportaient après avoir tout refabriqué grâce à des matériaux d'époque. L'équipe chargée des costumes avait monté des ateliers de teinture, de broderie, de couture qui employaient cinquante couturières vietnamiennes et sous-traitaient avec deux cents fabricants. Souvent la créatrice des costumes se rendaient à la frontière du Cambodge, pour aller chercher quelques mètres de soie laquée qui feraient un costume, une robe, une étole, un foulard."

[Assistants, assistant directors had been living in Vietnam for several months. They cleared the terrain in Cochinchina, opened bank accounts, requested authorizations for filming, submitted the screenplay to the censors, contacted the militia and the water patrol; they surrounded themselves with historical advisers and convinced customs to allow them to import all of the equipment. The team in charge of the film sets had built a gigantic hangar to accommodate rickshaws, tilburies, bicycles, a country bus, antique cars, oxcarts, wagons, old chassis, items brought, as the weeks passed, by the last autochthonous artisans, who had rebuilt them with period pieces and material. The team in charge of the costumes had set up dyeing, embroidering, and sewing workrooms where fifty Vietnamese dressmakers worked, subcontracting to two hundred manufacturers. The designer of these costumes would often travel to the Cambodian border in search of a few meters of lacquered silk that could be used to make a costume, a dress, a stole, a scarf] (in *L'Amant*, Grasset, 1992, 21–22).

26. Jean-Jacques Annaud, "L'Amant," *Le Point*, no. 192: 62.

27. Annaud may have succeeded in translating onto the filmic image the writerly quality of Duras's novel in the credit title sequence. The gold nib of the black pen moves sensually on the surface of parchmentlike paper; the distinctive sound of writing is superimposed with the deep voice of Jeanne Moreau. Then the

paper becomes skin, the skin of the lovers. This beautiful sequence is not without precedent nor is it entirely original. It echoes the opening shot used by Alain Resnais in *Hiroshima mon amour*. The bodies of the entwined lovers are first seen as body parts, framed by the camera; later on, the same shots frame the bodies of Japanese victims of the atomic bomb, and still later, that of the French heroine's first lover, a German soldier.

28. David Robinson, "In Bed with an Ingenue," *Life and Times*, Thursday, 18 June 1992, 3.

29. Annaud writes that after the end of the filming in Vietnam, "la jeune fille et le Chinois se sont retrouvés huit jours plus tard dans un studio parisien, transformé en garçonnière pour sept semaines" [the young woman and the Chinese man met eight days later in a Parisian studio, which was turned into a bachelor flat for seven weeks] (34). He ends his narrative thus: "Au Viêt-nam, j'avais montré le refus d'une jeune fille d'adhérer à la morale d'une communauté qui la méprisait. Dans la garçonnière, j'ai eu envie d'amener le spectateur au spectacle du plaisir, de lui faire aimer sans retenue l'image du désir, l'image de l'amour." [In Vietnam, I had shown the young woman's unwillingness to adhere to the morals of a community that had rejected her. In the bachelor flat, I wanted to suture the spectator to the spectacle of pleasure, to make him/her love unrestrainedly the image of desire, the image of love] (in *L'Amant*, Grasset, 1992, 35).

30. Ibid., 12.

31. Dien Bien Phu premiered on 4 March 1992.

32. Pierre Schoendoerffer, *Dien Bien Phu: de la bataille au film* (Paris: Fixot-Lincoln, 1992), 127. Subsequent citations appear as page numbers in text.

33. Jean-Luc Macia, in *"Dien Bien Phu, notre Apocalypse Now," La Croix L'événe-ment* (Friday, 6 March 1992), 3.

34. In ibid., 2, Jean-Luc Macia uses "docu-drama" or *"film-vérité"* to describe Schoendoerffer's movie. The documentary or *"vérité"* refers to a variety of elements: the shooting on location with the collaboration of the Vietnamese, the fact that Allaire became the "military adviser" for the movie, the use of war equipment from the period, the Vietnamese extras, etc. The distinction between "journalistic report" and "fiction" is blurred further by the overlapping plot lines (or, as Macia writes, "two films in one"). Schoendoerffer also depicts the lives of two journalists—one French, the other American—in search of information for their daily column. One could argue that Schoendoerffer's movie questions its own representational practice, how and what journalists are able to cover within the constraints of military blackouts, and, perhaps unwittingly, cover up, undermining its own authority in elaborating a transparent and "accurate coverage" of the war in Indochina.

35. Stephen Heath, "Narrative Space," in *Narrative, Apparatus, Ideology*, ed. Philip Rosen (New York: Columbia University Press, 1986), 404.

36. I am indebted to Colette Bouillon, "L'offensive télévisuelle," *La Croix L'Événement* (Friday, 6 March 1992), 3. Former enemies have also been given the opportunity to tell their version of the story. In her television program, the historian Danièle Rousselier attempts to balance the views of French military personnel, colonial civil servants, and politicians on the Indochinese question with those of the Vietnamese. She interviews peasants, writers, and leaders such as General

Giap, the commander in chief of the Vietminh forces during the battle of Dien Bien Phu, giving her "televised documentary," a dialogical aspect that other television programs lack. Thus we learn that the Vietnamese call "the Indochina war" the "first war," which gave rise to an even more dreadful "second war." One of the highlights of this program is "the dialogue between colonel Allaire—sub-lieutenant during the Indochina War—and the writer N'guyen Dinh Thi—a renowned poet who fought against Allaire at Dien Bien Phu" (see also Macia, "*Dien Bien Phu, notre Apocalypse Now*," 284).

37. These benefits were extended to other movies—all three movies were shot on location, thanks to the intervention and support of the French government.

38. Eric Hobsbawm and Terence Ranger, *The Invention of Tradition* (New York: Cambridge University Press, 1983), 4.

39. See Pascal Ory's essay, "De la République à la Nation," in Pierre Nora, ed. *Les Lieux de mémoire. 1. La République* (Paris: Editions Gallimard, 1984), 652.

40. This official gesture of recognition for their sacrifice is, however, deflated by the following news commentary on French national television, describing the battle of Dien Bien Phu: "Mais déjà la place forte s'était transformé en piège. Les Français étaient *minoritaire* dans les rangs d'une armée composée surtout de recrues thaïs, annamites, ou même, sénégalaises, moins motivées que les 40,000 guerriers du Vietminh avec leurs troupes d'élite et leurs commandos suicides qui leur faisaient face." [But the fortified camp had transformed itself into a trap. Frenchmen were *in the minority* in the ranks of an army made up essentially of Thai, Annamites, and even Senegalese recruits, men who were less motivated than the forty thousand Vietminh warriors with their elite troops and suicide commandos who faced them] (my emphasis) (France 2, 10 February 1993).

41. Jean Laplanche and J.-B. Pontalis, *The Language of Psychoanalysis*, trans. Donald Nicholson-Smith (New York: W. W. Norton, 1973), 485.

42. Ibid., 60.

43. Sarah Ferguson, "Return to Dien Bien Phu," *Sight and Sound* 1, no. 8 (1 December 1991): 28.

44. Schoendoerffer, *Dien Bien Phu*, 125.

Third Cinema or Third Degree

E I G H T   *The "Rachid System" in Serge Meynard's*
L'Oeil au beurre noir

Mireille Rosello

*De même que des cinéastes français "de souche" nous ont
montré qu'ils savent filmer, et plutôt bien, des beurs et des
immigrés (Serge le Péron avec* Laisse Béton, *André
Téchiné avec* La vie est un long fleuve tranquille, *Agnès
Varda avec* Sans toit ni loi, *etc) il devrait être possible
pour un cinéaste issu de l'immigration de filmer à leur
façon les Français (c'est d'ailleurs ce que fait Charef dans*
Camomille *et Maroun Bagdadi dans son téléfilm sur*
Marat).

*[Just as directors of French "stock" showed us that they
know how to film, and rather well, Beurs and immigrants
(Serge le Péron with* Laisse Béton, *André Téchiné with*
La Vie est un long fleuve tranquille, *Agnès Varda with*
Sans toit ni loi *[Vagabond], etc.), it ought to be possible
for a director who is born out of immigration to film the
French in their way (this is as a matter of fact what
Charef does in* Camomille *and what Maroun Bagdadi
does in his telefilm on Marat).]*

ABBAS FAHDEL, "UNE ESTHÉTIQUE BEUR?"
CINÉMAS MÉTIS, *CINÉMACTION*

*Un Arabe sauve une jeune fille agressée par deux blancs,
c'est le monde à l'envers.*

> *[An Arab rescues a young girl attacked by two White guys,*
> *this is the world upside down.]*
>
> L'OEIL AU BEUR̶R̶E̶ NOIR

What if someone asked you to give the title of one recent French film made by a Beur or Arab director? Would you be puzzled? Would you remain speechless? Would you immediately and perhaps triumphantly pull Mehdi Charef's *Le Thé au harem d'Archimède* out of some postcolonial hat? And what if someone asked you to make a list of *thirty* of the films made by Beur directors during the 1980s? Would you suspect that you were having a rather unpleasant dream about a *Jeopardy*-like game show in French cinema studies? Or would you wonder if the interviewer really meant Beurs (loosely defined as the children of immigrants of North African origin) or rather Maghrebian directors (working in North Africa or even in France)?

In reality, more than thirty films were made by Beur directors between 1980 and 1990. Doesn't that seem slightly improbable to you? Of course, the number of movies made by Maghrebian directors has been on the increase for the last decade.[1] And in 1982, the issue of *CinémAction* titled "Cinéma de l'émigration: émigrés et déracinés à l'écran" featured a list of five hundred films, but they were about the representation of immigrants, including Arabs, not films authored by Arab directors residing in France.[2] Thirty films? Probably not.

Then again, consider the following list:

1980	Abdelkader Dellas, *Les Corons*
	Okacha Touita, *Rue Tartarin*
	Mahmoud Zemmouri, *Prends dix mille balles et casse-toi*
1981	Farida Belghoul, *C'est Madame La France que tu préfères?*
	Fitouri Belhiba, *Mauvaises graines*
	Karim Idriss, *Esquisse pour un portrait de famille*
	Saad Salman, *En raison de circonstances . . .*
	Salah Sermini, *En marge d'événements réels et d'autres imaginés*
1982	Hamid Amzal, *Le Cercle*
	Reski Harani, *Le Taxicomane*
	Farid Lahouassa, *L'Oued*
	Okacha Touita, *Les Sacrifiés*
1983	Lakdar Lahcine, *Trois garçons sur la route*
	Farid Lahouassa, *Le Fourgon*
	Saad Salman, *Il était une fois Beyrouth*
	Mahmoud Zemmouri, *Les Années folles du twist*

1984   Abdelkrim Bahloul, *Le Thé à la menthe*
        Aïssa Djabri, *La Vago*
1985   Mounir Bekka, *Barberousse pas de chance*
        Farida Belghoul, *Le Départ du père*
        Mohamed Benayat, *L'Enfant des étoiles*
        Mehdi Charef, *Le Thé au harem d'Archimède*
        Farid Lahouassa, *La Poupée qui tousse*
        Malika Yacine, *En plein coeur*
1986   Abel Bennour, *Poésie en images-condamné*
        Abdelkader Dellas, *L'Image de soie*
        Reski Harani, *Da Mokrane*
        Okacha Touita, *Le Rescapé*
1987   Mehdi Charef, *Miss Mona*
        Abdelkader Dellas, *L'Escargot, le profil perdu*
        Bourlem Guerdjou, *Ring*
        Salah Sermini, *La Mémoire et le coeur*
1988   Mehdi Charef, *Camomille*
1989   Hamdi Abdallah, *Mes Nuits sont vos jours*
        Cheikh Djemaï, *La Nuit du doute*
1990   Okacha Touita, *Le Cri des hommes*
        Abel Bennour, *Khettana*

Naturally, a list is always a rhetorical coup de force, and my intervention is nothing but the playful invention of a new litany.[3] In fact, if my
little trick has annoyed any serious reader, let me recant on the spot and
declare that I am not terribly interested either in defining Beur cinema or
even in proving that it exists (and has been made invisible by the canon). If
some readers are already involved in the tempting enterprise that consists
of adding other titles to the list,[4] of challenging my right to call *Camomille*
(1988) a Beur movie,[5] or Mahmoud Zemmouri a Beur director,[6] I should,
in all fairness, warn them that I agree with everything they say in advance
or, as the saying goes, that I will not be available for comment. If you are
already convinced that Beur cinema does not exist, I will not contradict
you. I am perfectly aware that the list I just produced forgets that it rests
on the premise that we agree it is desirable to attach the label "Beur" to
any film, or even to a whole culture, let alone to individuals.[7]

Having confessed that the beginning of this article is in bad faith, I will
hasten to say that the controversial and irritating practice of the list (it is
powerful and simplifying, it is a discourse of truth that hides its arbitrariness and political bias behind the sheer strength of its immediacy) was not

a random choice. The list is not only incomplete, it is also inaccurate, but it serves a purpose. Because it can only be repeated, recited, because it suffers from amnesia (its own logic of fabrication and ideological structure craves oblivion and transparency), a list is not unlike a stereotype. As Jean-Marie Touratier puts it:

> Il y a du stéréotype quand il y a interdit sur le questionnement de la répétition. Mieux, lorsqu'il y a oubli, scotomisation de toute répétition, leurre pour faire miroiter qu'il n'y a pas, qu'il n'y a jamais eu répétition.
>
> [Stereotype is present when the questioning of repetition is forbidden. Better yet, when there is forgetfulness, suppression of any repetition, a lure to make it seem as though there is none, that there has never been repetition.] [8]

A list, like a stereotype, counts on the hypnotic power of repetition. It hopes that each repetition will confirm its incantatory charm. [9] Repetitive and formulaic statements, of the textual, oral, or visual kind, tend to build up around so-called politically sensitive issues ("immigration," "race," and of course "racism"), and this article is as much about a hypothetical "Beur" cinema as about a cinematographic discourse that may be capable of opposing the immediacy, predictability, and discouraging unanswerability of lists and stereotypes. If this form of cinematographic discourse, for historical reasons, happens to coincide with a number of films that have been called "Beur," let the coincidence become a form of ambiguous alliance and coalition rather than a definitional problem.

The film from which I poached the list strategy and the theory of ambiguous alliances is titled *L'Oeil au beurre noir*. Directed by Serge Meynard in 1987, it is a commercial feature, a mainstream comedy about a young White bourgeois woman, Virginie (Julie Jezequel) and two young men: Rachid (Smaïn), a "Beur" who lives in a typical "*cité*" and whose White friends are "*loubards*" and thieves, and Denis (Bernard Legitimus), a middle-class Black artist who has to move out of his apartment unexpectedly. Throughout the movie, the two men are completely absorbed by a double and impossible quest: find an apartment and seduce the heroine.

I have not even included the film in the list because it may well be the case that we could find as many reasons for insisting that *L'Oeil au beurre noir* is a Beur movie as for insisting that it is not. The plot is obviously not about lists, but it is about the uses and abuses of repetition, and the film as a whole never ceases to demonstrate the ambivalence of the representation of any identity. In other words, the movie seems to doubt that it is possible to construct a "Beur" or "noir" identity and examines the possibility of creating an alliance between two nonrepresentative characters, while at the same time devoting much energy to the reappropriation of stereotypes. Nothing prepares the Beur and the *noir* to cohabit harmoniously or even peacefully within this movie. In fact, nothing authorizes me to even suggest that there is such as thing as "a" Beur and "a" Black character, let alone a relationship based on such terms between them. And the ambivalence of the tandem is already made clear in the title of the movie.

Like the ambiguous "*beurre noir*" of the title, whatever is "Beur" about this movie is never autonomous, it is always attached to other connotations, other communities, other problematics. And if we were looking for a strong gesture of affirmation of Beur culture, we would find that it is always undermined by the movie's disrespectful tone and strong element of derision. The title suggests that the film will not decide whether or not it wants to be identified as a "Beur" movie. On the poster, the presence of a "Beur" entity is visible because the last two letters of "*beurre*" have been crossed out. It is due to a manipulation that modifies the original phrase (itself a graffito on a wall). The word "*beur*" appears in the title as the result of the fictional intervention of an anonymous hand that introduces a double entendre in the set phrase. The pun itself is not brilliantly original, but it is significant that the revelation of a "Beur" factor within the title should be the result of an act of tampering that some authority pretends to have overlooked rather than a deliberate decision to take liberties with the spelling or the traditional association of words (why not call the movie *L'Oeil au beur noir*, for example?). I suggest that the extra mark, that both erases and preserves the end of the word "*beurre*," is emblematic of the film's ambivalence toward what could be a solemn affirmation of Beur culture. The pun does not go all the way; it points to certain intertextual references but denies the importance, rather than celebrates the value, of a hypothetical "Beur" identity. Implicitly, the title responds to those critics and journalists who have been eager to hail the birth of a "Beuritude," perhaps because it was more convenient to remember familiar stories and conjure up recognized intellectual figures (Senghor, Césaire) than to examine what was new about the Beurs' ambivalence toward identity and community culture.[10]

The poster of *L'Oeil au beurre noir* is not the only example of facetiousness in the genre of recent French cinema posters. Jean-Luc Godard has been known to indulge in similarly self-parodic experiment: the advertising campaign that launched his latest movie (*Hélas pour moi*) played with the director's amused discovery that "there is God in Godard and Dieu in Depardieu." But even if the intention is obviously ironic, what is being parodied is a megalomaniac statement, whereas Serge Meynard's decision to let the title of the movie look like scribbled-over graffiti, a sloppy version of what was not even a slick design to begin with, is a more humble allusion to his film's lack of reference and origin. The graffiti also refuses to take sides: it neither adheres wholeheartedly to a supposedly new Beur identity nor denies altogether the possibility of having something to do with the "Beurs."

The association between "butter" and Beur is almost a mockery of more conventional political gestures. I wonder if, in 1987, it did not sound like a self-conscious rewriting of recently heard slogans like "Blacks, Blancs, Beurs," the rallying cry of the militants of the 1984 march (Convergence), which invented the flag of a new imagined nation. The allusion to the *"beur(re) noir"*[11] is the opposite of a serious declaration, and the title as a whole, with its reference to a form of latent violence and unmotivated threat (who will have "a black eye"?) remains unexplained. Yet, the chance encounter between *verlan* (a politically charged slang) and butter (arguably a most down-to-earth and apolitical matter) is at the same time completely meaningless, obvious (it is not subtle, it is not even a good pun) but a tentative sign of recognition.[12] In 1990, Azouz Begag seems to remember the pun in his "Lexique des idées arrêtées sur des gens qui bougent . . . dans le désordre" [Lexicon of stopped ideas about people who move . . . in disorder]:

> Beur: mot désignant une substance alimentaire grasse et onctueuse (voir Petit Robert). De plus en plus écrit de cette façon par les journalistes (grosse faute d'orthographe! cf. *La Disparition* de G. Perec). Voudrait maintenant désigner une population issue de l'immigration maghrébine . . . on a eu *Pain et Chocolat* . . . manquait le Beur. Décidément, l'immigration ça se mange bien au petit déjeuner!

> [Beur: word designating a greasy and creamy food substance (see Petit Robert dictionary). More and more often written this way by journalists (huge spelling mistake! cf. *The Disappearance* by G. Perec). Would like now to designate a population born out of Maghrebian immigration . . . there was Bread and Chocolate . . . butter (beurre/Beur) was missing. Indeed, immigration goes well for breakfast!][13]

The distantiation from a "Beur" community is not the only instance of ambivalent positioning in this movie. The dislocation of the original set phrase—*beur(re)/noir*—also functions like a prediction at the level of the plot: it announces that the solidarity that will slowly develop between the

Beur and the Black characters will owe as much to chance and necessity (to parody Jacques Monod) as to a supposedly shared minority status. No theory of race and culture will come to the rescue of the heroes. Once the spectator realizes that the *beurre noir* of the title meant more than the sum of the literal meaning of the words, s/he may imagine new forms of multiculturalism: the original linguistic arbitrariness of the set phrase becomes an apt metaphor to express the cohabitation between Beurs and Blacks in those far-off *banlieues* or *cités*. The alliance between the Black and the Beur is not forced into the narrative as a form of cosmic destiny (as in Stanley Kramer's *The Defiant Ones* [1958], where two prisoners are handcuffed to each other and have to learn to accept their hybrid and collective self). If a "culture" is represented in this movie, it may be close to what the press and the media are beginning to call *la culture des banlieues* (the culture of the suburbs), a patchwork of different cultures, which, unfortunately, may end up functioning more like a Benetton ad (a mere juxtaposition of communities) if a new discourse does not emerge soon. *La culture des banlieues* is at the same time an interestingly de-ethnicized and de-essentialized paradigm of coalition between communities and a reassuringly re-universalized entity for the dominant culture, which seems to welcome the reluctance with which some "Beurs" refuse to embrace a Beur identity. In the past few years, the media have seemed to consider that it is a reasonable, intelligent, and sophisticated point of view to side with those representatives of the Beur (non)-community who emphatically declare there is no such thing as Beur culture.

A recent special issue of *Le Nouvel Observateur* was thus titled "Les Beurs tels qu'ils se voient" [The Beurs as They See Themselves]. The title seemed to hesitate between a desire to be catchy and a determination to be moderate in its sensationalism, but at one level, it certainly implied that there was such a thing as *les Beurs* and that they had a self-image. Strangely enough, that statement was proposed only to be immediately withdrawn by the conclusion of a (reassuring?) series of interviews among Beur celebrities. The question was, "Y a-t-il une culture beur? Smaïn, Mehdi Charef, Amina . . . Ils occupent la scène artistique. Veulent-ils pour autant revendiquer leur identité? Débat." [Is there a Beur culture? Smaïn, Mehdi Charef, Amina . . . They occupy the artistic stage. Do they want to claim their identity for this reason? Debate."] And François Reynart's conclusion was the following:

Acceptons l'idée qu'il n'y a pas de "culture beur" en tant que telle, en France. Certes, il existe une culture des banlieues, le rap et le verlan, mais elle appartient à tous les habitants des cités, où vivent autant de blancs et blacks que de beurs.

[Let's accept the idea that there is no "Beur culture" as such in France. Indeed, there exists a culture of the suburbs, rap and *verlan* (backwards talk), but it belongs to all the inhabitants of these neighborhoods, where as many Whites and Blacks live as Beurs.] [14]

Interestingly enough, in this document, Smaïn, who plays a Beur character in *L'Oeil au beurre noir*, occupies a rather ambiguous place. On the one hand, his popularity as an actor and performer is such that it was apparently unthinkable for *Le Nouvel Observateur* not to include him as a guest of honor even in the title. Not only is Smaïn one of the most prominent artists among those identified as the children of immigrants from North Africa but his work is related to his ethnic and cultural background: the parts that he has accepted so far and the texts he writes for his shows are often directly inspired by the adventures of the first generation of immigrants and their children's predicament. He often attacks French xenophobia and racism, and he portrays older Arabs with more tenderness and complicity than most Beur writers (*"le président beur . . . t'en veux?"* [The Beur President . . . do you want one?]).

Consequently, his absence from such a *débat* about Beurs would have stood out as a glaring one. It is the case, however, only because we have already internalized a mental list of so-called Beur artists. And when one reads *Le Nouvel Observateur*, it quickly becomes obvious that this preestablished list exists independently from how Beurs see themselves. In spite of the well-intentioned desire to let Beurs define their own image (*comment ils se voient*), Smaïn's refusal to participate in the debate is not respected. After citing a few sociologists and other artists whose position is neatly categorized as either "for" or "against" the use of the word "Beur," the author must explain:

Reste Smaïn. Lui fait bande à part, parce qu'il préfère, fait-il dire "ne pas figurer dans un dossier sur les beurs". On peut le comprendre, Smaïn. Il choisit d'être radical pour ne pas se retrouver dans un ghetto. Il n'a pas envie non plus d'être à la France des années 90 ce que Sidney Poitier fut à l'Amérique des années 50—le cache-misère commode d'une réelle discrimination.

[As for Smaïn. He makes himself an outsider, because he prefers, he has people say, "not to appear in a study on beurs." One can understand him, Smaïn. He chooses to be radical so as not to find himself in a ghetto. Nor does he feel like being in the France of the 90s what Sidney Poitier was in the America of the 50s—the convenient smoke-screen of a genuine discrimination.][15]

What I find striking in the journalist's interpretation is that Smaïn's absence is never authorized. He is quoted as having someone else say that he has nothing to say, and yet this third-degree quotation is abundantly commented upon and recuperated. Not only is Smaïn's decision *de ne pas figurer* [not to appear on the list] completely dismissed but his difficult desire for what I have called elsewhere *departenance* [unbelonging] is heard as a transparent, unambiguous statement. Someone who has made a very clear choice not to be cited within a certain context finds that his silence reverberates in an echo chamber and that his absence has turned him into a public performer as surely as if he had been pushed out onto a balcony in front of a crowd. The moment is a remarkable instance of ventriloquism and puppet-master string pulling. When Smaïn does not say anything, yet *on peut le comprendre* [one can understand him]: he wants to be "radical" (whatever radical means here), he embraces hegemonic myths about ethnicity (community equals ghetto), he is afraid of being identified with Sidney Poitier. Naturally, I am not saying that it would be impossible for Smaïn actually to endorse this image of himself, but I find the assumption rather annoyingly hasty. It may be that the reason certain Beurs refuse to be associated with "Beur culture" results precisely from the media's tendency to carve a undesirable mold within which they are then forced to cast themselves. And the press then praises them, rather hypocritically, for their pro-integration stance.

In the end, two groups repeat (apparently) the same thing: they object to the very idea of Beur culture. The repetition is of course motivated by very different reasons. This profound difference, however, ends up sounding like a happy consensus. Whenever the media suffer from a "Beur" attack, it really does not matter that each Beur may have a different reason for not wanting to be associated with the word because the foregone conclusion of every debate is that of course a Beur culture cannot exist in France because a Beur culture would be an Anglo-Saxon vision and because French Beurs (unanimously?) object to the model.

When Stéphane Bouquet reviews Malik Chibane's recent *Hexagone*, he seems happy to let the director confirm that the question of his relationship to his community is a rhetorical one:

Malik Chibane se voit-il en porte-drapeau du cinéma beur? "Le cinéma beur fait référence à une grille de lecture, à une tradition communautaire plutôt anglo-saxonne, ça véhicule un peu un côté ghetto, et la société française fonctionne avant tout sur l'idée d'intégration. Il y a peut-être une fibre, une sensibilité beur, mais cette sensibilité est française aussi, puisqu'ils veulent ça, être français. Après tout, Pagnol a surtout filmé le sud de la France. Chacun a son propre univers."

[Does Malik Chibane see himself as the representative of Beur cinema? "Beur cinema refers to a mode of reading, to a rather Anglo-Saxon tradition of community, it expresses somewhat the notion of ghetto, yet French society functions with the idea of integration. There is perhaps a Beur fiber and sensitivity, but this sensitivity is also French, since they want that very thing, to be French. After all, Pagnol above all filmed the south of France. Everyone has his own universe."] [16]

If I do not find Chibane's remarks altogether convincing, it is because his desire to avoid the "community" model is finally expressed in a rather paradoxical way: if the reference for his definition of identity within France is Pagnol's "universe," not only is the model of the community still present but it is, precisely, universalized. Pagnol's cinema is not seen for what it was, the portrait of a culture that perceived itself as different, recognizable, and that did not wish to lose its regional perspective. I am not so certain that what is culturally interesting about Pagnol's work was his desire for "*intégration.*" And by identifying Pagnol's "universe" as "*le sud de la France*" (the south of France), Chibane also dismisses crucial historical and sociological differences between turn-of-the-century Southern French culture and Beurs. The reason it is difficult to describe what the Beurs share (is there a Beur community? is there a Beur culture?) is precisely that they cannot be territorialized. No geographical area can be said to be a Beur domain except for limited, fragmented, and stereotypical microspaces, such as certain neighborhoods, the *cités*, their stairways and basements. The problem is that even such places, in their diversity, have become stereotypes, as if all *cités* were alike, all *banlieues* comparable, all HLMs interchangeable. Unlike Mehdi Charef's *Le Thé au harem d'Archimède* and Abdelkrim Bahloul's *Le Thé à la menthe*, which were criticized for their representation of the Beur hero as a predictable delinquent, Chibane's *Hexagone* is a unique attempt in the sense that this movie presents a whole gallery of portraits: Slimane (Jalil Naciri), unemployed and depressed by his unsuccessful job search; Nacera (Faiza Kaddour), a young woman who is described by critics as "in search of her independence"; Samy (Farid Abdedou), who dies of an overdose at the end; Ali the intellectual (Karim Chakir); and Staf, called "*le sapeur*" (elegant dresser) because clothes are his only passion (Hakim Sarahoui). But this commendable effort at counteracting the simplification of the Beur-as-young-delinquent image does not successfully solve the problem of stereotyping: I suggest that the multiplication of images and the representation of diversity within a community may miss its goal because it fights one manifestation of a larger stereotyping system and not its actual process of fabrication. It is true that the strength of stereotypical images often comes from their unicity, because unicity begs for simple equations: community X = delinquency, but the grammar or syntax of the stereotype can survive even if plurality is introduced ("All Arabs are . . ." can be followed by several adjectives or nouns). When the grammar of stereotyping ("All Arabs are . . .") is combined with diversity, a list obtains, and the list adds the force of the litany to the rhetoric of formulas adopted by stereotypes. Abbas Fahdel wonders if it is fair or even an improvement to *"enfermer les Arabes du cinéma dans le tiercé suspect victime-délinquant-flic"* [to lock Arab film characters into the suspicious victim-delinquent-cop trio].[17] It may be that Chibane's decision to multiply roles will be recuperated as a stereotypical list: Beur intellectuals, Beur junkies, unemployed Beurs, Beur women ("Beurettes") are not necessarily free from stereotyping as long as the grammar that produces them as a predictable and recognizable list is not questioned.

What I find interesting in *L'Oeil au beurre noir* is the film's attack on the syntax of stereotyping rather than its manifestation at the level of the representation of characters. The question that seems to be asked by all the characters is not how the Beurs or Blacks will achieve integration but how a French society, in which they are already active participants, describes them. In a sense, integration is not even an issue; it already exists, and the current debate about whether it is possible or not is implicitly criticized as a rearguard and anachronistic preoccupation. How French language and culture integrate the presence of Beurs and Blacks in their images, metaphors, and rhetoric is, however, the slightly different question asked by Meynard in this movie. In this film, Smaïn/Rachid is neither the token minority, the unique representative of a hypothetical Beur community, nor a character whose position as a Beur is completely erased. For him, being "Beur" means being confronted with the grammar of list and repetitions, and the film is a very specific case study: *L'Oeil au beurre noir* is not about identity in general, nor even about stereotypes in general, but about three characters who learn how to analyze and recuperate the power of two very specific stereotypical statements that can either ruin their lives or allow them to fight back: "I will not rent to a foreigner" and *"Insécurité* [a right-wing buzzword] is due to the presence of immigrants."

To a rather conventional set of situations is added an interesting rhetorical and discursive parallel. The film suggests that the two heroes will never be in a position to sign a lease because they are the victims of an endless and unstoppable form of repetition: the repetition of maddening racial stereotype, which supposedly disqualifies them as tenants. But through a careful alternation of scenes, the movie also shows that the way in which Rachid and Denis endeavor to fight the system is also a form of systematic repetition, the "Rachid system."

The intolerable effect of repetition on people's lives is the point of the very first scene of the movie. A series of leitmotivs, which will accompany the Black hero in his endless quest for an apartment, are immediately presented to us as a given. The specter of homelessness is discreetly alluded to (the very first image is a close-up of a piece of cardboard, from under which emerges an old man who obviously spent the night under this precarious shelter). A little farther away, prospective tenants, standing in a ridiculously long line, are shown to be alienated from each other, the scarcity of places to rent creating an atmosphere of fierce competition. There is almost no communication and no solidarity among the individuals, whom the camera observes as if they were some exotic spectacle. Moving slowly from the end of the line to the front, the camera shares its powerful gaze and freedom with the spectators, allowing us to cut in line and putting us at a distance from the immobilized human beings: it is clear that we are not part of the line, that what we see is not limited to the back of the person ahead of us, and that we have the immense privilege of actually entering the apartment without waiting in line. When the door of the apartment is finally revealed at the end of a comically long panning, we realize that our hero is first in line, a few remarks and his half-asleep silhouette indicating that he must have spent the night on the street to be there first. The fact that he is first in line, however, cannot protect him from the barrage of stereotypes that greet him inside: the look of intense surprise on the landlady's face, who apparently cannot reconcile her client's face with the name she reads on her list (Denis Saint-Rose, such a "French" name, the movie ironically implies), and the subsequent refrain of lame and contradictory excuses (all revolving around some version of the implausible "the place has already been rented").

From an ideological point of view, the episode is so simple in its violence that there is little left to say. And from a narrative point of view, this scene is a bit of a paradox: it is, at the same time, a first scene and an "always already" scene, which wants us to know it for what it is. By definition, a first scene is not supposed to be a repetition—we perceive it as unique and original—but here this scene must point to its repetitive nature so as to make the spectator aware that it is out of the question to interpret the incident as unique, exceptional, self-contained. In other words, the film starts off with a denaturalization of stereotypically repetitive situations. The spectator discovers a new situation, a new hero, a new story, yet the point of the confrontation is to give Denis Saint-Rose a chance to let us know how much individuals suffer from the relentless repetition of unformulated assumptions: Denis Saint-Rose is systematically turned down by real estate agents because he is Black; his story is reduced to a minimalist statement. For him, no "first time" is ever possible because he is always greeted by the same implicit statement. In spite of his efforts to play the game of the bourgeoisie (he manages to arrive first, a punctual early bird, he is impeccably dressed up, his exquisitely old-fashioned manners betray an exaggerated degree of formality), the very first second of encounter with the real estate agent is always determinant, a premature closure.

The originality of the movie is to suggest that the infuriating episode is also a crisis for storytelling: If everything becomes predictable, how does one tell a new story? How does one find an apartment when the encounter with the real estate agent is an endless list of similar and predictable microdialogues that get repeated ad nauseam? And therefore, how does one make a film when a first episode cannot exist because it is the repetition of the last scene and the rehearsal of the next scene? The very first scene of the movie establishes very quickly that some individuals suffer from the relentless repetition of stereotypes and immediately makes it every spectator's problem by suggesting that we will be deprived of stories if repetition continues to dominate our culture. Even if we do not identify with the character (that is, regardless of our identity), the Black character's problem becomes ours in our capacity of audience waiting for a story.

The very next scene is apparently completely unrelated, and in this unrelatedness (and therefore unpredictability) lies the clue to the overall organization of the movie. When repetition threatens to kill stories, one has to re-appropriate the power of lists and repetitions by depriving the Other (us, the spectator, the maker of stereotypes) of their stereotyping grammar. Surprises (one of the conditions of storytelling) have to be stolen from the dominant discourse, to which lists will be repeated from a completely unexpected position. The second scene of the movie will eventually appear to the spectator to be a very symmetrical version of the first one, but at that point we are under the impression that the first episode is finished and that an unrelated narrative has started. Exit the Black character and his unsuccessful attempts at renting a place, his long wait, and repetitive failures. This time, everything happens very fast. Smaïn is sitting on his moped (the valiant steed of the modern knight), looking at women walking on the street. Suddenly he notices that two punks are harassing a vulnerable-looking young woman, whom they terrorize and trap inside a telephone booth. A Zorro-like Smaïn rushes to her rescue and courageously challenges the two punks, who turn against him, yelling racial slurs and trying to hit him. The rest is easy to guess. Smaïn defeats his unworthy opponents, grabs the hand of his pathetic victim, who by now is sobbing and screaming, drags her out of harm's way, allows her a second to recover from the shock, and proceeds to deliver the punch line: "Un Arabe sauve une jeune fille attaquée par deux blancs. C'est le monde à l'envers!" [An Arab rescues a girl attacked by two White guys. This is the world upside down.] Exchange of niceties, Smaïn suggests a drink, the young woman says she lives next door and invites him in. The camera follows them to the door of the building, but this time it does not have more power than the characters it follows. The couple disappear behind a closed door, and the camera does not intrude on their privacy. We are left outside, reduced to guesses as to whether Smaïn "sort vainqueur d'un combat dont Chimène est le prix" [emerges as the winner of a battle whose prize is Chimène]—a reference to a well-known seventeenth-century play by Corneille, Le Cid. (Needless to say, given what we will find out about Smaïn's propensity to make up stories, we will never know for sure what happened inside.)

The problem is, of course, that the camera has not really lost its power to cut in line and enter apartments. Like Smaïn, it is lying to us. For just as the spectator is beginning to think that this second episode is a rather moralizing bit of poetic and misogynistic justice (the minority knight in his shining armor has defeated the forces of evil and racism, and he gets the woman as prize), just as we are beginning to wonder if the film was simply going to trade off women for minorities, the door reopens, and the camera, which has not moved at all, finally and reluctantly gives us the key to the whole episode. Smaïn, standing with the door behind him, remains immobile for an inexplicably long time, a look of deep concern on his face, while the camera, from across the street, moves to the right until we realize that the two punks are still there, waiting for him to come out. When the camera has completed its rotation, the front of the screen is occupied by the back of the two punks. Their point of view becomes the spectator's reference: we now see Smaïn from the same angle as they do. If I suggest that the camera "lies" to us (rather than simply maintaining a element of surprise), it is because the long seconds during which Smaïn seems to hesitate before finally crossing the street toward the two punks are retro-spectively unjustifiable, for, suddenly, a brutal anticlimax relieves us of our fear of a second streetfight. In a childish, whining voice, one of the punks complains to Smaïn that he should really be more careful next time and not hit him so hard because he broke the cup, and by the way did he sleep with her?

In other words, and in spite of appearances, this second scene is quite similar to the first one: it is based on the repetition of a stereotype. Only, this time, the stereotype is used by the person who would otherwise suffer from anti-Arab prejudices. Playing on the implicit "All Arabs are . . ." Rachid uses racist fears and anti-immigrant hostility to win the woman's sympathy. He uses what he knows to be his Otherness as a trump card in a game of mirror strategies that nicely complements the different tactics used by his future friend and rival, Denis Saint-Rose. Whereas the film gives the Black character a name that traps the real estate agent into ac-knowledging her prejudices against him, the Beur character loudly pre-sents himself as an "Arab" even before introducing himself as "Rachid." Whereas Denis Saint-Rose seems to hope that his "Frenchness" (which apparently includes a class element, as shown by his instinctive increase of the level of formality) will be more significant than his skin color, Rachid's identity as an excluded and supposedly non-French minority is cynically performed in an attempt to seduce his victim. When the two White men pretend to attack him, they make sure to insult him as an Arab, and when Rachid comments on the situation, he also takes great care to insist on the "Whiteness" of the two offenders and on his own "Arabité" [Arabness] (and not "Beuritude" [Beurness], by the way).

In other words, the grammar of lists and repetitions is also at work in this second scene, although the camera has taken great pains to make us believe otherwise. What seemed like an exceptional scene (as the woman puts it: "Il ne m'arrive jamais rien" [Nothing ever happens to me]), a one-of-a-kind incident ("le monde à l'envers" [the world upside down]) is now revealed to be a well-rehearsed routine, a scenario, a film within the film written and directed by Smaïn and his two accomplices. As the infamous trio retreats to a public rest room, they squabble about who will be the next victim and who will sleep with her this time, and it becomes obvious to the audience that they have been at it before, that many women have been duped, and that, as spectators, we have been taken in, too. We have been deceived by the trio and their manipulation of repetition. In a sense, we are in the same position as the woman until it is too late: only after Smaïn comes out of her apartment again do we realize that our fear, anger, or frustration (the poor woman, poor Rachid) was unnecessary. At one point, the camera shows us the point of view of the woman, trapped inside the telephone booth by the two *loubards* (complete with leather jackets and bandannas), whose threatening faces look like distorted masks as they press their lips to the glass windows. Just like her, we were the victims of a hoax, and of our lack of competence as interpreters: we did not recognize that the scenario was a bit too perfect, that the terrifying images of threatening punks were a visual quote, and that the situation itself was a stereotypical narrative. The episode seems to suggest that there is a price to pay for our inability to identify repetition (including the repetition of stereotypes). If we fail to suspect that the whole scenario is a sort of quotation, that we are, just like the woman, at the mercy of an unscrupulous stereotype thief, we cannot escape what can be stereotyped in our identity (our ethnic origin or, here, our gender).

But the theft of stereotypes is not an infallible game: a first element of disorder sneaks into the well-oiled routine when one of the White men (the one whom Smaïn pretends to kick in the balls during the fight) is suddenly overwhelmed by a rush of inspiration: he wants to rewrite the script. He suggests to improve the dialogue by adding what he thinks will be a realistic detail, the finishing touch: "Et si je disais, en m'écroulant, 'Ah, les Arabes, c'est des fourbes!'" [And if I said, in tumbling down, "Ah, Arabs, they are treacherous!"] To which Smaïn, who was about to leave the room and go back into the street, very quickly and seriously retorts: "Oui, mais pas comme ça, parce que là, tu vois, tu me fais peur." [Yes, but not like that, because that way, you see, you frighten me.]

This first element of discord among the three friends is an intriguing moment because Smaïn's fear remains mostly unformulated. It is not clear why this addition to the scenario is more threatening than the rest of the prepared dialogue (why, for example, does Smaïn not feel threatened by some particularly cruel remarks in the original scene, which contains unambiguously violent racial slurs?). For the first time, he sounds in earnest and seriously concerned. His fear is motivated by something that he does not explain: apparently, he does not object to the content of the sentence, but to something else, to something indescribable in the way in which his friend pronounced it: The "Oui, mais pas comme ça" [Yes, but not like that] opens up the possibility of a crack in the Rachid system: suddenly, even in the rehearsed exchange, something invisible and mysterious becomes threatening and cannot be contained or exorcised by the principle of repetition. Even if both men agree to the formulation, there is a little something that escapes their control, and Rachid's "pas comme ça" [not like that] points to the risky nature of their game of make-believe. Even if Rachid controls the principle of repetition, thus becoming the master of the stereotype, the possibility of drifting into real violence against himself as an Arab is not so far away, hidden in the potential difference between two apparently identical statements. As it turns out, Rachid's warning, "Oui, mais pas comme ça" is prophetic, a harbinger of impending catastrophes.

The next attempt at using the aggressor-savior scenario in the hope of impressing and seducing Virginie, who is about to become one of the film's main characters, fails miserably and causes a series of grotesque misunderstandings as well as the implosion of the Rachid system. What should have been a simple repetition of the previous scene does not work: nothing happens as planned and the spectator's superiority (we think that this time we know what is going to happen) is as shattered as Rachid's confidence in the repetitiveness of the system. When Smaïn pounces on the two would-be aggressors, a red car suddenly appears out of nowhere and screeches to a halt in the middle of the staged fight. To everyone's surprise (the spectator's included), Denis Saint-Rose makes a spectacular entrance, adding a completely unexpected twist to the Rachid system: his own version of the chivalric knight. Obviously, the original script does not easily accommodate the new part. This is a case of too many saviors spoiling the denouement of a good play. Rachid/Zorro gets hit by Denis before being given a chance to explain, "Mais je la sauvais moi" [But it is me who was saving her] (ironically, he is now the victim of a bad reader of scenarios), and, in order to save what can be saved of appearances, he cannot go through the prearranged moves (the fake kick-in-the-balls trick). The two White men get rather badly beaten up as the result of the unexpected intervention of noise in the Rachid system. Once the Beur, the Black, and the woman have left the scene, one of the White men mutters, from under a car, as though for his own benefit: "Ah, les Arabes, c'est des fourbes" [Ah, Arabs, they are treacherous] to which his brother adds: "Ouais, et les noirs aussi." [Yes, and Blacks too.] At one level, the announced punch line is amusing because it now functions as a line in spite of the *loubard*'s intention and because it is true that the two *loubards* are indeed the relatively innocent victims of a misunderstanding in this case. As Rachid had anticipated, however, their eagerness to repeat stereotypes drifts dangerously because it replaces a more accurate description of the situation: rather than voicing their understandable resentment at having been betrayed by their friend Rachid, who sacrificed them to his scenario, they stupidly resort to the prepared statement about "Arabes" in general, making it even worse by their inclusion of "*noirs.*"

In fact, their analysis is completely off the mark as the new, apparently multicultural, team that has suddenly formed, will not function easily according to gender or ethnic category: from the very first meeting, the Beur, the Black, and the woman will be a tongue-in-cheek variation of a thousand Starsky and Hutch routines.[18] Their encounter inaugurates a whole series of misplaced quotations, ironic redoublings that end up completely discrediting the very principle of repetition. Deprived of his original script, Rachid is forced to improvise, and he does not prove very successful at patching up his secondhand stereotypical narrative. If we examine the reason that his system collapses once Denis intervenes, we realize that the film is slowly making the point that lists, repetitions, and therefore stereotypes can be defeated by the combination of two factors: the presence of noise in the stereotypical system and the presence of a good reader. Not only is it a pessimistic point of view and a mistake to imagine that we live in a world where there is no resistance to stereotypes, it is an even more serious mistake to underestimate the power of readers to see through the logic of lists and repetitions.

That there is spontaneous resistance to, for example, street violence against a woman is, in itself, an answer to the stereotypical "nobody ever does anything." Denis ruins the scenario because the Rachid system is predicated on the assumption that only an actor (himself) will interfere: the scenario includes the prediction that everyone else will be indifferent to the plight of a young woman bullied by two thugs. The noise in this system is the element of generosity and disinterestedness in Denis's impulse (even if he soon jumps on the "drague" bandwagon).

Denis also creates noise by refusing to play along with the binary logic (White versus Beur) and ethnic assumptions of the Rachid system's punch line. When Rachid, Denis, and Virginie meet in a café for the first time, Rachid and Denis compete for her attention and put her in the annoying position of having to decide who is the more clever suitor. Rachid's first attempt to strike up a dialogue with Virginie is a failure because Denis continues to mess with the script. Because he must slightly modify the original punch line ("Un Arabe sauve une jeune fille" [An Arab saves a young girl] becomes "Un noir et un Arabe sauvent une fille attaquée par deux blancs c'est le monde en l'envers" [A Black and an Arab save a girl attacked by two White guys, this is the world upside down]), Rachid is immediately challenged by Denis, who strongly reacts to his essentialist declarations. He objects to being brought into the system as "*un noir*," starting a grotesque and apparently irrelevant quarrel between the two men: Denis interrupts Rachid's pickup line with an unexpected "Elle aurait été agressée par un beur je serais intervenu aussi" [Had she been attacked by a Beur I would have intervened also] (the meaning of which remains unclear: does he object to Rachid's racialized discourse or to his implication that only White men can be aggressors?), to which Rachid furiously responds: "Et si ç'avait été un black?" [And if it had been a Black?]

The scene slips dangerously close to first-degree racism again. Refusing to be involved in Rachid's theft of stereotypes, Denis sabotages the script, both of them temporarily losing track of their original goal (they were supposed to court the woman). Virginie is forgotten (except by the camera, which watches her eyes following the ideological ping-pong game), the two men are trapped in a hostile debate about ethnicity, until Virginie herself intervenes, a straight-faced ironist whose caustic joke puts a sudden end to the argument by giving a name to the dynamics of the whole conversation. Having carefully listened to the silly inflation of the words "aggressor," "Black," and "Beur" in the men's conversation, she suddenly interjects: "Un black tout seul c'est pas possible. Il faut vraiment qu'il y ait un Arabe qui l'entraîne pour que ça arrive . . ." [A Black alone it's not possible. There must really be an Arab who drags him along in order for this to happen . . .] Dead silence, enjoyed by the woman who has suddenly won their undivided attention, and, after a pause, ". . . et vice-versa" [and vice versa].

For Virginie is the good reader in this story, the reader who does not let repetitions fool her. And as the two men look hurt and surprised, confirming that the Rachid system and its reappropriation of stereotypes had been engulfed in a sudden flare of first-degree racialization, she finally moves from the endless repetition of identical statements to a description of the type of language she has been using: "Non mais c'est une blague, c'est du deuxième degré" [My word, this is a joke, it's of the second-degree type"]. The noise that she introduces in the system is a level of self-consciousness about the genre of discourse. Her comment is a form of interruption that announces her role as the much-needed competent reader in the story, and her introduction of the notion of "second-degree" not only gives a name to the whole series of episodes that have been unfolding before our eyes, it also makes a series of important points: Virginie's attention to "degrees" of meaning invites us to be more attentive to the ways in which statements are used, and to the context. Her "Non mais c'est une blague" [My word, this is a joke] recalls Rachid's mysterious "pas comme ça" [not like that] and his unformulated fear to fall back into first-degree stereotypes. The fact that she has to reassure her shocked audience that it was a joke suggests that nothing in her use of stereotypes about "Blacks" and "Beurs" makes them intrinsically funny. "Deuxième degré" is neither innocent nor harmless because it puts the other at the mercy of whoever has the right and power to suddenly declare "c'était une blague" [it was a joke]. Her own use of "second degree" also demonstrates that the power of such tactics is unstable; in a sense, she does to Rachid what he did to all the other women, and what the film did to us by lying about what Rachid was up to.

If her statement about Beurs and Blacks is misconstrued as first-degree when it is, according to her, "du deuxième degré," her own critical intervention is yet another level of interpretation, which I will call here "third-degree reading." What the "third-degree" reader must do is remember quotations and expect repetitions, be able to start looking for meaning beyond the content of repeated statements. The third-degree reader is trained to see difference through sameness. Symmetrically, third-degree discourse, of which I suggest that *L'Oeil au beurre noir* is an example, can be imagined as a series of self-conscious and ironic audiovisual echoes (rather than as a form of intertextuality or intervisuality), as a constant and conscious reference to previous images or dialogues. Third-degree discourse always suspects what has already been seen or said to have become a prepackaged sound bite or a visual quote that irony now displaces and modifies.

Third-degree discourse, in the movie, is on the side of Virginie, some narrative power or voice having evidently decided not to let her be the victim of a limited and sexist alternative (why should she choose either Rachid or Denis?). When the three of them meet in the café, the film portrays the female character as amused and entertained by the two men's performance. Not only does she listen carefully to what Rachid and Denis say, but she is able to take into account apparently irrelevant elements of the environment: she controls the frame of meaningfulness. Refusing to be controlled by the point of view of the camera (which focuses on Rachid, then on Denis, then on both), her eyes wander away from their table, apparently by chance, looking elsewhere for signs that the camera does not show us at first.

Only later, as though reluctantly, will the camera follow her gaze, moving away from Rachid, distracted by other resonances, other noises until the whole café starts functioning like an echo chamber, providing Virginie and the spectator with third-degree grids of interpretation: when Rachid makes the mistake of quoting *Quai des brumes*, the special bond that he tries to establish between Virginie and himself is shattered. Appropriating the lines of a famous Don Juan from such a famous movie might be a blunder in any case (since the female character seems sensitive to the negative power of repetitions), but he rather poorly chooses his reference: the arch-famous "T'as de beaux yeux tu sais" [You got beautiful eyes, you know] is such a cult pickup line as to have become exclusively ironical, especially among young people. At best, the quote from *Quai des brumes* would function as a secondhand statement, dwarfing Rachid in his appeal to supposedly timeless, classical, monumental figures. And for the spectator, the sentence is both a symbolic and a literal second-degree, a double repetition, since we know that it is part of the Rachid system; literally, we have heard it before, when the three accomplices were rehearsing their lines in the public bathroom after the first episode. But the camera shows that Rachid's attempt at appropriating another kind of stereotype is defeated by his inability to eliminate undesirable redoublings from his own voice. The camera pivots to another table in the café, where an older man is sitting alone, slouched over his food, looking at no one in particular, using his fingers to push bits of food into his mouth without removing his cigarette. Trembling, mumbling to himself, a picture of senility and alienation, the old man apparently repeats Rachid's words in a much more convincing imitation of Gabin's rough tone "T'as d'beaux yeux to sais, embrasse-moi . . ." [You got beautiful eyes you know, kiss me . . .] The ridiculous echo emphasizes the stereotypical nature of Rachid's chosen sound bite and proposes to the spectator and to the trio a nasty version of Rachid himself, a portrait of the hustler as aging Don Juan, doomed to the ironic repetition of once successful lines.

For in a world governed by the tyranny of repetition, only the first two episodes of the movie would get endlessly repeated: the opening scene where the Black character is denied a lease on account of his skin color, and a mirror episode in which the potential victim uses the same form of racism against us (spectators) and against apparently helpless female victims. If nothing more was added to this pattern, the film would confirm that people's identities are always governed by what others consider meaningful about them (gender, or ethnicity, or class, etc.). Throughout the movie, Virginie would be only "a woman," Denis "a Black man," Rachid "a Beur." And if the film's only contribution was to suggest that negative stereotypes can be counteracted by other stereotypes, I would not have found its discourse powerfully seductive.

What occurs, however, after the two initial scenes, is a more optimistic series of experiments, and the tentative invention of what I have called third-degree reading. If the first scene represents the first degree of stereotypes, based on the harmful power of their literal meaning, Rachid's reappropriation of anti-Arab prejudices is a form of second-degree (which still implies a gullible reader: someone has to be taken in by the reappropriation of stereotypes). What the rest of the movie demonstrates, however, is that we are not reduced to this alternative. Among the three main characters, a new form of relationship develops as they become an interestingly conflictual trio. Each of the heroes is both quite aware of the existence of stereotypes and of their double-edged nature, but they also know that the other members of the team share their knowledge. This complicity enables them not only to take into account the existence of ethnic origin or gender but also to treat these elements with a tactically effective ironic distance.

A third-degree discourse emerges, and we are invited to respond with a third-degree reading that would transcend the repetitive nature of stereotypes, whether used by malicious real estate agents or clever poachers. "Third degree," in this sense, does not, should not refer to any content in particular; rather, the phrase is supposed to generate a number of echoes—echoes perhaps of all the "third" parties that dialectize our binary world. A third-degree reading would be the kind of skill achieved by a hybrid "tiers instruit" [informed third person], as described by Michel Serres, in what Homi Bhabha calls a third space[19] and it also evokes what has been called "Third Cinema," as long as we carefully maintain the distinction established in 1986 between Third Cinema and Third World. As Paul Willemen puts it, "The notion of a Third Cinema was first advanced as a rallying cry in the late 60s in Latin America and has recently been taken up again in the wake of Teshome Gabriel's book *Third Cinema in the Third World, The Aesthetics of Liberation* (1982)."[20] The phrase was also used as the title of a 1986 Edinburgh conference, which set out to study "a cinema no longer captivated by the mirrors of dominance/independence or commerce/art, but grounded on an understanding of the dialectical relationship between social existence and cultural practice."[21]

For what we discover, as the story unfolds, is that the so-called Rachid system, based on the belief that repetition is a matter of rehearsed scenarios, is far from infallible. Controlling the repetition of situations is not always possible when one tries to re-appropriate stereotypes, and this may be one of the most optimistic statements of the movie, as we are led to suspect that repetition may not be possible even in the case of first-degree stereotype. In the real world of narratives and stereotypes, the same causes will not always produce the same effects because the Rachid system cannot work without a reader: his victim must be a naive misinterpreter. The Rachid system would work only in a noiseless system (where stereotypes could not be opposed), in a universe where every ideological variable is predictable. That is not the case in the movie. Rather than insisting that the repetition of stereotypes is morally undesirable and that the stereotype thief is just as bankrupt because his strategy is guilty of the same short-comings as first-degree stereotyping, the film suggests that the Rachid system is threatened by its own (pessimistic) belief in the absolute power of repetition. There will always be an element of resistance in the world of repetition, and the stereotype thief will be betrayed by his lack of control over repetition.

Serge Meynard's *L'Oeil au beurre noir* will not easily be integrated into a "Beur" cinema category, but it contributes to the celebration of a certain cinematographic "esprit Beur" (where "esprit" conveniently means both "mentality" and "wit"). A third-degree discourse is neither universal nor necessarily acquired as part of one's genetic inheritance and ethnic origin. Linking "esprit Beur" and "third degree" is not the same thing as saying they are interchangeable; it is saying that their cohabitation is as much a necessity as an art.

NOTES

1. See Mouny Berrah, Victor Bachy, Mohand Ben Salama, and Ferid Boughedir, eds., "Cinémas du Maghreb," *CinémAction* 14 (1981), with a foreword by Mostefa Lacheraf and Paul Balta. See also Mouny Berrah, Jacques Levy, and Claude Michel Cluny, eds., "Les Cinémas arabes," *CinémAction* 43 (1987), with a preface by Tahar Ben Jelloun and Ferid Boughedir, and Lizbeth Malkmus and Roy Armes, *Arab and African Film Making* (London: Zed Books, 1991).

2. Christian Bosséno, ed., "Cinéma de l'émigration: Emigrés et déracinés à l'écran," *CinémAction* 24 (1982).

3. See also Hedi Dhoukar's series of interviews with nine directors (Mohamed Benayat, Abel Bennour, Mohamed Charbagi, Mehdi Charef, Aïssa Djabri and Farid Lahoussa, Idriss Karim, Saad Salman, Okacha Touita, Mahmoud Zemmouri) and the author's essay "25 Cinéastes *plus ou moins* beurs" (my emphasis), in *CinémAction* 56 (July 1990): 161–191.

4. There is of course no reason to restrict Beur cinema to the 1980s. Even if the word "Beur" appears in the 1970s, an analysis of the phenomenon should not forget that it is one of the cultural consequences of the Algerian war and that it cannot be completely dissociated from two hundred years of French colonial presence in Algeria, Morocco, and Tunisia. For a history of the evolving relationship between cinema of French expression and the Maghreb as (represented) colonies or (represented and representing) independent countries, see Susan Hayward, *French National Cinema* (London: Routledge, 1993), especially 40 and 252 ff. Nothing ends in 1990, either. For critics in search of some sort of unambiguous cultural territory, a recent movie may be hailed as a true "Beur" product. Released in 1993, *Hexagone* is Malik Chibane's first film, and it is presented by the critics and by himself as "le

premier film français 'où cinq Beurs ont les rôles principaux'" [the first French film "in which five Beurs have the main parts"]. It is noticeable, however, that Stéphane Bouquet, the author of the article on Chibane, feels that he must immediately qualify the statement with a parenthesis: "Il ne voudrait pas le revendiquer constamment mais quand même il en est fier" [He did not want to constantly claim it, but all the same he is proud of it] (Stéphane Bouquet, "Portrait: Malik Chibane," *Cahiers du cinéma* 476 (February 1994): 11); see also a critique of the film by the same author on p. 75). It is also worth mentioning Nicolas Klotz's *La Nuit sacrée* (an adaptation of Tahar Ben Jelloun's *La Nuit sacrée* and *L'Enfant de sable*), starring Amina, whose reputation as a singer is already solidly established. Amina had already played in Bertolucci's *Un Thé au Sahara* and in a British film titled *The Year of the Pig*, by Leslie Megahey (she plays an Egyptian woman suspected of being a witch, whose pig is accused of devouring a child).

5. Critics have been prompt to notice and comment on the fact that while Mehdi Charef's second movie, *Miss Mona* (1987)—the story of a strange and short-lived alliance between an aging transvestite and Samir, an illegal alien—may still be identified as (or reduced to) a film about a Beur character, his latest work moves away from a Beur context. *Camomille* (1988) is about the relationship between a young suicidal drug addict, Camille, and Martin, his benefactor/kidnapper, and *Au pays des Juliets* (released in 1993) tells the story of three women (played by Laure Duthilleul, Marie Schneider, and Claire Nebout) who come out of prison together.

6. Mahmoud Zemmouri was born in 1946 at Boufarik, Algeria, and has lived in France since 1968. Would the comparative belatedness of his arrival in France disqualify him? What about his 1980 film, *Prends dix-mille balles et casse-toi*, a film about the sobering experience of an Algerian family's return to their native village. Should we emphasize the fact that it was shot at Boufarik and not in France, or can we suggest that the provocative title, a direct and rebellious reference to the so-called *aide au retour* decrees (the ten thousand francs promised to each immigrant willing to go back to the would-be native land at the time of the "Stoléru" decrees) is a typical example of Beur humor? About the Stoléru decrees, see Olivier Mizla, *Les Français devant l'immigration* (Paris: Éditions Complexe, 1988), 160 ff.

7. For an interesting attempt at a historical distinction among three stages of Beur cinema, see Christian Bosséno's "Immigrant Cinema: National Cinema: The Case of Beur Film," in *Popular European Cinema*, ed. Richard Dyer and Ginette Vincendeau (London and New York: Routledge, 1992). See also Carrie Tarr's "Questions of Identity in Beur Cinema: From Tea in the Harem to Cheb," *Screen* 34 (1993): 320–342. The author argues that "the emergence of a putative Beur cinema has to be seen in the context of [a] particular conjecture of socioeconomic and political circumstances. New popular cultural forms did not benefit from the underpinning of a strong united political Beur movement, but rather emerged at a time of defiant yet defensive attempts to negotiate a recognition of the Beurs' right as French citizens and to create a climate of tolerance that would enable them to be more fully integrated into French society" (324). Thank you to Carrie Tarr for her comments on the first draft of this article.

8. Jean-Marie Touratier, *Le Stéréotype* (Paris: Galilée, 1978), 10.

9. See also Bhabha's "The Other Question: Stereotype and Discrimination and

the Discourse of Colonialism," in *The Location of Culture* (London and New York: Routledge, 1994): The stereotype "is a form of knowledge and identification that vacillates between what is always 'in place' already known, and something that must be anxiously repeated . . . as if the essential duplicity of the Asiatic or the bestial sexual license of the African that needs no proof, can never really, in discourse, be proved" (66).

10. One of the most striking differences between the word "*nègre*" and the word "*beur*" is that their respective status within the dominant language is practically opposite: "*beur*" is a very recent creation and it was never an insult, it never functioned like the word "*nègre.*" It is not a derogatory word that a community decided to re-appropriate as a gesture of rebellious affirmation. Even if some individuals are proud to call themselves Beurs, there is no consensus about the desirability or even any necessity to be named. And I think it would be a gross simplification to assume that 100 percent of those who object to the word are craving assimilation into the French dominant culture.

11. Originally "brown sauce," but mostly used figuratively in the expression "*l'oeil au beurre noir*" to refer to the bruised face of someone who was involved in a fistfight.

12. *Verlan* is one of the highly visible features of the language used in the *banlieues*. Words are formed by inverting the syllables of the original French word, or at least this is how people who usually do not speak *verlan* explain words such as "Beur," "*meufs*," "*keufs*," etc. "Beur" is supposed to be an inverted version of "Arabe" (some contortions and a certain degree of arbitrariness are necessary to explain the desired result, which may suggest that *verlan* functions like a language rather than like a strict mathematical secret code. "*Meufs*" and "*keufs*" are respectively derived from "*femmes*" and "*flics.*"

13. Azouz Begag, *Ecarts d'identité* (Paris: Seuil, 1990), 10–11.

14. François Reynart, "Y a-t-il une culture beur? Smaïn, Mehdi Charef, Amina . . . Ils occupent la scène artistique. Veulent-ils pour autant revendiquer leur identité? Débat," *Nouvel Observateur* 1517 (December 1993): 34.

15. Ibid.

16. Stéphane Bouquet, "Portrait: Malik Chibane," *Cahiers du cinéma* 476 (February 1994): 11.

17. Abbas Fahdel, "Une esthétique beur?" *CinémAction* 56 (1990): 143–144.

18. The relationship between Virginie, Denis, and Rachid will prove unusually volatile and difficult to fit into traditional models as the film unfolds. The last scene shows the two men having breakfast together in Virginie's kitchen, a very intimate homosocial atmosphere whose ambiguously erotic potential is denied by the men's discussion about the forever elusive apartment. For their presence in Virginie's kitchen marks the end of their rivalry only because the film eliminates her from the team: she is in her own room, with a third lover. For a comparison with other male teams and for an analysis of the role of gender in such constructions, see John Fiske's "British Cultural Studies and Television," in *Channels of Discourse, Reassembled*, ed. Robert C. Allen (London and New York: Routledge, 1987), 284–326. The author suggests that in *Starsky and Hutch* episodes, "any woman who attracts the hero has to be rejected at the end of the episode. Male bonding, on the other hand, allows an interpersonal dependency that is goal-centered, not relationship-

centered, and thus serves masculine performance instead of threatening it" (295). See also Appiah's analysis of the Black hero as saint in Anthony Appiah, "No Bad Nigger: Blacks as the Ethical Principle in the Movies," in *Media Spectacles*, ed. Marjorie Garber, Jann Matlock, and Rebecca L. Walkowitz (London and New York: Routledge, 1993), 77–90.

19. See Michel Serres, *Le Tiers Instruit* (Paris: Bourin, 1990); and Homi Bhabha, *The Location of Culture*.

20. Teshome Gabriel, *Third Cinema in the Third World: The Aesthetics of Liberation* (Ann Arbor: UMI Research Press, 1982).

21. Jim Pines and Paul Willemen, eds., *Questions of Third Cinema* (London: British Film Institute, 1989), 2.

Decolonizing Images

NINE   Soleil O *and the Cinema of Med Hondo**

Madeleine Cottenet-Hage

AN ACCULTURATED SUBJECT IN SEARCH OF A PLACE

When Med Hondo is asked to talk about himself, he will insist that he is an *acculturated* African who, as such, shares the plight of millions of Third World migrants displaced and dispossessed by neocolonial economic necessities. He came to cinema, he says, in part to find his place in the world and to make a place for images of Africa that will inform the world about the painful reality of Africa past and present.

Born in Mauritania to a Mauritanian mother and a Senegalese father, Hondo traces his forebears to the migratory journey of Sudanese slave workers. At age eighteen he went to Rabat, Morocco, to become a chef. His native language had by then been replaced twice, by Arabic and by French. One of the many cruelly comic scenes in *Soleil O* (his first full-length feature film, made in 1970) shows recent African immigrants being taught the French language reduced to the few vocabulary items that they will need to function in their menial tasks, one of which is *le balai* (the broom). An "assimilated" Black man directs the class to mindlessly repeat the word, which as any Parisian viewer would know, is the main tool of their future trade as street and Metro sweepers, and therefore a sign of their oppression.

Hondo was fortunate in that he was spared this fate, but the jobs he found when he came to France in 1959 were not better in terms of either salary or treatment: dockworker, farm laborer, cook in the back kitchen of a Marseilles restaurant, delivery man at the Paris Halles, and later, waiter.

These menial jobs gave him an insight, however, into the French scene, in particular the French bourgeoisie, which he came to understand, he says, "just by watching them eat."[1] More important, this period of his life would provide him with his inspiration for *Soleil O*, a loose narrative about the trials and tribulations of an African looking for a position as an accountant in Paris. The feeling of alienation, the experience of racism that he encountered during these years, the exploitation of cheap, imported manual labor, and the living conditions of immigrant communities all became the material for this film and the following one, *Les Bicots-nègres, vos voisins* (1973). These experiences made him a very angry young man, and it is his anger that gives Hondo's films an exceptionally biting edge.

While working at these various odd jobs, Hondo, under the impression that drama would provide him with a way to express himself, began taking acting courses. He soon discovered that the French repertoire was far removed from his own experience. He therefore decided to assemble his own theatrical company in order to direct or act in plays that spoke to his own concerns, mostly plays about the Black experience, by the Haitian Depestre, the Congolese Guy Monga, and the Martiniquan Daniel Boukman, whose play *Les Négriers* he freely adapted in his film *West Indies ou les Nègres marrons de la liberté* (1979). During that period, he also worked under the direction of avant-garde stage director Jean-Marie Serreau and held parts in Bertolt Brecht's plays.

Hondo's training in acting and stage direction led to his direct involvement in film. Like many film directors of his generation, he received very little formal cinematic training and taught himself by "doing," convinced that "if one is able to speak and express oneself, one is capable of making a motion picture."[2] But, like Truffaut and the other *Cahiers* critics, he sharpened his own critical sense by seeing as many films as possible, sometimes seeing the same one two or three times in succession.[3]

When Hondo finally decided to move behind the camera, his double exposure to the avant-garde theater of the sixties and New Wave cinema were to have a direct impact on his filmwork, inasmuch as both avant-garde playwrights and New Wave directors pursued objectives similar to his own: to challenge traditional modes of narration and representation. But for Hondo, taking up the challenge was a more clear, more pressing political act than for Western artists. His imperative goal was to create filmic images out of a number of traditions and traditional genres as long as they were meaningful to African audiences and relevant to their experience. "My work and that of other African film-makers, in our different ways, evolves and revolves around the question of colonial history," he said to Don Ranvaud in 1978.[4] He was therefore determined to make films that had to be different because their content was different, films that would adapt a cinematic language developed by the West—there was no quarrel about that—to speak to and about Africa in a language Africa would recognize as new, yet rooted in its culture and traditions. Only a man as tenacious as Hondo, however, would have been able to overcome, no matter with what difficulty, the financial hurdles that have brought many a Third World filmmaker down.

HONDO AND THE ECONOMICS OF FILMMAKING

Hondo's script for *Soleil O* was ready as early as 1965. After gathering a crew of technicians and a team of African actors, he was able to get processing companies to donate some raw film. The film was made on a very small budget of $30,000 and took one year for completion because his actors could play only during their spare time. His subsequent films, shot with the direct participation of African and Maghreb migrant workers living in Paris, and of people involved in the fight for freedom in Western Sahara, were also made on small budgets. But when in 1979 Hondo decided to film a version of Boukman's play, he was faced with hard choices about funding sources. The story is that he "refused a $2.5 million offer from an American film producer because the latter wanted him to use Black American actors instead of a lesser known West Indian cast."[5] Then, too, he "wanted African producers, not because they would be more aware or more motivated . . . but so that they would produce images [for their own people]."[6] Eventually, with help from African backers in Mauritania, Senegal, and the Ivory Coast, as well as the French Centre National du Cinéma, he was able, after seven years, to put together $800,000. One-fourth of the budget went to the building of the slave boat replica, a symbolic icon of slavery both past and present, in which the musical epic is staged. That he could spend $2.5 million for his latest film, *Sarraounia* (1986), is a tribute to his enterprising spirit, his persistence, and also the efforts of the government of Burkina Faso, which, at the time, was committed to helping to develop an African film culture. Hondo himself went into debt for half a million dollars and, once again, took seven years to make the film.

Hondo's difficulties in finding backing for his films are in no way unique, but they illustrate a state of affairs that the Mauritanian filmmaker has been denouncing repeatedly—the colonization of Black Africa by Western cinema.[7] In many ways, Hondo is less bitter about the lack of

interest shown in the West for African films than he is about Western distributors' inundating African nations with images—and often bad images
at that—made in Hollywood, Paris, or London. But the imperialistic dom-
inance of big distribution companies, which makes it very difficult for
independent filmmakers and producers to show their films on regular cir-
cuits, is not the only reason that Hondo's films have been kept out of
Africa.[8] His refusal to toe a party line has also made him persona non grata
in some circles. One scene in *Soleil O* takes union officials to task for not
supporting the cause of immigrant labor more actively. In this and other
films, especially in *West Indies, ou les Nègres marrons de la liberté*, Hondo
denounces the corruption of African "kinglets" with their lust for power,
the squandering of money on lavish embassies abroad, and more generally
the lack of concern of African nations for their exploited citizens. These
are images that African rulers would rather not have shown on African
screens.[9] To make matters worse, Hondo's position on the Negritude
movement is reserved, if not outright critical. Only *Sarraounia*, Hondo's
latest full-length feature, steers clear of controversy by celebrating the
African past rather than a grim postcolonial present. In this film the lines
are drawn very clearly—some critics would say a little too clearly—
between the good Black "guys" and the bad White "guys." So, not surprisingly, it was his first film to be shown in Congo, Burkina Faso, Mali, Senegal, Mauritania, the Ivory Coast, and Benin. (Even so, Hondo had to go
and present his film himself.)

SOLEIL O: IMAGES OF POSTCOLONIAL DISPLACEMENT AND SELVES

Hondo's films are remarkably different from each other, and while drawing upon many genres, each shows another facet of Hondo's creative ways
with images. Rather than touch briefly on each of them, though, I will
concentrate on his first experiment with long features, *Soleil O*, which
many critics pronounced the best African film at the time.

The film explores, as *Les Bicots-nègres, vos voisins* and parts of *West Indies*
will do later, the condition of African immigrants in France. But whereas
Bicots is more extensively documentary, and *West Indies* wholly theatrical,
Soleil O is essentially an autobiographical and fictional film, in which a central character, played by the West Indian actor Robert Liensol, is invested
with both individual and collective significance. The narrative is sparse,
and the film can be seen as a collage of scenes whose sudden shifts in tone
and style create a sense of constant ruptures, a fitting mode for a film

concerned with exile and alienation. So one way of approaching it is to look at how clusters of images and the camera work together to frame the central theme of displacement and its concomitants—marginalization, emptiness, loss of identity, forced ingestion of "alien," unwanted nourishment, and rejection (or *vomissement*)—motifs that all are paradigmatic inscriptions of the postcolonial migrant condition.

The poetic title, *Soleil O*, masks the theme of displacement, yet encodes it. It was borrowed from a song that the Haitian slaves would sing on their way to the West Indies and America: "Soleil O moi je ne suis pas né ici / Moi je suis nègre d'Afrique" [O sun, I was not born here / I am a Negro from Africa].

After a prologue, to which I will return, a sequence establishes the theme. A Black man gets off a train in a Parisian train station. The angle is low, so the man looks tall and somewhat assured. We will later learn that he has every reason to be confident: not only is he a qualified accountant in his country but he has also been indoctrinated and believes that France will welcome him with open arms. A close shot of stickers on his suitcase suggests that he has traveled to several African countries before coming here. The shot nicely illustrates the complexities involved in reading an image depending on one's racial and class identification as well as ideological positioning. A sympathetic viewer might interpret the various stickers, bearing the names of Ghana, Benin, Senegal, Mali, among others, as signifying brotherhood and solidarity. A less sympathetic viewer might, on the other hand, construe them as signs that he is from nowhere in particular; that he is "just" a wandering, rootless African, one in a "homogeneous swarm of grasshoppers," as Hondo puts it with bitter irony.[10]

The image, however, invites yet another reading as one remembers that all these names inscribe the legacy of a colonial past when lands were carved into national entities irrespective of African historical, geographical, and tribal realities. The single close shot of the suitcase therefore becomes a metonymy of imperialistic control. As the different layers of meaning are unpacked, the train station sequence engages the viewer in a sort of dialectical seesaw in which he/she is constantly having to shift positions and gazes, alternately reading from a White and a Black point of view, a Western and an African position, which is very much at the microlevel what Hondo's film is about at the macrolevel: not just about shifting individuals from continent to continent but about shifting and unsettling gazes, and challenging ready-made interpretations. About learning to view the Other and one's Self as engaged in a historical process in which responsibility for the Other must be accepted.

THE WANDERING BLACK

After the sequence at the train station, we follow the immigrant in search of a job and a home. Even though the search will end up in his finding temporary occupations and lodgings, Hondo's montage deliberately underscores the message of his film: that there is no successful insertion of postcolonial subjects into the dominant social structure. That externality, marginalization, and rejection define their experience. Hondo's nonlinear narrative is therefore particularly suited. He has assembled sequences suspended in medias res, without origins and ends. And if they tell a story, it is a very elliptical one, made up of fragments that do not construct a fully developed whole. The inability of the African immigrant to account for his own existence in toto in the White world finds its visual equivalence in the truncated, fragmentary narrative in which he is thus caught.

Hondo's use of an essentially static camera further stresses his message. What was an economic liability—he could not afford expensive filmic equipment—was turned into an aesthetic asset. The absence of long tracking shots, varied angles, panning shots, except in a couple of instances, including the long final sequence, means that the view we have of the protagonist's life—and that of all the other characters as well—is incomplete and distant. Therefore the individual is made to appear transient, passing but never touching our lives profoundly. So, paradoxically, the lack of mobility of the camera is pressed into serving a thematics of non-rootedness, disconnectedness, and not, as in the old, classical cinema, a thematics of stolid stability.

In a similar fashion, the positioning of the camera outdoors and at some distance from the events it narrates results, too, in highlighting the immigrant's social *exteriority*. Thus when the man tries unsuccessfully to get a job or a room, the camera is not "allowed" inside but merely records from the outside his being expelled. The first time, we see from a courtyard a concierge chasing away the man, who has come to apply for an advertised position. The second time, we witness his being rudely kicked out of an apartment building by another concierge. The same scene being repeated farther down the street, this time accompanied with sound effects, transforms the whole sequence into a visual and sound gag. Such Chaplin-esque use of comedy to clothe tragedy is particularly effective in this context because it catches the White viewer in his/her own contradictions: between laughing at the Black character and feeling sympathy for his plight. But as the film progresses, and the Black man experiences more rejection, rejection takes on surreal and anxiety-laden connotations. At one point, he comes to a garage that has advertised a position for an accountant. Again from the streetside, he asks a mechanic at work under a car whether the job is available. In place of the expected verbal exchange all he and we hear are silences and monosyllabic negatives uttered by a voice—that of the boss—somewhere in the darkened garage. The sense of distance, of non-engagement, is made eerily visual and aural.[11]

From that point on, the theme of rejection spills out, so to speak, to encompass other destinies, embrace other transitory characters. On the streets of Paris, we see Blacks in suits, while a voice-over reads statistics on the "Black invasion" in France since 1944. We see African women in traditional dress, we see chance encounters of Black people who come from nowhere and vanish from the screen forever. None of these characters enter our lives, nor do we connect with theirs, the filmic replica of life in which Blacks remain transient ciphers.

Underscoring his message that these are people who have no place in the White society, Hondo has chosen to film them in public rather than private spaces: in cafés, restaurants, a classroom, and, of course, the streets. When he does film them in private spaces, the camera captures the fact that they are exiguous and filled with signs of impermanence. Furthermore, such spaces are always, in one way or another, the setting in which White ignorance and prejudices are tested and exposed. In one such case, a blonde wakes up in bed with the protagonist, whom she had propositioned the night before. Unfortunately, her partner was unable to confirm the legendary sexual overendowment of Black men. In another scene, the same woman and a companion visit their creole colleague's newborn baby. But they discover that genetics work in wondrous ways, since the white-skinned Antillean has fathered a black child!

To return to what we said earlier, then, both thematically and formally, transience and marginality are established. Short segments, rarely lasting more than two minutes, showing lives cut off from their beginnings and their destinations, translate visually the fact that these migrant workers, while necessary to the economic well-being of France, have no existence as unique subjects. Hondo's very sparing use of close-up shots underscores this feeling of nonrecognition. At times, faces move across the screen but are never held steady long enough for the viewer to identify with one. Even the main character is seen mostly in long shots, and generally on the side of the frame rather than dead center, which, of course, keeps his emotions at a distance from the viewer. Hondo is not trying to make us feel sorry and manipulate our sympathies. Rather his camera reproduces the harsh, distant gaze with which the Whites view the immigrant community. The one scene in which the main protagonist is seen looking at us and is framed in the center is at the train station. A low-angle shot at that point gives him a status he will never regain until the very end: that of a man in the process of freeing himself. The next full close shot will turn up in the very last sequence. But before we come to it, let us return to the prologue, which is about history and the process by which African subjects have become ciphers in it.

THE NEW SLAVE: EMPTYING AND FORCED INGESTION

The colonized subject is one that has been divested of his/her identity and invested with a new, borrowed one. This, the long prologue—more than fifteen minutes long—establishes in a form that is totally dissonant with the rest of the film. In five sequences using, in turn, animation, theatrical techniques that draw upon Brecht, guerrilla theater, and symbolic realism, Hondo paints a schematic picture of African history, from precolonial times to the postcolonial era. We see how proud peoples, with a rich and varied culture, technical skills, and facility with multiple languages, were turned into puppets, thanks to the joint efforts of the Catholic Church and the colonial army. The longest and possibly the most emotion-packed scene of the whole film, the third scene, takes place in a church. Africans from all nations are confessing to a priest for speaking their tribal languages. Then they are baptized and given a new Christian name. Changing names—which is tantamount to changing one's identity, particularly in an African culture where naming is giving life to—is the apex of a process of acculturation through which the Black man must pass in order to be "whitened" and "proud of it." We do note that as each newly baptized individual pronounces his name he spits out toward offscreen in a symbolic yet futile gesture of rebellion. Futile, since in the next prologue scene we see the Africans leave the church dressed in white surplices, lined up in military fashion and carrying crosses, which, when turned upside down, become swords. The camera then cuts to a deadly fight between two Senegalese soldiers supervised by a sarcastic-looking and cynical French corporal. The soldiers drop to the ground but are momentarily revived by being given French franc bills until they die for good. The whole prologue tells it all in uncomplicated but powerful skits: the African has been robbed of his culture and his self; he has become an object, a pawn in a new slave trade.

RESISTANCE AND REBELLION

So, with the protagonist pursuing his dream of becoming a full-fledged citizen on French shores, the film follows his gradual descent into despair. In many ways, the binding cement of the filmic patchwork is an interview that he conducts with a sociologist for an organization that employs him temporarily. The use of interview sequences interspersed at various points in the film may point to an unacknowledged Godardian influence over Hondo, for, as we know, in the sixties Godard frequently used interviews in his own films.[12] The interview provides the theoretical, Marxist foundation for the narrative: It makes clear Hondo's belief that the responsibility for the new slavery rests not, certainly not solely, with individual racism and bigotry but with powerful and inescapable economic forces that create a demand for cheap labor. So, armed with the conviction that there is no hope for him as an individual nor for his "brothers," the protagonist chooses the last resort—to flee.

Thus begins one of the longest sequences in the film. Abandoning all pretense of realism, Hondo plunges headlong into an eerily symbolic meal scene, almost in anticipation of Peter Greenaway, in which he settles accounts with his own past experience. As the protagonist runs through a forest, he meets a White union official—whom we have already encountered in another scene—and his family. They invite him to share a meal at their country home. But the meal turns into a nightmare. The children refuse to eat the food they are given and begin using it as projectiles, later climbing onto the table and wildly trampling on it, while their parents watch with mild reproach. The African stares with dismay. What can this rather unnerving scene possibly mean? How does it cap the various messages previously encoded? According to Hondo, "The meal is the image of the West. I imagine it as a big meal in which nothing has any meaning any more."[13] Certainly this scene gives support to that assertion. It makes abundantly clear that the refusal of food is scandalous in a world in which so many are starving. It also suggests that in Hondo's view the Western family as an institution symbolized in the ritual of togetherness around the table, its values, and its traditions has crumbled. Third, and perhaps more important, it throws into question the meaning of refusal and rebellion, particularly when we connect this scene to an earlier one in the film.

In it, we saw a little girl (ingenuously?) offer the newly arrived immigrant a sandwich. The man refused it. The film left the viewer clueless as to why he did so. One can therefore only surmise that for the Black man the offer is construed as a demeaning act of charity. Refusal, in this instance, shocking as it might be to good souls, becomes an assertion of dignity and an exercise of freedom.[14] By contrast, in the later scene, the children's rebellion is presented as an example of misguided freedom, precisely because it is not framed in the context of oppression. The children's refusal of food makes a mockery of freedom and of resistance as an empowering act. Furthermore, it is the sign of a society that has lost its sense of the sacred, vital relationships between human beings, and between them and the economic processes—including the production of food—that make their lives possible. To the extent that Third World laborers are involved in this production, trampling on food becomes symbolically trampling on them.

This farcical sequence ultimately makes a powerful statement by exposing the humanistic values—respect, decency, control, education—that are supposed to define the Western culture. What hope is left? None at this point, and the protagonist resumes his flight. This time, however, he is no longer the one that is being rejected: *he rejects*, and he does so in a long scream, akin to a *vomissement*—he throws up everything he has endured.[15] Thus the cycle of ingestion/rejection is completed. Significantly, language, the medium of his acculturation, is what is being thrown out. The man returns to a state of infancy—literally of not speaking. In the last shot, he is filmed in the fetal position at the base of a very large tree, a baobab lookalike, while nearby three portraits are aflame: those of Malcolm X, Ben Barka (the Algerian leader), and Che Guevara. Is it a dream or the foretelling of a revolution, of a general conflagration, death or resurrection? The film ends with the title "To be continued." But the wandering Black man has come home. He has literally and figuratively returned to his roots, to the base, to the center of the frame.

DECOLONIZING CINEMA AND THE RECEPTION OF AFRICAN CINEMA

It is ironic that at the beginning of this decade, representatives of European filmmakers at the GATT meetings should again be fighting the same battle as the one Med Hondo—and other Third World filmmakers—have been fighting in the last twenty years. It is a battle against the hegemony of Hollywood cinema, based upon the premise that whoever controls the images controls the ideology. Of course, for Med Hondo, the battle must be fought against other White national cinemas as well.[16]

But perhaps as important as the "decolonizing" of images is the decolonizing of film criticism. Again, I shall return to *Soleil O*. The film reviewers were exceptionally laudatory. "*Soleil O* seems to me to be the film that, to this day, best expresses Africa," wrote Bernard Trémege in *Jeune Cinéma* (39). It is "an extremely modern work on the aesthetic level and strikingly powerful on the political level," according to the critic for *Jeune Afrique*. It is a fascinating film that will deal a masterly blow to the Europeans, his former "masters," according to Jean-Louis Bory, the film critic for *Le Nouvel Observateur*.[17] Bernard Cohen, in *Positif*, is struck by its creative wealth and turbulence, while the critic for *Les Lettres Françaises* states that this "scream of protest, filmed with remarkable mastery, makes *Soleil O* one of the very best African films today."[18]

Even though Hondo's subsequent films would not always draw such unanimous praise, the critics would seldom fail to comment positively on his originality, his creativity and vision, the beauty of his images—which, in fact increases with time—and the power of his convictions.

Interestingly, one of the sources of disagreement has been how well Hondo's militant camera has avoided the pitfalls of ideological didacticism. In view of the French taste for political readings of artistic works, it is surprising that didacticism should have acquired such a negative connotation among French reviewers, and, I must add, irrespective of their political affiliation. How militancy articulates with didacticism, and how didacticism impacts on aesthetics, are questions too broad to be taken up here but that Hondo's films beg.[19] With regard to this point, the films that most invited such criticism were *Les Bicots-nègres, vos voisins* and the two on the Polisario freedom fighters (who have been trying to secure independence from Morocco in the Western Sahara for more than two decades). In his 1973 film, Hondo, fearing that his political message in *Soleil O* had been overshadowed by the existential dimension of his protagonist's fight and flight, decided to sharpen it with the theme of Black and North African laborers in Paris. Inevitably, the risk of didacticism increased with the need for clarification. The risk was there, too, in the following works on the Polisario, because of the need to inform a generally uninformed viewer of the historical background, and the difficulty of avoiding "preaching" on an issue that so directly involved Hondo the Mauritanian.[20]

But Gilles Colpart's praise of *Nous aurons toute la nuit pour dormir* (1977) as "A just and honest film," in which an "attentive" and "unobtrusive" camera was all the more effective as it avoided sentimentality, would suffice to illustrate how subjective judgments can be when it comes to measuring didacticism in a film, or any work of art, for that matter![21]

Another theoretical issue that Med Hondo's work brings to the fore is that of the relationship between "modernity" and "Africanism."[22] At first glance, there is something unexpected in associating the two terms, as we tend to link African aesthetics with traditional forms, in contrast to modern aesthetics. Among the traditional features commonly stressed in African literary and filmic texts figure orality (or oralitude), the presence of nonlinear narratives, and, of course, any inscription of an African culture, history, symbology, and mythology.

Certainly, to the extent that Hondo's films are solely concerned with chapters of African colonial and postcolonial history, no one can dispute their "Africanism." His inventive use of the sound track can easily be related to an oral tradition. The use of songs, of tribal languages, the intensity of verbal exchanges and of the sound level on the track—particularly noticeable in *West Indies*, even his stream-of-consciousness voice in *Soleil O*, can all be related to an oral culture. They certainly make the White reality represented in his films sound strangely lifeless. Nonlinearity, too, is a common trait of Hondo's films, with the single exception of *Sarraounia*, to this day his most conventional film and conventionally African for its content.

Yet, even *Sarraounia* is touched by modernity. With its strong linear narrative, beautiful and controlled images, a unifying African theme, alternation of grandiose battle scenes and intimate ones (as of the queen being groomed for battle), its subversive intent may not be as evident as in previous works. Its patterning after the Hollywood epic genre is contradicted, however, by a reversal of viewpoint: the film speaks from the position of the colonized or the aggressed, not that of the aggressor. The film's modernity, therefore, lies in its thematic rather than its formal treatment.

Where modernity and Africanism may be seen in a somewhat less easy relationship is in a film like *Soleil O*. The sense that the two orientations are dichotomous runs through Albert Cervoni's review of the film, which he criticizes for being "too excessively Rive-gauche/Left Bank."[23] True, Hondo's use of animation, theatrics, symbolic theater, masks, songs, and dance—which he also used extensively in *West Indies*—is reminiscent of Western avant-garde theater. But here is a case in which criticism is marred by Eurocentrism. To claim these features as Western property is to forget to what extent twentieth-century avant-garde theater was influenced by non-Western theater, developed in the East as well as in Africa. The theater that Antonin Artaud envisaged, with its expressionistic forms, its display of raw emotions through dance and sound, this "visceral" and ritualistic form of drama, was indeed a Western reinvention of Eastern and African realities. So instead of arguing that Hondo is too acculturated to Western forms, I would like to argue that his work is situated at the confluence of two traditions: his own native tradition and the one he acquired in the West, one that itself had borrowed heavily from artistic forms more familiar to an African artist. In a sense, *Soleil O* and *West Indies* reclaim, in their very modernity, the African heritage buried beneath the veneer of the Western avant-garde.

Cervoni's criticism points to the dangers of critical misappropriation and monocultural interpretations.[24] Decolonizing images means taking them back from their exclusive appropriation by a culturally dominant group; but images must also be freed from the viewers' monocentric and monocultural appropriation. How much each of us remains imprisoned in his or her own epistemology is illustrated in Michel Ciment's otherwise sympathetic and intelligent interview of the film director after the release of *Soleil O*. In it, Ciment asked Hondo to define his style, a notion that directly reflects a Western concern—and certainly a very French one—with formal unity and artistic integration. Significantly, Hondo rejected the concept of style and concentrated instead on the role of "visions" as inspiration for his film.

Hondo's dream is to educate people about the "richness of the African heritage," to "explain Africa and the crucial burning issues faced by Black people in Africa and abroad."[25] Hondo likes to end his films on a note of hope. I wish I could do likewise here. Yet none of Med Hondo's films are distributed in the United States at the moment. The one most likely to appeal to a wide audience, *Sarraounia*, saw its career on Parisian commercial screens curtailed, and no American distributor stepped forward despite "strong, positive reactions from blacks and whites" when it was shown in Alberta, Chicago, Washington, and Philadelphia.[26] The decolonization of images may begin with a talented individual's fight. It will perhaps have a chance of succeeding with the decolonization of the film industry. But as long as audiences continue to demand films that show "colonial adventurism" and leave no space for reflection about the implications of living in a postcolonial world, it is difficult to be very sanguine about the future of Hondo and filmmakers like him. Yet, Hondo is busy making another film![27]

*I am indebted to Robert P. Kolker for his critical comments.

NOTES

1. Quoted from an interview of the filmmaker in Françoise Pfaff, *Twenty-five Black African Filmmakers* (Westport, Conn.: Greenwood Press, 1988), 157.

2. Quoted in ibid., 159.

3. He worked briefly as an apprentice assistant on several sets and had minor parts in television series.

4. In Don Ranvaud, "Interview with Med Hondo," *Framework* 7–8 (Spring 1978): 28–30.

5. Cf. Maryse Condé, quoted in Pfaff, *Twenty-five Black African Filmmakers*, 160.

6. In Marcel Martin, "Brève rencontre avec . . . Med Hondo," *Ecran* 79 81 (15 June 1979): 25–26.

7. Cf. in particular Med Hondo, "Cinémas africains, écrans colonisés," *Le Monde*, 21 January 1982, 12.

8. Hondo founded his own distribution company, Soleil O, in 1970.

9. Hondo's criticism of African rulers ended up keeping his films out of the Carthage Festival.

10. Cf. Pfaff, *Twenty-five Black African Filmmakers*, 161.

11. Hondo's interesting work with the sound track would merit a long discussion.

12. To my knowledge, Hondo never mentions Jean-Luc Godard as a possible influence on his cinema. As a matter of fact, he goes to great lengths to disclaim any influence by a French filmmaker, acknowledging only Glauber Rocha, the Brazilian master of Nuovo Cinema, and Luis Buñuel.

13. In Michel Ciment, "Entretien avec Med Hondo," *Positif* 119 (September 1970): 22–26. My translation.

14. The notions of gift, refusal, dignity, and independence take on a particular meaning in the context of a postcolonial economy and Western "assistance" to the Third World.

15. Hondo uses the term in a number of interviews that he gave journalists and critics about the film.

16. Hondo has raised questions, for instance, about the appropriateness of using neorealist aesthetics, as the Senegalese filmmaker Ousmane Sembene has done, to represent an African reality.

17. Quoted in the press release. Jean-Louis Bory, "Les pièges du catéchisme," *Le Nouvel Observateur* 421 (4 December 1972): 81.

18. In *Positif* 119 (September 1970): 18, and *Lettres Françaises* (5–6 May 1970).

19. On this issue, cf. Thérèse Giraud's discussion of *Les Bicots-nègres, vos voisins*, in *Cahiers du Cinéma* 245–255 (December 1974–January 1975): 41 ff.

20. The two films were *Nous aurons toute la nuit pour dormir* (1977) and *Polisario, un peuple en armes* (1979).

21. Gilles Colpart, *Cinéma* 77 223 (July 1977): 103.

22. The modernity/tradition opposition was a key structuring element in colonial ideology, where the West's supposed modernity served as a rationale for colonization. By borrowing from both traditional and modern formal codes, Hondo is consciously subverting this opposition and therefore the whole discourse that was founded upon it.

23. In Albert Cervoni, "Un film rive gauche," *CinémAction* 8 (Summer 1979): 81–82.

24. There are notable exceptions to this critical monoculturalism. One is Guy

Hennebelle, who wrote in *CinémAction:* "Mise en scène délibérément moderne, *sans être pour autant d'inspiration occidentale*" [purposely modern mise-en-scène without, however, being inspired by the West] ("Med Hondo: Mon Film est un vomissement," *CinémAction* 8 (Summer 1979): 80–81). My emphasis. See also Guy Hennebelle, "Dans *Soleil O* je dénonce les "nègres-blancs . . . ," *Les Lettres Françaises* 1333 (6 May 1970): 17–18.

    25. In Pfaff, *Twenty-five Black African Filmmakers*, 161.

    26. Cf. Tony Rayns, "African Queen," *Time Out* 906 (30 December–6 January 1988): 36.

    27. In 1994 Med Hondo made a new film entitled *Lumière noire*.

Post-Tricolor African Cinema

TEN   *Toward a Richer Vision**

John D. H. Downing

I do not propose to produce a travesty in this essay—namely, a claim to cover, or to distill the essence of, African[1] postcolonial cinema. The literature on the subject is thankfully substantial and growing; readers may refer to the notes at the end of the essay and to references in the text in order to deepen their knowledge. Furthermore, for an Anglophone audience generally unable to make use of screenings in Paris, Ouagadougou, Carthage, Milan, or Montreal, access to the films that are my focus here is limited to the few outlets that have had the vision and determination to begin to distribute these works.[2] I myself have been able to see only a fraction of the creative work that exists, and additionally I am dependent upon the French or English subtitles, or French dialogue when it takes place, since at this point I do not know any African language.

What I propose to do is different: first, to give some sense of the variety of African cinematic responses to the postcolonial era; second, to touch upon the political economy of film production in a neocolonial setting; and third, to analyze a number of films in a little depth for their portrayal of precolonial, colonial, and postcolonial society, focusing especially on the work of Ousmane Sembene. If in the process I succeed in arousing the reader's appetite to search out more about these vigorous cinematic developments, I shall be delighted.[3]

THE PLURALISM OF AFRICAN CINEMAS

By "pluralism," I do not have in mind the artificial pluralism of a continent chopped into fifty and more arbitrary pieces by the armed arrogance of an imperial conference in Berlin, even though the repercussions of those divisions have been and will be tenacious. I rather have in mind both the variety of themes addressed in African cinemas and the variety of structures for production and distribution.[4]

It would be a little dry to list themes here, and in any case Françoise Pfaff has already proposed such an inventory for sub-Saharan Africa.[5] Nonetheless, what stands out in this cinematic corpus is the very intense pluralism of African cultures, from the exploration of Sufi Islam and its responsiveness to women's dilemmas in *Bab Sama Maftouh* (Door to the Sky) by Moroccan woman filmmaker Farida Belyazid, to the ferocious attack on power structures' claiming the mantle of Islam in Ousmane Sembene's *Ceddo* and his *Guelwaar;* or from the meditation on magical power in *Yeelen* (Brightness/The Light), by Souleymane Cissé (Solimani Sise), to the intensely erotic sequence in Désiré Ecaré's *Faces of Women*.

Regarding the portrayal of colonial and anticolonial realities, there is the same variety. Perhaps the most famous African anticolonial film of all, *Battle of Algiers*, although based upon an Algerian novel and using Algerians as actors and as some crew members, was directed by Gillo Pontecorvo and financed by a private Algerian company, Casbah-Film. Rachid Boudjedra rather sourly noted the company's proclivity for Hollywood-style spectacle and consequently for using expensive foreign technicians, with the result that vast sums of money were poured into one internationally successful movie (*Venice Golden Lion*, 1967), while young Algerian film-professionals-in-the-making in every category were deprived of funds, experience, and opportunity.[6]

In part, perhaps, because of the success of *Battle of Algiers*, and over the longer term in order to try to legitimize its power through creating and dwelling upon the myth of its origins, the Front de Libération National (FLN) government of Algeria poured a great deal of its film budget until the mid-1970s into making films about the anticolonial struggle. This phenomenon has been commented upon widely[7] and has a certain resonance with the former Soviet regime's crushing emphasis on funding films about World War II. (As recent history demonstrates in both cases, neither hegemonic strategy could substitute for appropriate political and economic policies.)

For some Algerian filmmakers, this avoidance of the present became impossible. Perhaps the best known outside Algeria itself is Merzak Allouache,[8] whose *Omar Gatlato* (1977) depicted everyday realities: the chasm between macho ideology and male nervousness relating to women, the threat of street crime, the popularity of Hindi movies, the banality of office life, the overcrowded living conditions of the majority. With the recent appearance of Saïd Ould Khalifa's *Ombres Blanches* (White Shadows), which premiered at the Carthage Festival in 1992 and which addresses the dilemmas of a woman single by choice and the problem of anti-Black racism in Algeria, perhaps those voices may yet be heard more loudly—though the protracted agony of Algeria at the time of writing leaves but a small space for hope in this regard in the near future.[9]

Other films address colonial and anticolonial themes in more nuanced and less militaristic ways than earlier Algerian cinema did. There is, for example, a group of films that address the presence of African migrants in France, notably *Soleil O* (1970) by Med Hondo (discussed by Madeleine Cottenet-Hage in Chapter 9), and equally *La Noire De . . .* (Black Girl) (1966), by Ousmane Sembene. These stand side by side with the evolving Beur cinema, and indeed there is a growing interpenetration between the two, in part because of the pressure on dissident filmmakers to emigrate.[10] Others refer in passing to colonialism as a device to address contemporary issues, as Cheick Oumar Sissoko does in *Finzan* (1990). There, the small boys trying to support a widow against the village leaders' insistence that she marry her drunken and stupid brother-in-law put tree slugs in his beer to disrupt his digestive system so he cannot engage in sex with her. One says he learned the trick from his grandmother, who used to do the same to colonial tax collectors. This is the sole reference to colonialism or neocolonialism, yet the allusive parallel of despotic power and sly resistance, in this instance on the level of gender power, is evidently present.

Styles of cinema, too, vary widely. For some, neorealism has clearly been a potent influence; for others, linear narrative and suspense are totally unimportant. For some, extreme precision in lighting and sound is obviously de rigueur; for others, the tradition of "imperfect cinema"[11] is paramount, in other words a cinema that does not wait for all the technical and financial means to be in place in order to address pressing realities. For some, an intensely political mission is evident; for others, a commitment to exploring the vagaries of the human condition. Yet even this summary of variations does violence to the creative work available, which quite often draws upon several strands in world cinema simultaneously, without being captive to any particular one.[12]

For example, folkloric and theatrical traditions also make their presence felt in many African films, in a mode that sometimes evokes Brechtian *Entfremdung* approaches and at other times touches upon the magical realism of some Latin American literature and cinema. Yet again, although it would be no harm for either or both of these to be the cultural sources of these narratives, the real sources are overwhelmingly within African traditions. Sometimes the characterization may seem stilted to those steeped in contemporary U.S. cinema, and sometimes an element in that impression may be derived from the quite frequent use of nonprofessional actors. Yet the highly structured roles of traditional villages, and the confluence of drama and ritual in the history of African theater, also play their part in these performances—as does the satirical tradition, which somehow in the minds of non-African film critics is permitted to lampoon and caricature outside, but not inside, Africa. European dramas may be expressionist, or Shavian, or Mozart's opera plots may be totally absurd, yet those are acceptable deviations by the indisputably great: but woe betide an African filmmaker who experiments with canonical forms.

THE POLITICAL ECONOMY OF AFRICAN CINEMAS

The standard accounts of African cinemas, as of "Third World" cinemas in general,[13] correctly and inevitably lay stress on the problem of distribution as the nub of the economic problem faced by African filmmakers. No distribution or poor distribution brings minimal receipts, which in turn destroys the financial basis for the next film. Most independent film and video artists in metropolitan countries face much the same problem, the difference being that in metropolitan countries at least some version of national life and culture finds its way onto the screen, whereas in African countries the choice is generally between no version and an imported racist version, subtle or unsubtle.

The sources cited above note the series of obstacles placed in the path of African filmmakers by French cinematic and cultural institutions. This pattern has persisted from the colonial days, when Africa was effectively an exotic backdrop to narratives about Europeans but Africans were kept from producing their own filmic discourses and images, through to the domination of the French cinema chains over distribution, screening, and profits. Unfortunately the statist solution to the problem, as with Algeria's Organisation Nationale du Commerce et de l'Industrie Cinématographique (ONCIC) and its predecessor bureaus before 1968, tended to create new problems of government censorship and policy inertia in the process of solving the initial problems of funding and distribution. It is for this reason that the Declaration of Filmmakers in Niamey in 1982 began a move toward combined public and private organization of film production.[14]

The impact of these dilemmas has been visible first and foremost in the tiny number of films made. It is not unusual for an African creative artist to get to make just one or two films, often a decade or more apart, even when the first film has received critical acclaim. Meanwhile the Hollywood machine churns out its mammoth dross at mammoth expense, and our human cultural heritage is accordingly unbalanced and disfigured.

The festivals of Carthage and Ouagadougou are vital nodes in such distribution as does exist and, increasingly, metropolitan countries' film festivals have been giving more space to Third World contestants. The "Three Continents" festival at Nantes is virtually alone in the metropolis in focusing strictly upon Third World cinemas, however, and the more prestigious festivals seem often to have a courtesy space for three-quarters of the world, with the rest reserved for "real" movies. The Third World films that win prizes in these festivals, such as the Argentinean film *The Official Story* or the Chinese film *Farewell My Concubine*, outstanding as they certainly were, are generally framed within the production and narrative codes taken as givens in contemporary Hollywood.

The full story of African/non-African coproductions has yet to be fully told, as the most recent study (Diawara) takes the story only to the early 1980s. The chief protagonists in the non-African world have been to date the Ministère de la Coopération, the Ministère de la Culture and the Centre National de la Cinématographie in France. More recently television channels such as Canal Plus and some of their British and German counterparts have also been playing a role. There have been continuing critiques of French coproduction policy as a prolongation of colonial assimilationist policy,[15] with African filmmakers forced to be somewhat dependent upon the hand that feeds them, or at least to have to be prepared to risk biting it, because of its owner's urge to control film production, either through the initial choice of projects to fund or by refusal to distribute. The situation is further complicated by the different policies of different French administrations, with the Mitterrand administration—especially in the person of its intermittent minister of culture, Jack Lang—representing a more pro-African policy than that of his conservative peers with the same portfolio.

At the time of writing, however, two further developments heralded a new period of uncertainty in this realm. One was the vigorous attack by the French government in 1993–1994 on the "open doors" cultural trade policy proposed by other metropolitan nations in the context of the Uruguay GATT (now WTO) negotiations (1987–1994)—launched with some success in that cultural trade was cordoned off from inclusion in the final agreement. The other was the untying of the CFA franc from the French franc in early 1994, which had the instantaneous and predictable effect of devaluing the CFA franc by a factor of four or five. Whether the French insistence on cultural autonomy would extend into any form of continued support for the cultural autonomy of those African nations that it had sought so hard to retain within its sphere of influence after the tricolor had been run down still remained to be seen following this economic casting adrift.[16]

One plausible scenario was that it would make African governments even more dependent upon French favor in the short term, in which case the opportunity for French hegemony in any coproduction decisions would be enhanced. For some filmmakers, this would simply be the new reality; for others, the opportunity to spit out the sugared bullet would be timely, albeit tough. For others still, there would likely issue an even stronger search for multiple sources of support from TV firms in different lands, perhaps in the hope that no one company would be too deeply invested to worry about political corns being stepped on.

What would not change in the foreseeable future would be the sensitivity of many African governments to critical film portrayals of their policies and inadequacies. Sembene's *Emitai* (1971) took six years to be distributed in France because of its direct attack on French colonial policy, and many of his other films aroused political hackles and were blocked from distribution or cut. The depiction in Gaston Kaboré's *Zan Boko* (1988) of the squelching of an independent journalist by fiat of a tiny clique of top government officials outraged at his critical media interventions represents a continuing political reality.[17] In the film the journalist at least seemed to expect to stay alive, even though his career was obviously dead in the water. Such a moderately beneficent outcome could certainly not be assured in every country.

AN ANALYSIS OF CERTAIN FILMS

I will now turn to the analysis of a number of films, based primarily on their treatment of colonial realities but also by necessity comparing their treatment of pre- and postcolonial realities, since the latter clearly have a major bearing on the former. Within this analysis I will also pay particular attention to representations and discourses about women, both for their intrinsic importance and because they often play a significant part in the best of these films.[18] I will also pay special attention to the work of Ousmane Sembene, both because of its major weight and because at the time of writing his work is more accessible to viewing than the work of many others. I will begin by discussing Sembene's films, especially *Emitai, Camp de Thiaroye*, and *Guelwaar*, and then will conclude with an analysis of Souleymane Cissé's *Yeelen*.

Sembene's films that focus specifically on the colonial era are *Emitai* (1971) and *Camp de Thiaroye* (1988), codirected with Thienno Faty Sow. *La Noire De . . .* (Black Girl, 1966), *Mandabi* (The Money Order, 1968), *Xala* (1974), and *Guelwaar* (1992) deal with neocolonial themes, and *Ceddo* (1976) with the early colonial era. *Yeelen* (1987) is set in the precolonial period.

The importance of distinguishing earlier and later eras in an assessment of the treatment of colonialism in African films is derived from two considerations. First, the term "postcolonial" glosses over the issue of neocolonialism and the continuing sway of French economic and political power over African nations: an analysis of this continuing heritage helps us to understand the character of formal colonial rule and its consequences. Second, the "hoorah for the glorious past" attitude toward precolonial Africa, rather like the cozy romantic glow that some Europeans project concerning feudal Europe, masks a frequent inability to come to terms with the reality of the African present. The quality and honesty of depiction of that earlier phase in African development are important criteria for the conceptual integrity of a film project dealing with Africa and, again, important guides to appreciating Africa's present.

Colonialism

Emitai and *Camp de Thiaroye* virtually represent two chapters in the same tragic and shameful saga, beginning in the village of Effok in the Casamance region of southern Senegal, immediately to the north of formerly Portuguese Guinea. As a glance at the map will show, Senegal is one of the many nations of Africa in which colonial boundaries have created an absurdity, in this case an absurdity born of British-French rivalry. Gambia, for a period a British possession, is wedged into Senegal, so that without a passport it is impossible to go straight down the coast from northern to southern Senegal.

Casamance is also the region of Sembene's birth, where mostly Dyula (Diola, Jola) is spoken and not Wolof. Within this region lay the village of Effok, and it was there that in 1942 a detachment of French troops of the Vichy regime, confronted with the villagers' refusal to hand over their rice crop to support the war effort, shot down dozens of men (armed only with spears), women, and children in cold blood. Sembene's film *Emitai* addresses that atrocity.

The film moves slowly, especially for those reared on contemporary action-adventure movies, although as Sheila Petty notes,[19] the shot length becomes shorter and shorter in the final sequence leading to the climax.[20] The film's sound track[21] uses the sounds of birds, insects, animals, and humans "talking, behaving, ululating, dirging, chanting," rather than the musical score often regarded as required in Hollywood productions in order to gather up all the threads of our attention. Yet the action builds remorselessly toward the climax, incorporating not only the major theme of French army brutality but also significant critiques of overreliance on religious defenses against military repression and of the village elders' vacillation, as opposed to the steady resolve of the village women.[22]

The story is essentially as follows: First the young men are forcibly drafted by the French, and then the French return a year later to impound the rice crop. The women, whose primary responsibility is the rice, hide it. The French force them to sit directly in the tropical sun, hour after hour, without water or movement, in order to torture them into revealing the whereabouts of the rice. Meanwhile the elders pointlessly consult the gods in ritual after ritual in a spirit shrine and finally capitulate. They are about to deliver the rice to the army detachment when the women call upon them to stop. Upon obeying the women, they are shot down without further ado.

The *mission civilisatrice* is ripped to shreds, revealing its ugly naked body of rapacity and force. Over and above the main narrative, whose message offers a damning commentary on French colonialism, some significant exchanges in the film serve to underscore that message. Sembene himself, playing a minor role as a Senegalese *tirailleur*, expresses astonishment when the picture of Marshal Pétain is replaced by the picture of General de Gaulle. He asks how a two-star general can possibly replace a seven-star general and shakes his head bemusedly.

This scene represents the moment in 1942 when the colonial governors of French-held West Africa transferred their allegiance to de Gaulle. Yet the film makes it plain that the "pro-Fascist" Pétain and the "anti-Fascist" de Gaulle are absolutely indistinguishable in their colonial policy. Under the first, young men are drafted; under the second, rice is stolen with the aid of a bloodbath. Indeed, Sembene is pointing out with ineluctable logic that colonial policy and Fascist policy are indistinguishable if you are so unfortunate as to find yourself on the receiving end.

At the same time, the film is not simply a diatribe, however appropriate that might be under these circumstances. Its concentration on the stoic, unwavering resistance of the Dyula women—who are renowned in Senegal for their degree of social and economic power and whose completely spontaneous and effective unity under collective torture contrasts so sharply with the male elders' waffling—prevents the viewer from focusing on only one term of the colonial relationship. At the same time, Sembene wrote out of the film a woman character, An Sitoé, who was a protagonist in the original event and came to be venerated as a goddess, on the ground that she was too saccharine a character.[23]

Equally, traditional religion is stripped of all romanticism. The spirit shrine to which the elders repair for guidance is a characteristic feature of fused religious and economic expression in Dyula culture.[24] The supreme god, Emit, is a very remote deity who delegates management of the rice economy to the spirit shrines, and so to the *ai*, priest-kings of each community (hence the title of the film, *Emitai*). These spirit shrines are the guardians and protectors of the rice fields (ultimately owned by Emit) and the rice crop. This, however, is the zone of economic life managed by women, whereas the men focus on cattle rearing.[25]

Once the central elements of Dyula life are appreciated, the film's message comes into much sharper focus. The women's obduracy is spontaneous but grounded in their tradition of controlling the highly developed wet-rice economy (indeed, some of the spirit shrine *ai* are women). The men's gerontocratic power, buttressed by traditional rituals that are as powerless as their spears against the invaders, is shown to be hollow, outmoded (compare the dissection of gerontocracy in *Yeelen*, below). The women's secular collective resistance is far more powerful—and might have been ultimately successful had the men's resolve not cracked when their religious crutches proved useless.[26]

Sembene's typically ruthless honesty in portraying all sides of the issue did not, as noted, prevent the French government from delaying the screening of *Emitai* on French soil for six years or from persuading a number of other neocolonial regimes in West Africa to ban it.

Camp de Thiaroye, completed seventeen years after *Emitai* but set in time just two years after the Effok massacre, takes the story to its next, equally horrific phase. In this film the individual characters are more clearly drawn than in *Emitai*, where there is generally more emphasis on collective actors. The central character is Sergeant Diatta, whom we first meet escorting his troops off a ship in Dakar, having served in extensive combat in the European theater. They are dressed in loaned U.S. Army uniforms, and their military precision and professional bearing are consistently in evidence and emphasized. Among them are no doubt the survivors of the conscripts whom we saw being drafted in *Emitai*, although the troops' provenance in general is from all over the French colonies in West Africa.

On the quayside, Diatta meets his uncle and Bissoun, a young woman his village has sent to be his bride, and he introduces them to Captain Raymond, his commanding officer. Raymond, whose sympathies lie in part with the Africans, alongside whom he has fought many tough engagements under fire, immediately offers the relatives his hand, but his uncle refuses to shake it. In the general quayside enthusiasm, military marching band music, and cheering of the troops—although the cheering Whites are standing some dozens of safe meters apart from the Africans—this is the first definitively sour note, aside from the wounded on stretchers who are brought first down the gangplank.

Shortly afterward, it transpires that Diatta, Bissoun, and the uncle all hail from Effok and that the 1942 massacre, in which both of Diatta's parents were killed, had been totally unknown to him up until then. He initially receives the scarifying information with what seems to be surprisingly little overt emotion, but it operates on him like a slow burn throughout the narrative, gradually bursting into flame toward the denouement.

On one level the film simply reproduces the historical episode near Dakar in 1944 in which African soldiers briefly kidnapped a general in order to pursue their claim for the promised pay that was being denied them; then, after they released the general, a pre-dawn reprisal action by French tanks and machine guns that razed their military camp and obliterated most of them outright. Now that they were no longer risking their lives in some of the most intense engagements of the war, and now that they were home as colonized subjects rather than as fighting men with the duty to kill White enemy soldiers, the Africans' self-assertion was enormously dangerous to political stability in the colonies. It was more than a question of paying or not paying them their just deserts. It was a fundamental question of control. They had now served their temporary purpose and were dispensable. Their dispensability is underscored by the way at the film's close we see a huge new contingent of African troops embarking to continue to fight the war, obviously oblivious of the coldblooded slaughter of their recently returned fellows.

On another level, the film is a study in particular of the contradictions and development of Sergeant Diatta, which are played out both in relation to the events that swirl around him and in relation to a series of other characters: his corporal, Diarra; his *gauchiste* captain, Raymond; Raymond's antagonist, the echt colonialist Captain Labrousse; the psychologically damaged but clairvoyant Pays, struck mute by his experience of incarceration in Buchenwald;[27] and not least, Diatta's uncle Adjangor, his official village fiancée Bintoun, and Diatta's French wife and their daughter, whom we see only in a photograph and hear of through the words of a letter Diatta writes to her. (In *Camp de Thiaroye*, however, the women's roles are less significant than in any other Sembene film.)

On a third level, the film is also about collective identities, not only African and European but also the national identities imposed upon Africans by the colonial division of the continent, and the universal collectivist identity of African cultures. The troops call each other not by their names but by their nicknames, which are those of colonial territories such as "Gabon" or "Niger." The men are also barracked according to their colonial nationality. On one level, then, this artificial reality is seen in the process of being "naturalized," and yet on another level every time a major crisis erupts, especially when the general is seized, the military hierarchy imposed by the French evaporates and there is instantaneous *collective* discussion as to how to proceed, given the crisis.

Let us first of all identify Diatta's contradictions, which the film portrays with consistent respect—not with sarcasm, as in the case of Ibrahima Dieng in *Mandabi* or El Hadj in *Xala*. His conflicts are born of his experience within the colonial system as well as of World War II. On the one hand, he perfectly fits the official image of the *évolué*, the *assimilé*: someone whose English is almost as fluent as his French, someone who chooses to play a record of Albinoni, who has Aragon's poetry on his bookshelf, who is planning to return to France after the war to complete his university studies, who is an intensely proud and professional soldier in the French army,[28] and who has married a Frenchwoman, whom he clearly loves and respects (an action that represented serious overkill in view of the reality of French assimilation policy).

At the same time, he is equally au courant with and appreciative of the music of Charlie Parker. He is able to respond without malice to the African American military policeman who has mistaken him for a U.S. soldier absent without leave and has seized and beaten him. And in a memorable exchange toward the close of the film, when the French officers are standing by their refusal to pay the wages and benefits due the African troops, he reveals in a scorching indictment his detailed memory of the maltreatment and contempt experienced at French hands by Africans fighting on the same side: from the refusal to let them board boats to escape to England at the 1940 Dunkirk evacuation to the refusal to protest the slaying or bury the body of Captain Nichorere, who was shot by the Nazis at Buchenwald for refusing to detach himself from the White officers' group. It is clear that the details were all perfectly known to him, but seemingly psychologically buried.

We see the contradictions at their most complex in his reaction to the murder of his parents. He seems initially to react almost as though numb, and he appears to dull his response with his annoyance about his uncle's anger at his French wife—that is to say, about Diatta's choice to marry one of the colonizing people whose army killed his parents and slaughtered his village. Somewhat later, when he is translating from some U.S. soldiers' English for the benefit of his French officers, he is asked to translate one American soldier's remark that "These French are completely out of control—they've lost the empire." He pauses, allows himself a very slight private smile, and says, "It's nothing important, Captain."

Yet shortly afterward, we see him writing to his wife, telling her only as one element in a whole list of events that his parents had both died while he was away—not that they had been shot down like dogs by order of the French army. We are left to wonder whether he is gradually distancing himself from her, since he cannot seemingly express horror and grief and anger at their loss, or whether the information is still only gradually penetrating and challenging the carapace of French-ness that has been overlaid on him during his previous years of university education and military service.

But then we see him arguing, albeit quietly and peaceably, with Captain Raymond, who despite his respect for and sympathy with the African soldiers under his command, and despite his radical alienation from his fellow officers' blunt racism and their pointed ostracism of him, cannot accept that the Nazi massacre at Oradour was comparable to the French massacre at Effok. For Raymond, the comparison is too painful, inasmuch as it equates the French with the Nazis, and he is anxious to differentiate between decent French and colonialist French—a distinction that he himself has no ability to make when it comes to the Germans. For Diatta, the conversation serves as a reminder that even the most sympathetic White person has certain strict and powerful limits when it comes to applying the same criteria to Africans as to Whites. When Raymond is later detailed to negotiate with Diatta with regard to the general's capture, Diatta raises this with him—"Are there two rules, one for Whites and one for Blacks?"—and then tells him, "After we fought your enemies in Europe, now we're fighting for Africa."

Yet even by the end of the action, neither Diatta nor any of the others expect the French retribution for capturing the general to be so swift, or so merciless, or so annihilatory. Only Pays, whose speech faculty has been destroyed by the horrors of his Buchenwald experience—he constantly wears a Wehrmacht helmet to signify them—intuits what is going to happen, but even at the very last moment before the assault he cannot communicate it to his fellows, who naively assume that they are safe and he is crazy. We know that they will never leave the camp alive, for we have seen them from an elevated distance, at the outset of the film, proudly marching into the camp at the peak of their prowess, and we long to have them hear his message before it is too late.

But does Sembene mean to dwell on Pays's dumbness, expressing the inexpressible with his donkey's harsh bray, or to signify Diatta's and the others' deafness, somehow induced by having been temporarily treated seriously as human beings, as fighting men rather than as "natives"? Or are both of these symbols fused?

Nonetheless, Diatta has moved a considerable distance—if not far enough and fast enough to save himself and his fellows. He refuses to intervene to stop the general's being taken captive, even though Labrousse orders him to do so. Furthermore, when the Africans are in full revolt and rejecting French-imposed officialdom to the point of denying the authority of Diatta's sergeant, and they ask him bluntly, "So are you with us or against us?" he replies, "With you"—although even then only after a pause.

Corporal Diarra is a much more spontaneous character than his sergeant. We see him in action first of all leading an impromptu protest against the disgusting food served up to the troops. We know that his vigor and truculence have paid off when we see a huge side of beef being unloaded from a truck, meat that the men had previously been told was available only to the White officers. "Were the bullets a different size for the whites when we were fighting in Europe?" he demands.

A little later, when Diatta has been summarily arrested, badly beaten, and locked up by the U.S. military police detail, it is Diarra who puts together a commando unit to capture a U.S. soldier in reprisal. The tactic works, and there is a mutual release. As he frequently does in his films, Sembene leads us to consider that there is often much more wisdom below than above. And yet the "below" is itself already a distortion, for we also see Diarra cursing out a truck driver for driving recklessly—and doing it in rather fluent German.

In his portrayal of these two individuals, Sembene deepens his analysis of the *tirailleurs* in *Emitai*. In the former film, they are seen as the naive accomplices of French colonial rule, caught between loyalty to Africa and the process of mental colonization by French culture, a kind of historical bridgehead. But they are defined collectively and seen as a generation on whose shoulders the neocolonial elite stood, with its own split loyalties and consciousness.[29] Their dilemmas are more individually explored in the later film, which underscores that more personal reality by having the camera dwell for a moment upon the faces of those we have come to know as it pans over the corpses strewn about the ground after the massacre, and by emphasizing the terrible price they paid through superimposing their images over the scene of the new recruits embarking at the quayside at the film's close.

We have already noted the political ambivalence of Captain Raymond. Although on one level his primary conflict is with the knee-jerk racist and colonialist Labrousse and the other French officers, the primacy of that conflict is in his own thinking. They, in the end, are his peers, and he defines himself in relation to them, however angry he is with them and however much he despises their crude and ignorant stance. When he is negotiating with Diatta over the general's release, he tells Diatta that he will personally take their grievances to the governor-general. This is a level of naiveté that is simply stunning if assessed rationally, but absolutely on target as a delineation of standard White leftist psychology, which despite its critiques is always prone to believe that someone in authority will be on the side of justice. It is a psychology of doubtful veracity in social-class terms, but when it comes to race relations it is historically absurd.

The true focus of Raymond's conflict is thus the Africans, despite his respect and sympathy for the men with whom he has shared countless dangers and upon whose courage and tenacity in battle he has come to rely. He has not a hint of the racial-sexual jealousy and anger concerning Diatta's French wife that are evinced by the other White officers. Yet he seems unable to follow through to the obvious practical conclusions of his experience of European officers and of African troops. In this respect, he and Diatta are paralleled exactly, even to the ironic point of both being described contemptuously and angrily as "Communists" by the other French officers. In plain fact, they are both intellectuals, overconfident in the power of words and reason in political conflict and rendered politically impotent when appeals based on reason and equity merely spin off into space.

Captain Labrousse, by contrast, has no such complexities in his character. He is, sadly, not a cardboard cutout racist, simply a composite racist voice, of the unreflective and absolutist variety whom White liberals fondly like to think of as a throwback, a mossback. In a perverse sense his purity is a pleasure to watch, as when he says to Diatta, "Oh, you like serious music, not the tom-tom, do you?" Or when he notes sagely, "The Americans are really racist," although we have just seen him on the telephone groveling before the American officer with whom he is speaking. Or when he expresses his outrage that the captured White American soldier is having to spend the night with Africans in the barracks. Or when he repeats the slur that the francs the African soldiers have saved, they either stole from battlefield corpses or were given by the Nazis to cause runaway inflation and thus to "destabilize the Empire." Or, finally, when in tones of rage at Diatta's recital of French rejections of their African fellow soldiers and at his reminder of French collaboration with the Gestapo, Labrousse says: "Mr. Intellectual! You've given us a fine history lesson: now get out of here!"

One point at which Labrousse's totally racist attitude strikes a curious but effective chord in the narrative is when the troops are brought standard *tirailleur* military garb in the place of their U.S.-donated uniforms. Diatta protests that he is being given a rank-and-file *képi*, rather than that of an officer, and Labrousse comments, "They are big children." Yet Labrousse's slur is effectively articulated by one of the African soldiers, albeit from a totally different direction, when he observes the dejection on the faces of his fellows as they change into their normal uniforms. He upbraids them bitterly: "You're not Americans! White Americans, white French—white, white—the same thing. We're Africans, we're men, we fought the war, we slept next to corpses—why are you sad? We're not thieves, we have brought no shame on our families . . . we're crying because of American uniforms? Shame on you, shame on you, shame on you! *Why?*"

In many ways the most haunting character and the most complex performance in the film is that of Pays. He can only utter wordless, tormented sounds that grate violently on the ear and that act as grim heralds of the approaching doom. His experience in Buchenwald is constantly referred to: shortly after the troops have proudly marched into the camp, we see him wandering up to the barbed wire fence, looking at the wire strands against the open blue sky, running his hand slowly over the spikes, looking up at the sentry tower, all the while with fear etched in his face. The mawkish sounds of "Lili Marlene"[30] on a mouth organ play out on the sound track, both here and at repeated intervals when Pays is the film's focus of attention.

Corporal Diarra tries to comfort Pays by pouring some soil on his hand and telling him he is in Africa now, not Germany, but with no effect. A little later Pays, wearing his Wehrmacht helmet, stops a couple of soldiers who are going out of the gate for a stroll and utters his hideous groan to them. The film intercuts with the images in his head through newsreel footage clips of concentration camp corpses being dumped into mass graves, but the two men simply dismiss him as crazy. The film repeatedly emphasizes that his derangement, however agonizing to him, has locked onto the truth in a way that not one of the other African protagonists has succeeded in doing (with the partial exception of Diatta's uncle).

This intuition is at its most evident in two episodes toward the close of the film. One is where he violently protests the release of the general, shaking his head, running his fingers over his lips and making burbling sounds to indicate that the general is lying through his teeth when he guarantees to pay them the entirety of what they are due. When they disregard him, his whole body shakes with frustration and fury, he spits in disgust and emits further tortured groans, like the harsh brayings of a donkey. A little later, he is the only one who ascends the watchtower in the expectation that the French will be back in force, and hoping to warn them as soon as he spots them. Yet when he wakes them up—and the audience has seen the lights of the trucks and tanks, so we know the true score—they are irritated at him and once again dismiss him as demented.

Minutes later, the holocaust ensues.

The uncle and the cousin/fiancée play rather small roles (indeed, the fiancée, Bintoun, scarcely speaks), and the presence of Diatta's wife and daughter is entirely symbolic. The role of the former seems primarily to connect the audience to the earlier massacre that was the subject of *Emitai*, although Bintoun's presence seems also designed to underscore how far away from village life Diatta has moved mentally, in that her presence and expectation of marriage are merely an embarrassment to him. We see them finally at the close of the film at the quayside as the next consignment of African recruits boards the troop ship, the uncle reluctantly holding the large sack of coffee beans that Raymond had agreed to take to Diatta's wife. But the sack of beans stays in Adjangor's hands, his face expressing his distaste and anger at what is unfolding before him. It is probably implausible that he even knows yet of the massacre. And Raymond does not come to take the sack from him, presumably because he cannot face the reality of the situation.

Thus the film closes as it opens, on the colonial quayside, symbolizing the drastically asymptotic exchange between Africa and colonial France.

Yet France, quite definitely, is not the only target in view. Not only are Nazi Germany and French colonialism arrayed next to each other, but U.S. imperial policy is skewered as well. For when the U.S. army detail arrives to reclaim their captured soldier, one of their number tells the French, "If this man had been mistreated, our army would have been in here and leveled your camp and all your soldiers in it." Which the French military proceeds to do not very long after this incident. The disparity is in fact between the treatment of captives by Europeans and Africans. When Diatta is seized, he is badly beaten by four U.S. soldiers, his arm is broken, and the only soldier who comes to apologize is the African American. When first the White American soldier and then the French general are taken hostage, neither is physically harmed in any way. Yet these actions are viewed as reasonably paving the way to retaliation by mass extermination, Nazi-style.

Postcolonialism—or Neocolonialism?

Sembene's *Guelwaar* partially takes the form of a political mystery story: What happened to the body of Pierre Henri Thioune Guelwaar? Why was it buried in a Muslim cemetery, especially given that he was well known to be a fanatical Catholic? Why is the Muslim hierarchy in the town where he was buried conniving and covering up the fact of his gravesite with vehement refusals to allow the corpse to be disinterred, on the rationale that the cemetery is sacred ground—covering it up even to the point of trying to face down their own imam and accusing him of siding with infidels?

The answer becomes clearer piece by piece as we follow the efforts of Guelwaar's expatriate son, Barthélémy, and the police captain, Gora, to track down and then to disinter the body. Our first clue comes as they leave the police precinct and we see trucks driving down the street labeled "Food Aid" in large letters. The moment passes without further comment, but soon we are treated to Gora's flashback memory (which he does not share with Barthélémy) of Thioune's police file, which has the words "*Élément Incontrôlable*" (Disruptive Element) written on it in large letters. Then we travel with them as they meet the local leader, Baye Aly, in the town where Thioune is thought to be buried and shortly afterward as they meet the brother and associates of Meissa Cis, supposedly the person buried where Thioune is buried.

Mor Cis, the surviving brother, is a wiry, waspish individual who produces Thioune's death certificate when asked for his brother's. Neither he nor his friends can read French. Nonetheless, he instantly professes himself totally outraged at Gora's suggestion that he, as a devout Muslim, could have countenanced an infidel being buried in a Muslim cemetery—and in lieu of his brother. He and his cronies abuse Gora and almost physically throw him out.

We are quickly given strong further indications that Mor Cis is not to be given credence despite the strident tone of his protests, when we see Meissa Cis's two widows sitting in official mourning for their husband. One of them contemptuously describes to the other Mor Cis's shouted protestations as akin to the noise of a goat having its throat cut, and soon afterward we see Mor Cis begging her to take him as her husband, even promising her that he will divorce all four of his existing wives if she will only agree. It emerges that in the past they had had an ongoing adulterous relationship from which two children were born, but she had ended the relationship some time back. On top of a lengthy adulterous relationship with his brother's wife, urging marriage on her within forty-eight hours of his brother's burial and proposing to ditch four wives and leave them to fend entirely for themselves are hardly the marks of a devout adherent of Islam! (In the best tradition of women in Sembene's films, she gives him a no-holds-barred tongue-lashing from which he retreats in furious disarray.)

It is clear by now that the official version of Thioune's burial is extremely suspect. We also learn that he did not die of natural causes; the cause of death was a general internal hemorrhage, presumably caused by prolonged and violent assault. Further, we see him in the flashback already mentioned delivering a formal complaint to Gora concerning the harassment of members of the Association of Catholic Women. Gora queries him on the political character of the group, and Thioune replies that they discuss both religious and political issues, including the embezzlement of public funds. When Gora asks how it was that three young men in that neighborhood came to have their arms broken, Thioune denies any knowledge of the specifics but laughs deeply and tells Gora he should reframe the question to ask why they only had their arms broken. And then, to drive the nail home, we see Mor Cis and his cronies surrounding Baye Aly and threatening to publicize his diversion of public funds unless he backs their story about who is buried in the cemetery.

Thus it is equally clear that Thioune had succeeded in challenging some very powerful people in their systematic wrongdoing and that he almost certainly paid the consequences with his life. We see the most dangerous step he took in another flashback, when he addresses a crowd in a stadium and ferociously denounces the habit of accepting food aid from other countries. There is a huge pile of food containers labeled "Food Aid" in the stadium, and this is obviously an official event for the political elite to express publicly Senegal's gratitude to France for its generosity. Thioune inveighs, to strong applause from many parts of the crowd, against what he terms "begging": "drought, famine, diseases, are nothing for us to be ashamed of . . . we are at risk of uttering but a single word from generation to generation: thankyou; thankyou; thankyou."

We see during his speech the principals of the event, Deputy Amadou Fall and Yawar, Mor Cis's closest associate, conferring, with the deputy urging, "Shut him up," and Yawar assuring the deputy, "It's the last time he speaks in public." By this point we can safely be left to dot the *i*'s and cross the *t*'s in terms of why Thioune died and who was responsible, and why his murderers would have chosen to have him buried in a graveyard where there would be a powerful prohibition against the body's being disinterred and given an autopsy.

The film ends with Thioune's associates stopping their journey to take his body back to the Catholic cemetery, in order to intercept a truck laden with food aid. They clamber up on top of the truck, toss the bags of food onto the ground, rip them open, and scatter the contents. The truck had been heading for the Muslim town that they had just left; it was carrying sugar and powdered milk[31] ordered by Deputy Amadou Fall (the purpose of whose intervention will be clarified in a moment). Some of the older men are scandalized at the destruction of food, but Thioune's widow, Nogoy Marie, intervenes in the spirit of her late husband: "The sacrilege is not what the kids are doing—the sacrilege is what Guelwaar said it was!" And we are treated to a second flashback of Thioune in the stadium denouncing food aid and the corruption and false dependency it engenders. The film's final freeze is on the funeral cortege walking over the food scattered on the ground.

The core narrative engages, therefore, with this issue, challenging one of the numerous nostrums that people are content to accept, namely that food aid is somehow a pure and untainted component in the relationship between the Third World and the affluent nations. Weapons, no; tied aid, no; cultural imperialism, no; but food for survival, surely yes. No again, insists the film. There is no sacred ground—not even a Muslim cemetery!— exempt from the fundamentally corrupt relations that currently persist between the affluent nations and Africa.

In the process of telling this story, however, Sembene includes a series of other observations on the character of neocolonial society, especially on the roles of women, on the sources of religious conflict, and, not least, on the partial colonization of the mind by French hegemony. Let us examine each in turn.

The strongest woman in the film is Thioune's widow, Nogoy Marie. Earlier in the film we are privileged to look over her shoulder as, alone for a moment, she addresses her late husband's suit, laid out on their bed waiting for his disappeared corpse. She tells him, as she puts it, a few "home truths": the harsh conditions in which he has left her, with Barthélémy living in France, Aloys (his brother) seriously crippled with a leg injury, and Sophie (their daughter) working as a prostitute in Dakar. She recalls how over thirty years of marriage she had to put up with his bad temper and his totally stubborn refusal of compromise on issues. Implied is that if he had been prepared to bend a little, he might have avoided being murdered and leaving her widowed. We see him in a further flashback saying that he would much rather Sophie worked even as a prostitute than that she should beg for money. We are led to appreciate the shadow side of living with and supporting a convinced campaigner. Yet we also see how Nogoy Marie comes forward to pinpoint the key issue as her generational peers express horror at the destruction of food by the young activists.

Her daughter, Sophie, and Sophie's friend and fellow prostitute Hélène Sene, represent a different dimension. Their bearing is clearly marked out as tough and self-assertive. Sophie comes out to smoke a cigarette during the funeral reception and tells her accusing brother, Aloys, "It's the life I lead in Dakar that keeps you alive." Her friend Hélène comes out into the yard, picks up an unused chair from among a circle of men sitting down, without asking their permission or saying a word to them or even looking at them, carries it off, and sits down on it on her own. Her attire is not even notionally attuned to the funeral, but rather to the street corner or the bar where she works. She is wearing an outfit that merely drops flaps over her breasts, so that her movements or the movements of the breeze reveal them seductively. Most of the men at the funeral cannot take their eyes off her, one in particular standing still and staring obsessively at her body.

Yet it is in conversation with the priest, Abbé Léon, that her story emerges and reveals some of the bitter realities of neocolonial city life. They speak turned away or half away from each other, she in embarrassment, he in priestly decency. She tells him of her five brothers, cousins, and other family members that she supports, including one younger brother who attends medical school. She gets a medical checkup weekly and is terrified of contracting AIDS. After three months, and then six, in which it was impossible to find any professional work, she finally opted for sex work. But she points out that when the pope came to visit Dakar she was one of the first to turn out to his mass, and that Sophie's earnings had enabled her to pay for her father to make a pilgrimage to Jerusalem. It is by these means that Sembene establishes the integrity of both women and, simultaneously, the appalling pressures of the situation. And finally Hélène admits to the priest that she feels naked and ashamed in the gathering.

We see both women later, clad in the garments of the Catholic Women's Association, whose members have come to mourn Thioune; the two are seemingly at ease and accepted among them. It is a further signal that the desperate conditions of city life for many urban residents lead to behavior that is not approved of but is understood, albeit more easily by women than by men. Abbé Léon himself offers no criticism; he only urges Hélène to dress more decently, as befits the occasion.

Religion for Sembene has always been a target, whether Christianity (in *Ceddo*), Islam (*Ceddo* again, and in *Mandabi* a little), or traditional religion (in *Emitai*). Islam has received the most attention from him—predictably so in view of its overwhelming position in Senegal. Yet the target has typically been the institution, not the belief system itself. In *Guelwaar* the institution is actually accorded a measure of respect, insofar as both the priest and the imam—especially the imam—are treated in the narrative as individuals with integrity. Such was not the case in the portrayals of the power-hungry imam or the fatuous, ethically blind priest in *Ceddo*. Furthermore, Thioune himself was deeply religious and saw no conflict between his beliefs and his political activism, any more than did the Catholic Women's Association.

Indeed, to the priest's nonjudgmental approach to Hélène is added the depiction of the imam as a man of straightforward ethical principle, even in the face of the elite's angry opposition to him and their readiness to challenge his religious authority in the interest of protecting their conspiracy. He is the one who actually digs up Thioune's body and transfers it back to his Catholic mourners, and he is the one who endears himself to us by losing his aplomb in his fury at the manipulation of his town by its leaders and swearing to "motherfuck" anyone in the inflamed crowd who takes sectarian passions any further. He also slugs one of the elite's nasties with a club and lays him out, which, by the time he does it, seems a positively saintly action.

Yet there are two further interesting dimensions to the treatment of religion in the film. One, based on an actual incident of a mix-up in burial grounds that was the original spark for the film, is the eruption of a near riot between Muslims and Christians. The other is the syncretism of Catholicism and traditional religion espoused by Thioune's young activist followers and the suggestion of a deeper level of affinity and understanding possible beneath the overlay of non-African religious imports (Christianity and Islam).

The groundwork for the riot is initially laid by the deliberate burial of Thioune's body in a Muslim cemetery for purely political cover-up purposes. It is then fertilized by the town's elite telling the citizens that the Catholics are desecrating the cemetery, which instantaneously generates a large crowd of men armed with clubs, who race off to protect the graveyard and avenge the blasphemy. When the imam's courage succeeds in neutralizing the elite and defusing the tension, it is the deputy, Amadou Fall (whom we have seen in the flashback urging that Thioune be silenced) who proclaims that quelling the disturbance has been his own achievement and piously condemns religious conflict. As a reward, he announces the delivery of sugar and powdered milk, which is intended to further bolster his powerful position in the community. The crowd vigorously and naively applauds him, and we are perhaps reminded of the enthusiastic applause of the African troops, in *Camp de Thiaroye*, in response to the general giving his word that they will be paid in full.

In other words, the conflict arising out of religious divisions is fomented and manipulated in Sembene's view by the political elite. This conflict, in turn, he proposes, is capable of being overcome and indeed avoided altogether if Africans can only speak to each other with respect, bypassing the artificial barriers to communication set up by fundamentally foreign religious traditions.

We see this most clearly when Gor Meg, the Elder of Elders, whom we first meet requesting Abbé Léon for a requiem mass in Latin as Thioune had wished, is sitting on the ground talking with Birom, the imam, about the tense confrontation between Christians and Muslims. Gor Meg speaks of the unity of Catholic and Muslim male, both being circumcised on the same block of stone, of the problems they all face with embezzlement and theft of public funds, of the fact that the country is run by people who speak to each other by preference in French. He then describes the situation concerning Thioune and his burial, and they reach immediate consensus on what has to be done.

And at the close, when the Catholics receive Thioune's body back from the imam, Gor Meg thanks Birom: "You are a credit to humanity." Birom replies, warning him of how religious division can easily be fomented by the unscrupulous: "When the vulture eats the body of your enemy, it is eating you. Chase it!"

Thioune's militant young followers are clearly emphasizing the fusion of deeper and longer African traditions with Catholic beliefs. Etienne, their leader, at the head of his group, carries to the funeral a plain wooden cross with a thick copper-wire insignia attached to its front. The wire is cruciform, but in addition it has a large loop at a ninety-degree angle to the surface of the cross. This clearly does not represent Jesus' head, therefore, but holds some other significance.

In the religious symbolism of one of the most traditional groups of inner West Africa, the Bambara—and the overlaps between cultures in that region are not inconsiderable—the loop in the shape that we see it signifies certain very relevant themes for the film's overall message. A similarly shaped symbol literally means "stomach" (*kono*), and then by derivation "interior life," and then fire and lightning, and overall is a symbol that honors growers of food.[32]

This connection is plausible in the light of Thioune's overriding political message, but necessarily tentative. However, let me also comment on the significance of the use of copper.[33] Throughout the continent, copper was traditionally much more highly prized than gold, which was mostly a European obsession. Body adornment, sculpture, decorated weapons, instruments of aural art, were all made of copper—or sometimes brass, but more rarely of gold, outside of Egypt, Meroë, and Akan. Beyond any abstract beauty that they might have, their use was highly specific, tightly bound up with rituals signifying wealth, power, religious status, and age group, and they were also used as devices for protecting against danger, physical and spiritual. (As we will see in the discussion of *Yeelen*, the smiths who created this and other metals were figures of great spiritual power in society.) Thus the bent and shaped copper wire on Etienne's cross definitely signifies a commitment to traditional symbols and motifs.

What is interesting in the progression of the narrative is that initially the priest will not allow Etienne to bring this cross with its African motif into the house to express his formal condolences to Nogoy Marie. One of his group holds it as Etienne and his young woman friend go to do so. The camera dwells on the symbol fairly carefully at this point. But then in the final scene, where Etienne and his group are tearing open the food sacks, each young person in turn hands the cross to the person next to him and rushes forward to help, eventually leaving Abbé Léon holding the cross himself. It is a symbol of a certain transition in his political consciousness, even though the priest is one of the ones to call out to them to stop doing what they are doing to the sacks.

We see the same syncretic impulse in the name "Guelwaar," which Thioune has adopted. In the Fulani language, again not to be kept in quarantine among the region's languages, *gelowar* signifies someone of noble blood and correspondingly distinguished personal behavior, but without any accompanying aristocratic privileges.[34] Additionally, it carries with it the suggestion of supernatural powers—or what in a secular culture might be termed great force of personality, which is certainly something the charismatic public-speaking style of Thioune also evinced. Thus Sembene at a number of points does not so much criticize religious belief as try to suggest how it might be made more relevant to and effective in contemporary African conditions.

Indeed, to link this with the final theme, that of the colonized mentality as portrayed in part by Barthélémy, when the latter confronts the deputy and the town leaders, he takes pains to point out that the two most sacred shrines that both Christians and Muslims pay to make pilgrimages to are outside Africa—namely, Mecca and Jerusalem. (It is a point made in a different way, but with much more force still, in *Ceddo*.)

Barthélémy is also someone who changes and develops over the course of the film in interesting ways. When we first meet him, dressed in a suit and dark glasses, speaking only French and expressing disgust at every point with what he sees as the backwardness and foolishness surrounding him, it seems clear that he has sold his soul to France. When later he relieves himself against a *bani* tree, usually considered in West Africa as a communication site of the spiritual world, and when still more he insists to police captain Gora that he is French—European—and shows him his passport to prove it, it seems as though the case is closed. Indeed, even Baye Aly says of him, "What a pity—another copy!"

Gora begins therefore as his antagonist on a number of grounds. He is the servant of the state, who has to be aware that this is the educated son of a political rebel whose demise is clouded with intrigue. He is simultaneously deeply irritated with Barthélémy's attitude of national superiority and tells him if he does not like the way the case is being handled he is free to approach the French ambassador—"his" ambassador—knowing perfectly well, as does Barthélémy, that the ambassador would be totally disinterested in the plight of a Black French citizen. He also drops Barthélémy a long way distant from his mother's house when they get back to the city, telling him that citizens pay for the state's use of gasoline, so he must find a taxi for the remainder of the journey home.

As the action progresses, so Gora's points begin to work on Barthélémy in a positive direction. Not immediately—Sembene's interpretation of shifting consciousness and the operation of ideological hegemony gives no ground to Gramsci's in its subtlety and recognition of continuing psychological inconsistencies. Barthélémy, told by Gora that some idealistic young French people actually give up their summers to come help with agricultural projects in the countryside in Senegal, says cynically that he will be in tears soon. But then, almost instantly following that, Barthélémy is denouncing the way foreign aid money is diverted and ends up building and buying huge homes in France for the elite. He adds that young people throughout the continent are on the move for democracy. "Where do you stand?" Gora asks him, pressing home the point. "In exile?" Barthélémy does not respond.

But later, after Barthélémy has passionately attacked the religious leaders for allowing imported religious beliefs to divide Africans, Gora says to him, "Are you Senegalese now?" He replies, "I always have been." They smile at each other and shake hands firmly.

It seems that in this instance, rather as Sembene portrays the gradual but decisive change in the neocolonial mentality of El Hadj Abdou Kader Beye in *Xala*, but with less by way of satire, the character of Barthélémy is initially allowed to express his disgust with corruption in Senegal simply in terms of its being backward, not as advanced as France. In other words, his target and his motivation are sound—unlike El Hadj's—but his diagnosis is flawed, the product of French ideological hegemony at work. The seemingly detached, practical, professional, but deeply pro-African stance of Gora is one that works on Barthélémy to great effect.

It is a new experience to see Sembene give a state employee a role that displays such integrity—contrast the neocolonial regime's officials in *Mandabi* and *Xala*. Yet in *Guelwaar*, Sembene sharpens still further his critique of the neocolonial elite in those earlier films, which portrayed the elite as thieving, arrogant, and incompetent but did not suggest that they would resort to political assassination as a method of controlling dissidents. Both Gora and the Préfet are clearly privy yet unsympathetic to the real reasons for Thioune's altered burial site, and they seem equally unable to do more than grimly acknowledge to each other the full truth of the matter, a truth completely tied into the neocolonial relation of Senegal to France.

Precolonial Africa

With the exception of Sembene's depiction in *Ceddo* of the rituals and procedures of a Wolof royal court, and of Christian and Islamic missionaries as equally the scourges of precolonial Africa, the era before colonial consolidation has not been part of his work. Nor has it been part of the work of most other African filmmakers, Med Hondo's *Sarraounia* (1986) being one of the few exceptions. Gaston Kaboré's *Zan Boko* depicts a rather idyllic contemporary African village seemingly straight out of the past and shows how it is ground to pieces by the greedy ambitions of the urban rich (whom he rather indirectly defines as "the city"—in other words as operating by a particular lifestyle, rather than by their socioeconomic position). Other filmmakers have portrayed traditional village life, sometimes without real reference to the encroachment of the modern world, and not necessarily in the idyllic terms of *Zan Boko* (compare Idrissa Ouédraogo's *Yaaba* and his *Tilaï*), but never unambiguously before colonial contact.

Souleymane Cissé's *Yeelen* (Brightness/The Light) is in that respect a unique creative offering in the history of African cinema, at least up to the early 1990s. The film is distinguished in many other respects as well, perhaps especially by its treatment of patriarchy. Unlike the Freudian tradition, which sees small sons as raging to avenge the father's sexual possession of and displacement of their own relation with the mother, *Yeelen* concentrates on patriarchy as it blights the life of the younger generation, especially male in this narrative—since the lead is male—but female as well. In this sense, it addresses a dimension of patriarchy less often addressed in recent Western feminist writing, which has been prone to focus the term purely on the gender dimension of male supremacist institutions and processes.

The story is situated within the ancient and complex Bambara culture, focusing mostly on a father (Soma Diarra), the father's twin brother (Djigui Diarra, played by the same actor), a further brother (Bafing Diarra), and Nianankoro Diarra (son of Soma, in his early twenties). Soma's appearances in the film are always those of a man incandescent with rage against his son. His explosive fury never slackens. His twin brother, Djigui, by contrast, whom we encounter only toward the close of the narrative, is a serene and positive figure. He is, however, blind, having been robbed of his sight when younger by his own father, who in response to his request to share the secrets of the Komo had punished him by abruptly bringing out in front of his son's face the eye-searing Wing of the Korè (see below).

When we first meet Soma at the outset of the narrative, we have already seen four shots. The first and third are of a breathtaking equatorial sunrise that offers one level of meaning—that of the brightness of the film's title— the second the violent screech of a live white rooster set on fire in sacrifice, flaming out of the screen at us.[35] The juxtaposition of these two images sets the scene for what follows and initially defines the tension between positive and negative energies that dominates the film. A longer, fourth shot follows, of a little boy leading and then tethering a sacrificial white ram to a human-size statue. The image recurs later in the film and alludes directly to the myth of the very first white ram sacrificed at the beginning of creation in honor of the rainbow, perceived in Bambara belief as the summation of all knowledge.[36] The ritual site depicted is the later scene of a solemn benediction, by the Komo cult's ritual leaders, of Soma's all-devouring punitive crusade against his son.

It is an extraordinary outpouring of ferocity that then cascades from Soma's lips as he invokes Mari, god of the sands and rocks, god of the brush, god of the earth:

> Let me catch Nianankoro, wherever he is. If he is hiding in the distant bush, burn it! Dry the lakes, bare the trees, so I can search them. . . . Destroy towns and buildings, find Nianankoro for me that men and women may see him in my hands. Rip him from heaven and earth and give him to me. Break the sky, break the earth, be their master! Make the heavens tremble! Shake the earth!

He then hangs a long, narrow, cream-colored cloth on the long, heavy pestle upright in the ground, before which he has been sitting, and carefully and delicately—quite in opposition to the violence of his words—wraps the cloth around the pole. But this is no ordinary piece of wood: this is the *Kolonkallani*, which the film's opening credits have told us has been used for millennia[37] in Mali as a huge divining rod to find lost objects and to discover and punish robbers, thieves, criminals, traitors, and perjurers. With it borne by two serfs who continually stagger under its shifting direction, Soma sets off in search of his son, who is guilty in Soma's view of the same extreme hubris as Djigui once was in wanting to know the secrets of the Komo cult. The film's action spans the long pursuit by foot, covering five hundred miles from the center to the south of Mali, and traversing the territory of the partly nomadic Peul people (customarily known as Fulani in Anglophone Africa).

The film's suspense consists in whether the father's fearsome magical powers will, when combined with his politically inspired and religiously sanctioned rage, succeed in exterminating his son. The duel of wills between father and son is played out against the immense spaces of the Sahel savannahs south of the Sahara, against the exquisite soft golden light of the dawn hours—Cissé shot much of the film from five in the morning each day—and is framed within the age-old rituals of the Bambara people.

For those of us who have learned our signals of suspense from hurtling cars, flying swordsmen, and creepy lower-register clarinet on the sound track, the pace of *Yeelen* may seem to deny all sense of tension. As modern social beings, we feel that we no longer believe in magic, we are accustomed to the agitated speed of the shots and cuts in TV advertising or shows like *NYPD Blue*, and suspense for us is ingrained as rapidity— though the brilliant movement photography of Nianankoro's capture by the Peuls shows clearly what Cissé could have produced in that vein had he so chosen. We need, therefore, for this film to think ourselves back into the epochal drama of this eternal battle for power between generations and to adopt the cultural vision of the protagonists, if we are to pick up on the charged intensity of the narrative, its own slow, concentrated burn into flame.

After its doom-laden opening, the film proceeds by way of the following basic episodes: (1) Nianankoro's warning from his mother to flee and her preparation for his defense against his father's magic; (2) Soma's brief but significant stop at the blacksmith's forge; (3) Nianankoro's subjection to a prognosticatory address by a hyena figure sitting in a *bani* tree;[38] (4) Nianankoro's series of adventures as he travels through Peul/Fulani country—a major and constitutive section of the film, with its own subsections and insertions;[39] (5) the gathering of the Komo rite elders, in flashback, to bless Soma's crusade against his son; (6) the ritual washing in the sacred Bango spring by Nianankoro and his new Peul bride, Attu, and their meeting with Djigui; (7) the final apocalyptic confrontation between Nianankoro and Soma; (8) the new dawn for Nianankoro's young son, miraculously transported to the Saharan north and invested with symbols of hope for the future.

The shifts between these segments and sub-segments are often virtually as abrupt as jump cuts, frequently, it seems, with the intention of indicating simultaneity of the actions depicted. At the same time, the long takes and abundance of medium and long shots draw us—once we can shake our minds free of the tropes of contemporary Hollywood—into the basic rhythms of interconnected life, namely life and the land, collective life with allies and enemies, life and the spirit world, life and light. Both space and time are redefined for an urban audience, but the film's ultimate symbolic connecting thread is indeed light, which in Bambara belief enables the existence of the two worlds of earth and heaven.[40]

Before I comment further upon the narrative, let us briefly note some key aspects of traditional Bambara culture that are important for understanding the film. We have already made reference to the Komo cult or rites. The film's opening credits tell us that the Komo is information about divine knowledge and that its teaching is based on signs that embrace every aspect of life and knowledge, both natural and supernatural. This formulation may give an initial impression that the Komo is a thing; in actuality it is a social group into which males are initiated, beginning with a formal postcircumcision retreat. Its seventh[41] and supreme initiation group is the Korè, whose symbol is Mawla Duga, the vulture, bird of the great spaces of hunting, of war, of knowledge, and of death, whose scepter is a carved plank known as Korè Kaman, or Wing of the Korè.

Bambara cosmogony is extremely elaborate, embracing no less than 266 signs, divided into a variety of numerically ordered categories.[42] These signs are held to encapsulate all knowledge. At the same time, this knowledge is both sacred and secret, and the rituals and beliefs of Korè are the most jealously guarded of all. Anyone divulging them is regarded as the most heinous of criminals. This social organization of knowledge by way of a masculine secret society based on age effectively props up a male gerontocracy, and this aspect of Bambara history is indeed what the film rather accurately portrays. Even though the Bambara in general were among the most resistant peoples to Muslim or Christian missionaries, part of Islam's attractiveness for some younger Bambara men was precisely that it held no brief for this gerontocratic secret society—in which respect Tukulor colonial policy also anticipated French colonial policy and postindependence government policy.[43]

In this context, Soma's grinding fury against his son becomes comprehensible. At the same time, it is not acceptable, because even within that framework, Soma and his fellow initiates have completely overstepped all limits. As Nianankoro faces off against his father in the film's penultimate scene, a voice-over pronounces: "Soma, your ancestors were priests of the Komo, but for centuries they've misused their powers. . . . Your lust for revenge, your contempt and hatred of people have gone too far . . . you are one of those who use their power only for evil and injustice." Indeed, his uncle Djigui's blindness is terrible testimony to the totalitarian impulse of the Komo initiates.

The other elements within the culture that need preliminary comment are the vulture, the hyena, and the blacksmith. The figures of the vulture and the hyena are so commonly thought repulsive that their prime place within Bambara culture comes as something of a surprise. Yet they have been defined in that culture as emblematic of positive forces much more than of negative ones. It was to them as representatives of day and night that Faro, instructor of the universe and master of water, entrusted the knowledge he had been given of the full meaning of all the 266 signs.[44]

What the vulture does not eat by day, the hyena completely finishes off by night: "the 'old beast' is [lives] in the night; the night is darkness; what is the darkness but the secret, the mystery of the original nothingness and the mystery of the final nothingness?"[45]

The hyena enjoys, among other qualities such as innocence—like the vulture, he does not kill but only eats carrion—and guardianship of the soil, infallible foresight. The vulture is possessor of "white knowledge," the daytime's knowledge, and is master of the priesthood and of death.

The blacksmith has been widely defined throughout West Africa as someone with special mystical powers, and indeed blacksmiths have often been socially organized there as a hereditary caste. The mysterious nature of the work they do, discovering mineral ore in the ground and then transforming it into metal, especially copper, was seen as powerful and magical.[46] The Komo, in one version, was founded by seventeen blacksmiths.[47] Furthermore, the blacksmith has the capacity to be ubiquitous if he needs to be, and even to transform himself into a hyena,[48] whose nocturnal presence and powers are seen as analogous to the smith's.

The adjoining scenes of Soma with the blacksmith and Nianankoro with the hyena figure[49] in the *bani* tree are illuminated by knowing the significance of both figures. Soma, who wears a head covering of hyena skin for much of the narrative, with hyena paws hanging down on either side of his face, is greeted by the chief blacksmith with the words: "A hyena in daylight! Ill omen!" He listens without comment to Soma's tirade against his son for having fled the land with ancestral fetishes of the Komo. After Soma is seen leaving the village, the camera closes the scene with a second-long focus on the blacksmith's craft, with red-hot metal being hammered into shape.

The scene that straightaway follows has Nianankoro addressed by a speaking hyena in a tree in broad daylight—and we can tell from Nianankoro's face that initially he too finds this a very frightening omen—who tells him his road will be good, his destination happy, his life radiant, his death luminous.

I would suggest that two communications are being fused in this scene. One seems to be the infallible foresight of the hyena, assuring Nianankoro and the viewers that whatever we see playing itself out—though we realize now that it will involve Nianankoro's death at some juncture—will be for the best, and not the worst that seems to be menacing him. The other message may be that this hyena figure is a positive force, as contrasted with the destructive force of Soma, whose wearing of the hyena-skin head covering is radically at odds with the hyena's mythical role as a constructive element in the creation. It is even possible to surmise that the hyena figure may be the blacksmith we have just seen, who has been magically relocated and reincarnated to reestablish the principles of good and of harmony, in order to establish the ultimate driving forces in the ensuing chapters of the saga.

In this connection, Imperato notes that a key member of the Bambara pantheon, Ndomadyiri the divine blacksmith, the main stabilizing force in society, was often seen as "symbolized in trees, fixed and powerful living beings. . . . Some see him as a tree and thus as a master of herbs and remedies and a healer, a characteristic of all blacksmiths."[50]

The role of magical powers in this saga is obviously a central one. At the same time, it seems to be a role that more obviously incorporates magic into the texture of daily life than is customary in Latin American magical realism, in which magic tends to arrive abruptly and unexpectedly, in a manner that sharply skews off the otherwise predictable course of the narrative. In African epics, it is rather common for the heroes to have supernatural powers.[51]

In *Yeelen*, the drama is centered on the escalation toward the cataclysmic confrontation of rival magical powers. All the Diarra have such powers: Djigui knows, bereft of sight, that Attu is bearing Nianankoro's son; Uncle Bafing and Nianankoro himself are completely immune to harm from attack by the Peul, whose bodies freeze as they try to attack them; Nianankoro is able both to disperse the enemies of the Peul village with a miraculous swarm of bees and a brushfire and to make the Peul king's youngest wife fecund; the *Kolonkallani* unerringly guides Bafing and Soma along Nianankoro's path; the hyena speaks from the *bani* tree; Nianankoro's mother's self-purification in millet milk[52] and her gift of a fetish to her son help to protect him against execution by the Peuls on suspicion of rustling. We are in a world where the secular tradition has no toehold.

Indeed, in one scene, as Soma's two serfs hide terrified behind a tree, he summons up first a dog and then an albino, both walking backward toward us and him, and swears to sacrifice both in order to discover Nianankoro. Both are potent images in context. The dog in Bambara culture was traditionally the prime symbol of humans' domestication of the nonhuman world (being the animal most frequently brought into a personal relation with humans), as well as of land, fertility, fidelity, and sexual activity.[53] The figure of the albino has a variety of possible senses, from rarity and oddity to quasi pariah status.[54] Together, their summoning-up reinforces our sense of Soma's extraordinary powers and total ruthlessness.

Let us turn now to examine the role of women in *Yeelen*, certainly a minor one compared to the roles of the four male leads and less explored than we might wish but nonetheless very significant in the narrative.

In sharp contrast to Soma's opening tirades, we are sent in one of Cissé's abrupt transitions[55] to the tranquil hut of Nianankoro's mother. Her face is a fascinating study in itself, the vicissitudes of her life etched on her cheeks and forehead. Traditionally, the relationship between mother and son has been extremely close in Bambara culture, and here we see her striving to warn and protect him against the fearsome danger to his survival posed by his father, yet at the same time chiding him for asking totally disrespectful and unfilial questions about why he was conceived. He is shamed into a double apology.

She gives him then a protective fetish to wear around his neck at all times, and the "eye" of the Wing of the Korè to take to Djigui. When reattached to the Wing, it may give him a magical force equivalent to that of Soma. They bid farewell to each other on the path out of the village, looking long at each other, knowing that this is likely to be their very last meeting, given her great age and the great peril in which he finds himself.

We see his mother once more only, praying for her son's safety, in the process of giving herself a ritual lustration in millet milk against a wondrously delicately hued rose dawn sky, standing and then sinking to her knees in a shallow rush-filled lake. She gradually lifts the bowl of milk high above her head and pours it in a careful, steady flow over her head, the camera quietly watching the moisture dripping off her naked upper body. To the goddess of the waters, water being a Bambara symbol of motherhood, she bares her breasts and utters her prayer: "Do you hear me, mother of mothers? Hear this helpless mother. Save my son! Keep him from harm! Save this land from harm! Don't let weeds overgrow the house of the Diarra." We observe the rushes all around her, choking the lake, and wonder whether her prayer has any chance of being answered, especially when the scene jumps to her captive son, licking his parched lips as his Peul captors share milk among themselves but offer him none.

The other woman in the narrative is Attu, youngest wife of the Peul king. Nianankoro is assigned to use his magical powers to restore her fecundity and enable her to give the king a son. In the event he both restores her fecundity and has consensual sexual relations with her. She is given by the king to Nianankoro and banished, not executed, though for a moment their very physical lives appear to hang in the balance. The child of their union will be not only their son but also the survivor-inheritor of Nianankoro after his confrontation with Soma.

Attu, like Nianankoro's mother, is in many ways a tragic figure, yet one of enormous resilience. Banishment from the clan was a social and economic death, something that came upon her with bewildering speed. Yet it is not long before she is again ripped apart from Nianankoro. Her role is to perpetuate his line, to give him victory in the future even though he, along with his father, is consumed in the inferno of magical force that they unleash on each other. That role is especially emphasized by the camera's tracking slowly, respectfully, over her frame as she bathes in the sacred spring; it is also stressed when she and Nianankoro sit with Djigui while he announces to them that she is pregnant with Nianankoro's son. Djigui also says that as a result he can now die in peace, that a constructive future is assured despite the threats and tumults he can also see ahead.

In both instances, the women appear to be playing the type of subordinate roles that have been a standard target of feminist media critique, protecting and servicing males so that the latter can continue to dominate the world. A version of this response is offered by Ratiba Hadj-Moussa and Denise Pérusse: "The premature disappearance of the first woman, [her] peaceful and powerless impact—she cannot save her son indefinitely from his father's vengeance—is replaced by the real powerlessness of Nianankoro's wife. The latter only follows the orders of her two successive husbands."[56] I do not dismiss this accusation (though as I argued above, the mother's prayers are implied to be effective in saving her son from execution by the Peuls), but I would suggest that it may helpfully be reframed in a wider context.

Perhaps the main issue to be borne in mind is the question of concern for the survival and continuity of life, which predominates in both traditional and contemporary African cultural expression, as contrasted with a more habitual exploration of psychological dilemmas in contemporary U.S. and European cultures. Djigui says of his clan, for example, that the Diarras have been "the placenta and the umbilical cord of the Bambara people," an image that, far from demeaning women, rather places their procreative role as central to history.[57]

In *Yeelen*, this gives the two women much more weight than a superficial reading of their roles might suggest. "The importance of consensus to the organization of African society," writes Kofi Agovi, "cannot be overemphasized. It is the key to its integrity and . . . its sense of stability, cohesion and continuity."[58]

It is the male elders, the seat of power and supposed wisdom, who generate the conflict and tragedy in the narrative. To be foregrounded is not necessarily identical with being enthroned, nor is to occupy a secondary role in a given narrative the same as being trashed. The demand sometimes voiced that every film should have at least one strong woman in it is a little too close to Socialist Realist filmmaking to be credible. The portrayal of the women as agents of stability must be read against the portrayal of the men, especially of Soma, but also of the Komo initiates who chug their shots of millet beer and burp their way into a holy high of vengeance and male solidarity with a father hell-bent on obliterating his own progeny. The blind seer Djigui and the somewhat merciful Peul king are the only male characters aside from Nianankoro with positive features. The fierce warriors who are bent on exterminating the Peul are reduced to abject ludicrous terror by the bees and the brushfire, hunched and doubled up on their faces on the ground. And Nianankoro, admittedly offering himself up to the Peul king for execution for his adultery with the king's wife, can only say in miserable self-defense, "My penis betrayed me"!

In particular, the two warlike male-on-male confrontations in the narrative, the first foreshadowing the second, present a discourse of gender that does not favor men. The first is the head-butting contest between the Peuls' chief warrior and the attacking tribe's counterpart. The Peul is pushed back beyond his line, which concedes the Peuls' total military vulnerability to the opposing side. As the other Peul warriors scatter in panic, he falls on his sword. There is no more "value" to the event than there is of two rams locking horns and battling it out with each other. This contest of physical power heralds the final contest of supernatural power between Soma and Nianankoro, in which indeed the film compares them explicitly to two charging buffaloes, and in which Soma's face is then dissolved first into an elephant's, then into a lion's.

In this connection, it is impossible not to pay attention to the *Kolonkallani* that figures continually in the narrative. Soma and Bafing track down Nianankoro with the aid of this huge phallic pestle,[59] which has such power that the two Peul warriors who try to grasp it in order to teach Bafing respect for their king are thrown bodily backward onto the ground and paralyzed until Bafing releases the spell. At the final confrontation between Soma and Nianankoro, it flies out of the hands of the two serfs and positions itself upright in the ground, to be overwhelmed only by the superior force of the Wing of the Korè, although both father and son are vaporized in the magical firestorm—with nuclear blast sound track—that ensues.[60] But the film's association of the phallus with unjustified vengeance and the arrogance of power is hard to escape. In this regard, at least, Freud was a cross-culturalist.[61]

Cissé's film has many other absorbing aspects that are not explored in this essay. He has indicated some of his objectives in the film.[62] Positively, he hopes to make younger African generations aware of aspects of Bambara culture and to communicate the commonalities of African experience, despite Africa's linguistic and cultural diversity. Negatively, he wants to make an "anti-ethnographic" film, namely one that does not offer a "voice of god" dissecting commentary from a European perspective, but one that is set inside Africa and inside an African narrative and does not stop to explain to a non-African audience the significance of the actions portrayed. Cissé expressed himself quite forthrightly on this latter issue, underlining that over many decades Africans "have made [an effort] in order to understand [Euro-American] cultures which they have sometimes forced on us." He continued that equally, "we have great riches, it is for [Euro-Americans] to show themselves keen to get to know them."[63]

There has also been commentary on the film's implied criticism of the contemporary African era's gerontocratic political leadership (such as Félix Houphouet-Boigny or Hastings Banda, at the time the film was made). Segun Oyekunle has noted in this context the significance of the choice of one ostrich egg over the other by Nianankoro's son in the final scene, along with his endowment with the Korè Wing and his father's garment.[64] It is common in African folklore to see the procreation of children as bringing forth both good and bad into the world, and the two eggs represent that perception, one being good and the other not, implicitly the transmuted future beings of the obliterated Nianankoro and Soma. The little boy, representing both the youngest generation and the future, freely chooses the good, and in so doing harks back to the little boy bringing the archetypal white ram to sacrifice at the beginning and in the middle of the film.[65] Hope remains for a return in the future to leadership based on shared knowledge, rather than domination by a secretive elite.

Africa is not the only continent living in such hope.

CONCLUSIONS

I hope in this essay to have given some sense of the riches available in African and Arab postcolonial cinemas, with a special focus on their treatment of colonial, neocolonial, and precolonial realities. I have selected four films for particular comment that are exceptional by any standard, that may need special cultural interpretation but are not in need of some special concessionary genre of Africanity or Arabism, or mark of the exotic, in order to be acknowledged as potent political cinema.[66]

I cannot end without observing once more the wretched disparity between the production and distribution resources available for feature films in Hollywood in particular, but also in other affluent nations, as opposed to Africa. For the pioneer of African cinema, Ousmane Sembene, twelve years elapsed between *Ceddo* and *Camp de Thiaroye*, and he has been able to be more prolific than almost anyone else. To be sure, there is a great volume of films made in Africa, but overwhelmingly they are government-sponsored documentaries and educational films.[67]

Cissé's problems in making *Yeelen* are emblematic in this regard.[68] It took three and a half years from its inception to its Cannes screening. Along the way it was plagued by the sudden death of the original principal actor (Uncle Bafing); by the need to fly the director of photography to Paris to treat a boil that was turning gangrenous; by the useless "gift" of 10,000 meters of film stock by Fuji that turned out to be old, with faded color and weak resolution; by weeks of sandstorms that halted initial shooting; by the difficulty of finding a Peul woman to act Attu, since Peuls mostly think of actresses as akin to prostitutes; and by the complete exhaustion of shooting funds halfway through the process. The stresses and strains of the mainstream filmmaking and distribution process in affluent countries indeed pale by comparison.

*I would like to thank office-staff members of the Department of Radio-Television-Film, Susan Dirks, Paul Johnson, Lillian Respress, and Cathy Simmons, for their splendid professional work, which enabled me to find time and concentration to write this essay during the exceptionally intense spring semester of 1994.

NOTES

1. By "Africa" in this essay, I refer to all the nations once colonized by France—in other words, I am not subscribing to the bifurcation of the continent into Africa and "North" Africa.

2. In the USA, the primary outlets have been New Yorker Films, 16 West Sixty-first Street, New York, NY 10023 (212-247-6110); and California Newsreel, 149 Ninth Street, #420, San Francisco CA 94103 (415-621-6196). Both have rendered tremendous service in enabling African cinemas to be widely known.

3. I cannot help but observe how little encouragement in this direction has been offered by the central redoubt of French cinema criticism, namely *Cahiers du Cinéma*. From 1981 to March 1994, aside from brief notices, significant attention to films from former African colonies was restricted to issues 402, 423, 431, 433, 435, and 465 (twenty-one pages in all). Of these, sixteen focused on a single (admittedly very gifted) director, Idrissa Ouédraogo, and three of his films: *Yaaba*, *Tilaï*, and *Samba Traoré*. Two pages were devoted to *Halfaouine* by Tunisian director and author Ferid Boughedir, and three to Souleymane Cissé's *Yeelen*. This is

despite the journal's very wide-ranging, non-insular coverage of cinema in India, Latin America, Taiwan, the Philippines, Japan, Hong Kong . . . even Egypt! It is hard to avoid the surmise of a certain postcolonial myopia on the editorial board of this worthy publication.

4. Cf. Nwachukwu Frank Ukadike, *Black African Cinema* (Berkeley: University of California Press, 1994), 9–13.

5. In the index of Françoise Pfaff, *Twenty-Five Black African Filmmakers* (Westport, Conn.: Greenwood Press, 1988), 329–330.

6. Rachid Boujedra, *Naissance du cinéma algérien* (Paris: Maspéro, 1971), 54–55.

7. Ibid., 68–84; Mouny Berrah, Victor Bachy, Mohand Ben Salama, and Ferid Boughedir, "Cinéma du Maghreb," *CinémAction* 14 (1981): 45–65; Iotfi Maherzi, *Le Cinéma algérien: Institutions — imaginaire — idéologie* (Algiers: Société d'Editions et de Diffusion, n.d.), 244–285.

8. John D. H. Downing, ed., *Film and Politics in the Third World* (New York: Praeger and Autonomedia, 1987), Chapter 8.

9. Gérard Grisbec, "Sale guerre en Algérie," *Le Monde diplomatique* 472 (August 1993): 1, 6–7; Lyes Si Zoubir, "Voyage au bout des peurs algériennes," *Le Monde diplomatique* 482 (May 1994): 1, 4.

10. Jean-Pierre Garcia, "Trente ans de cinéma algérien," *Le Film africain* 14 (1994): 20–22; Miriam Rosen, "Un Cinéma déraciné: Les Cinéastes arabes en exil," in *Les Cinémas arabes*, ed. Mouny Berrah, Jacques Lévy, and Claude-Michel Cluny, *CinémAction* 43 (1987): 106–113; Carrie Tarr, "Questions of Identity in Beur Cinema," *Screen* 34, no. 4 (1993): 321–342; Yves Thoraval, "Les cinéastes arabes scrutent leur société," *Le Monde diplomatique* 464 (November 1992): 15.

11. Julio García Espinosa, "For an Imperfect Cinema," in *Communication and Class Struggle*, ed. Armand Mattelart and Seth Siegelaub (New York: International General, 1983), 2:295–300.

12. Cf. Moumen Smihi,"Moroccan Society as Mythology," in Downing, *Film and Politics in the Third World*, 77–87, and Souhail Ben Barka, "A Cinema Founded on the Image," in ibid., 89–92.

13. Roy Armes, *Third World Filmmaking and the West* (Berkeley: University of California Press, 1987), Chapter 3; Férid Boughedir, *Le Cinéma Africain de A à Z* (Brussels: Editions OCIC, 1987); Manthia Diawara, *African Cinema: Politics and Culture* (Bloomington: Indiana University Press, 1992); Lizbeth Malkmus and Roy Armes, *Arab and African Filmmaking* (London: Zed Books, 1991), Chapter 2; Paulin Soumanou Vieyra, *Le Cinéma africain des origines à 1973* (Paris: L'Harmattan, 1975); Paulin Soumanou Vieyra, *Le Cinéma au Sénégal* (Paris: Editions OCIC/ L'Harmattan, 1983).

14. Boughedir, *Le Cinéma africain*, 26–32.

15. Ibid.; Diawara, *African Cinema.*

16. As of summer 1994, African filmmakers were noting that French coproduction money seemed to be abruptly swinging toward Eastern Europe (personal communication from my colleague Professor Lindy Laub).

17. Wolfgang F. Freund, ed., *L'Information au Maghreb* (Tunis: Cérès Production and Fondation Friedrich Naumann, 1992).

18. Cf. Sheila Petty, "La Représentation des femmes dans le cinéma africain," in *Films D'Afrique*, ed. Michel Larouche (Montreal: Guernica Larouche, 1991),

127–141.

19. Cf. Sheila Petty, "Le Geste plus important que la parole," in Larouche, *Films D'Afrique*, 18.

20. Some audience members have been extraordinarily confused and irritated by the fact that the credits appear only between the French army's initial foray into the village and its second appearance. Such is the religion of cinema.

21. See Jonathan A. Peters, "Aesthetics and Dialectics in African Film: Ousmane Sembene's *Emitai*," in *African Literature in Its Social and Political Dimensions*, ed. Eileen Julien, Mildred Mortimer, and Curtis Schade (Washington, D.C.: African Literature Association and Three Continents Press, 1986), 69–75; Petty, "Le Geste," 13.

22. Françoise Pfaff, *The Cinema of Ousmane Sembene: A Pioneer of African Film* (New York: Greenwood Press, 1984), Chapter 7; Downing, *Film and Politics in the Third World*, Chapters 2–3.

23. Peters, "Aesthetics and Dialectics," 71.

24. Olga F. Linares, *Power, Prayer, and Production: The Jola of Casamance, Senegal* (New York: Cambridge University Press, 1992), 15–51.

25. It is tempting to surmise that the strong roles assigned to women in practically all Sembene's films, and his frequent critiques of religious belief, may stem in part from this culture in which the supreme deity is so remote and women so strong.

26. I think Peters ("Aesthetics and Dialectics," 73) rhetorically overstates, however, when he describes the men's processions in the film as "death-defying and disastrous" in contradistinction to the women's processions, which he characterizes as "life-affirming . . . or culture-affirming." There is nothing death-defying about them.

27. The film plays a little fast and loose with dates at this point, but without significance for the narrative.

28. Indeed, at the outset of the film he could almost be the African soldier saluting the tricolor whom Roland Barthes made so famous in his essay "Myth Today."

29. Peters, "Aesthetics and Dialectics," 71.

30. Incomparably the favorite popular song among German troops and the German public in the latter days of World War II, its sentimental melody and words completely belied and displaced the stupendous horrors of the Nazi extermination camps, and of the imminent military defeat of the Nazi war machine by the Soviets and the Allies. In *Camp de Thiaroye*, the mouth organ rendition is as piercing and grating on the ear as are the wordless noises made by Pays.

31. Sembene does not expatiate on this point, but it should be recalled that an international campaign of more than a decade was needed to stop the U.S.–Swiss food transnational corporation, Nestlé, from selling huge quantities of powdered milk in Third World nations. The point was that it had to be mixed with either pure or thoroughly boiled water to be safe for babies. Such conditions were often unavailable to the poor, and the result was that legions of babies died who might have survived had they depended on their mothers' milk. Nestlé's advertising projected powdered milk as the "modern" way for mothers to feed their babies.

32. G. Dieterlen and Y. Cissé, *Les Fondements de la société d'initiation du Komo* (Paris: Mouton, 1972), 110.

33. Eugenia W. Herbert, *Red Gold of Africa: Copper in Precolonial History and*

Culture (Madison: University of Wisconsin Press, 1984). I am grateful to Professor Sandra Lauderdale Graham of the Department of History at the University of Texas for bringing this reference to my attention.

34. Marguerite Dupire, *Organisation Sociale des Peuls: Etude d'ethnographie comparée* (Paris: Librairie Plon, 1970), 373–374.

35. "A white cock was the master of the seventh heaven. . . . Because of the special place of the white cock in Bambara cosmology, the sacrifice of this animal was considered among the most powerful that could be made" (Pascal James Imperato, *Buffoons, Queens, and Wooden Horsemen: The Dyo and Gouan societies of the Bambara of Mali* [New York: Kilima House Publishers, 1983], 38).

36. Dieterlen and Cissé, *Les Fondements de la société d'initiation du Komo*, 37 n. 2.

37. The film's English subtitles wrongly translate "millennia" as "centuries." The film's U.S. subtitling presents a number of uncertainties and infelicities, such as Nianankoro's mother's description of Soma as "Your father is a terror," rather than "Your father is terrifying."

38. Also known as the silk-cotton tree (*ceiba pentandra*), the *bani* grows sometimes to 160 feet, with a trunk diameter of more than 6 feet. It is seen in Bambara lore as a kind of ladder, on which ancestor spirits descend to earth, sacrifices ascend to them, and the soul ascends to heaven at death (Imperato, *Buffoons, Queens, and Wooden Horsemen*, 28, 38).

39. This section subdivides into (a) Nianankoro's encounters and is captured by the Peul; (b) his mother prays for him in the shallow lake; (c) Nianankoro amazes the Peul king with his defiance and magical powers; (d) the Peuls are suddenly challenged to military contest by a neighboring tribe and lose; (e) the Peul king calls upon Nianankoro to use his magical powers to defeat the attackers, which he does by calling down a swarm of bees and creating a brushfire that together rout them; (f) the Peul king honors Nianankoro and asks him to cure his youngest wife's infecundity; (g) Soma is seen at nighttime and then at early dawn, silent except for reiterated threats and curses and magical spells directed against his son; (h) Nianankoro cures Attu, but they join their bodies in love and are both banished from the Peul kingdom; (i) Uncle Bafing arrives in pursuit of Nianankoro at the Peul king's, with the *Kolonkallani*, and overwhelms the Peuls with his supernatural powers.

40. Translated as "sky" from the French *ciel* in the English subtitles to the opening explanatory credits to the film.

41. According to various anthropologists, such as Dominique Zahan, *Sociétés d'initiation Bambara* (Paris: Mouton, 1960), and Dieterlen and Cissé, *Les Fondements de la société d'initiation du Komo*, it is the sixth. According to Imperato (*Buffoons, Queens, and Wooden Horsemen*, 25), there were seven. This discrepancy need not concern us for our present purposes. It probably issues from regional variations in Bambara culture in the first place.

42. Dieterlen and Cissé, *Les Fondements de la société d'initiation du Komo*, 63–213.

43. Imperato, *Buffoons, Queens, and Wooden Horsemen*, 21–22.

44. Dieterlen and Cissé, *Les Fondements de la société d'initiation du Komo*, 26.

45. Cited from a Komo ritual in ibid., 265.

46. Herbert, *Red Gold of Africa*, Chapter 2.

47. Dieterlen and Cissé, *Les Fondements de la société d'initiation du Komo*, 15, 43, 195.

48. Ibid., 28.

49. In Malkmus and Armes (*Arab and African Film Making*, 183) this figure is referred to as a leopard-man, presumably because of the dark blotches on the arms and torso, but I would venture to disagree with this identification.

50. Imperato, *Buffoons, Queens, and Wooden Horsemen*, 30.

51. Isidore Okpewho, *The Epic in Africa: Toward a Poetics of the Oral Performance* (New York: Columbia University Press, 1979), Chapter 3.

52. In Bambara culture, this liquid represents the very purest libation with which to celebrate the divine spirit (Dieterlen and Cissé, *Les Fondements de la société d'initiation du Komo*, 279).

53. Dominique Zahan, *Sociétés d'initiation Bambara* (Paris: Mouton, 1960), 68–73.

54. Cf. Bernice N. Ezeilo, "Psychological Aspects of Albinism: An Exploratory Study with Nigerian (Igbo) Subjects," *Social Science and Medicine* 29, no. 9 (1989): 1129–1131.

55. Segun Oyekunle, "A Review of Souleymane Cissé's Film *Yeelen*," *Présence Africaine* 148 (1988): 183–184, has noted the influence of Russian "associative editing" on Cissé, who received his formal cinematic education in Moscow.

56. Ratiba Hadj-Moussa and Denise Pérusse, "L'Arbre de la connaissance," in Larouche, *Films D'Afrique*, 118–119.

57. In fact, although this film is set in time long beforehand, from 1760 to 1862 a famous Bambara royal dynasty was the Diarra clan, in Segou (Imperato, *Buffoons, Queens, and Wooden Horsemen*, 15).

58. Kofi Agovi, "Is There an African View of Tragedy in Contemporary African Theatre?" *Présence Africaine* 133–134 (1985): 68.

59. Those who know Sembene's film *Xala* will recall the trouble El Hadj gets into through refusing to sit astride a large mortar and pestle before his wedding night with his third bride.

60. Despite Nianankoro's youth and his virtue, the masculinism of the final confrontation between him and Soma was partly evocative to this commentator of the confrontation of the two male nuclear-armed gerontocrats of the 1980s, Brezhnev and Reagan.

61. Certainly, to dissect patriarchal power is not in and of itself to open the public realm to women's power. That is a different chapter in human history, which Cissé's narrative does not address.

62. Jean-François Senga, "Souleymane Cissé, cinéaste malien," *Présence africaine* 144 (1987): 132–138; Antoine de Baecque, "Cela s'Appelle L'aurore," *Cahiers du Cinéma* 402 (December 1987): 25–27.

63. Senga, "Souleymane Cissé," 136.

64. Oyekunle, "There's Power in 'The Light,'" 183.

65. I would like to thank Segun Oyekunle for expanding on his comments in *Présence africaine* to me.

66. While there is no space to debate the issue here, I am inclined to argue that the leaky notion of Third Cinema (Teshome Gabriel, *Third Cinema in the Third World: Aesthetics of Liberation* [Ann Arbor: UMI Research Press, 1982]; García Espinosa, "For an Imperfect Cinema"; Fernando Solanas and Octavio Getino, "Towards a Third Cinema," in *Communication and Class Struggle* 2: 220–230; Paul Willemen, "The Third Cinema Question: Notes and Reflections," in *Questions of*

Third Cinema, ed. Jim Pines and Paul Willemen [London: British Film Institute, 1989]: 1–29) would be better simply recast as "political cinema" and that the undoubted insights and arguments of its proponents would then find a less constricting frame in which to be expressed. The critique leveled by Felix Thompson, "Metaphors of Space: Polarization, Dualism, and Third World Cinema," *Screen* 34, no. 1 (Spring 1993): 44–46, for example, at Gabriel's claim that collective life is a typical focus of "Third Cinema," as opposed to the attention given to individual psychology in other cinemas, seems very much to the point.

67. Nancy J. Schmidt, "African Filmmakers and Their Films," *African Studies Review* 37, no. 1 (1994): 175–181.

68. Senga, "Souleymane Cissé"; De Baecque, "Cela s'Appelle L'aurore."

Race Matters and Matters of Race

ELEVEN   *Interracial Relationships in Colonial and Postcolonial Films*

Dina Sherzer

In this essay I explore the intersections of culture and society with colonialism and postcolonialism as represented in films from two moments of French history, the colonial era of the 1920s and 1930s and the postcolonial era, from 1976 to the present. With regard to this second period, I discuss films dealing with life in the colonies as well as films set in France involving postcolonial subjects (Beurs, Blacks). The representation of interracial relationships immediately brings to mind love affairs with an exotic Other with amber skin taking place in a tropical setting with a vague feeling of sin, transgression, and pleasure. But in fact there is more at stake in these representations than just a sensual or forbidden relationship. In films and in literature, interracial relationships frequently serve to foster and reinforce racial stereotypes in French and European society, and such representations now provide a point at which controversial matters of gender, history, ethnicity, and class are determined and debated. Underlying and shaping my reading of films are the following concepts and orientations: Films are instruments that society has at its disposal to stage and display itself, and they are discourses participating in the creation and expression of the ideology of a period. They also channel the impact of social and historical changes, and they interrogate certain aspects of the past and render certain aspects of the present because of the problems that besiege a society at a particular time.[1]

COLONIAL FILMS: THE 1920S AND 1930S

Zou Zou, by Marc Allegret (1934), *Princesse Tam Tam*, by Edmond Greville

(1935), and *Pépé le Moko*, by Julien Duvivier (1937) are films that make interracial relationships a central feature of their narrative. To assess the full significance of these relationships, it is pertinent to place them within the discursive configuration of which they were a part and consider a field of various positions and practices having to do with politics, gender, and racial issues in the colonies as well as artistic fads in France at the time.

Recent research on the culture of empire[2] has shown that the categories colonized/colonizer were secured through forms of sexual control that defined the domestic arrangements of Europeans. The Europeans' obsession with White prestige, their racial and sexual anxiety, their fear of racial degeneracy, and their phobia of *métissage* (race mixing) led to the regulation of sexual, conjugal, and domestic life in the colonies. Mixed marriages were considered a paramount danger and the result of a regrettable weakness, and as such they were deemed incestuous, incongruous, and even treasonous. For instance, about Isabelle Eberhardt, living in Algeria and married to an Arab officer of lower rank, the French said: "S'allier avec un Arabe est une déchéance ou la conséquence d'un vice" [To marry an Arab is a sign of degeneracy or the consequence of vice].[3] Interracial relationships were political issues in colonial life, because it had to be determined which children could be citizens, i.e., could share power with the Whites. Indeed, sexual policies were really about maintenance of power and domination, the inheritance of White property, and the threat to the homogeneity of the social group. But, though mixed marriages were discouraged, the sexual exploitation of the native woman was a common practice in colonial society, as native women were frequently used as concubines, servants, and playthings for Europeans.

Back home in the metropolis, literature, popular entertainment, and films during the colonial period expressed the same double standard. They presented negative images of interracial relationships while at the same time suggesting the attractiveness of exotic sexual encounters. In an article titled "Vampire in the Mirror," R. L. Stevenson demonstrates convincingly that *Dracula* by Bram Stoker (1894) was not so much about fear of incest or the Victorian fear of women's sexuality as it was about fear of excessive exogamy. Dracula is represented as being a foreigner, an Other, and a threat to the White man's sexuality. Precisely at the time of the British imperial expansion, Dracula concretized the cultural fear of race mixing.[4] In 1922 F. W. Murnau's *Nosferatu*, an adaptation of *Dracula*, was an immense success in France. With its gothic horror it conveyed in a politically unconscious fashion the fear of racial mixing, the fear of the Other, sexually potent and capable of seducing the White woman.[5] Pierre

Loti, in *Le Roman d'un spahi* (1925), expresses the fear of the non-White in very racist terms. Jean, the French officer who has had a relationship with a Black girl, worries about "sa dignité d'homme blanc souillée par le contact de cette chair noire" [his White man's dignity soiled by the contact with this Black flesh].[6]

And yet negrophilia was the mood of the Paris of the 1930s and had been for twenty years. The year 1925 saw the triumph of Josephine Baker in *La Revue nègre*. She became one of those African objects that suddenly seemed beautiful to the Paris avant-garde. In 1931, in conjunction with the Exposition Coloniale, Baker sang about interracial relationships at the Casino de Paris. Her most famous song, "J'ai deux amours" [I Have Two Loves], was not about an American girl in Paris, as the later myth constructed it; rather, it was part of an elaborate sketch called "Ounawa," set in the equatorial jungle with the leopard Chiquita and depicting an African girl in love with a French colonist. He asks her to go to Paris with him, but her tribe prevents her from doing so. "J'ai deux amours" was about France and its African colonies and forbidden interracial love.[7]

From 1927 to 1929 popular novels set in Asia offered a particularly negative and dysphoric representation of individuals of mixed blood of both sexes. They were systematically presented as evil, dangerous, and perverted; thus interracial unions were tacitly discouraged.[8] Yet Baker sang "La Petite Tonkinoise" [The Little Girl from Tonkin] at the Casino de Paris. In this song the Vietnamese mistress of the French colonist expresses her love for the Frenchman.[9] Malraux's 1930 novel *La Voie royale*,[10] set in Cambodia, portrays several male characters having sexual adventures. Grabot, the Frenchman from Marseilles, avatar of Kurtz of Conrad's *Heart of Darkness*, had emigrated with the primary purpose of enjoying native women. Claude, the main protagonist, remembers his exotic and erotic adventure in Aden, and Perken, wounded and near death, asks that several native women be brought to him in the same casual fashion that he would ask for newspapers and a drink, for these women were supposed to be there ready and available to satisfy his needs. Thus at the apex of imperial power the Frenchmen and other European male tourists who attended the colonial exhibition and went to the Casino de Paris and those who read Malraux's novel were given the message that the colonies were the ideal place to satisfy their sexual fantasies.

In addition to literature and songs, films also conveyed mixed messages. The interracial relationships, with some exotic details and folklore, were the ingredients that gave *L'Atlantide* (1921), *La Maison du Maltais* (1927), *Itto* (1934), and *La Bandera* (1935)—all set in North Africa—a wide popularity. These films discouraged interracial relationships, however, by portraying them doomed to failure because bad luck and fatality brought about death and separation. *Zou Zou*, *Princesse Tam Tam*, and *Pépé le Moko* proposed the same message but in other ways. The basic plot of these films involved rejection of the Other. The native woman was in love with a White man, but this love was not reciprocated, for the White man fell in love or was in love with a White woman. In addition to this narrative structure, these films insidiously but very systematically constructed a negative image of the Other, of the non-French woman, through behaviors and characteristics assigned to her, the comments of other characters about her, and the actions and reactions of the French man toward her.

Zou Zou, which takes place in France, is the story of two orphans—Zou Zou, a little girl from Martinique, and Jean, a French boy adopted and raised by Papa Mélé, a circus owner. From the very beginning the film accumulates a series of negative messages about Otherness. Papa Mélé, an otherwise nice and friendly man of charitable character and demeanor, utters particularly damning statements to the children. He tells them they were born from a Chinese mother and a Redskin father who refused to recognize their children because they did not have the same color as their parents, thus blaming colored people for their behavior. As a little girl Zou Zou is reacted to as different, as having something wrong with her. When French boys her age peep into her room they say, "elle a une drôle de tête" [she has a strange head]. When she and Jean inquire about their birth, Papa Mélé says that a stork brought them but let Zou Zou drop in the chimney by mistake. In the theater an employee whom Zou Zou bites to get away from him calls her a cannibal.

The ending, the marriage of Jean (Jean Gabin) and Claire (Germaine Aussey), is prepared for by a series of facts that imply that Zou Zou (Josephine Baker) is not appropriate as a wife for Jean. Jean is made into a character who is indifferent to difference and exoticism. Already as a sailor in an undetermined tropical setting he is shown not even paying attention to the bare-breasted native girl dancing in a frantic fashion next to him. He just nods without looking when the French woman sitting with him notices and comments, "Ils ont la danse dans le sang" [They have dancing in their blood]. Back in Toulon, when Zou Zou asks him about Manila he answers, "Oh tu sais, Manille c'est Manille" [Oh, you know, Manila is Manila]. Zou Zou is too different from Jean. A kind of savage and strange beauty emanates from Zou Zou when she dances with triangular movements and unbounded energy,[11] and at the peak of her success she is presented as a beautiful exotic bird in a cage with an ethereal beauty that is in sharp contrast to the banal and down-to-earth Jean. Furthermore, Jean's actions toward Zou Zou are those of a caring brother, while his behavior with Claire is that of a man physically attracted to her. When Claire and Jean dance together, the camera focuses on the perfect fit, the togetherness of their bodies. Indeed, spectators are given the message that Claire, the laundry girl, and Jean, the electrician, the two French individuals, typical characters of films of the period of the Popular Front, are made for each other. They are a "natural" match; their names, their bodies, and their looks fit.

In *Princesse Tam Tam* the issue of race and of the inferiority of the non-French individual is brought up immediately at the beginning of the film when the writer, fed up by the nagging of his wife, declares: "Allons chez les sauvages, les vrais sauvages" [Let's go to the savage land, among the true savages]. Then, seeking inspiration for a novel, he tells his *nègre*/collaborator/confidant, referring to the young Tunisian girl he has met, "Une histoire de race ça peut faire un roman très à la page. Je vais dire que je suis amoureux d'elle." [A racial story can make a very fashionable novel. I am going to say that I am in love with her.] The racial story that the film presents repeatedly constructs the Other in negative terms. Alvina (Josephine Baker) is always represented as unsophisticated, childish, and naive. Not only is she associated with animals (she carries a sheep and she climbs a tree to reach a monkey), she is also referred to in terms of animality, especially by the French women at the picnic: "Tu ne vas pas nous imposer la présence de cette sauvage, l'odeur des fauves me coupe l'appétit." [You are not going to impose the presence of this savage creature on us, the smell of wild animals ruins my appetite.] In Paris, where she is given the role of a Black princess "qui a accepté de se civiliser" [who has agreed to become civilized], the reactions to her presence are stridently racist. The author's wife reports to her girlfriend: "Il [her husband] est arrivé avec une princesse noire et moi qui avait presque honte d'être courtisée par le Maharajah." [He has arrived with a Black princess and I was almost ashamed to be courted by the Maharaja.] People comment that Princesse Tam Tam "mange avec les doigts, c'est une sauvage, une cannibale" [eats with her fingers, she is a savage, a cannibal]. Yet when she dances in the low-class bar the song says that under the sky of Africa is a bewitching country where everything is desire and pleasure, and when she jumps onstage and dances a rumba with the drums beating she becomes a wild attraction. But in these moments for the spectators she was no longer Alvina/Princesse Tam Tam, she was Josephine Baker, the exotic Black beauty loved by the French. Again, the scenario has Josephine Baker as Alvina fall in love with the White man, but she is cast aside for the White woman and marries Tahar the Tunisian servant. The writer's involvement with Alvina is only a scheme to get his wife back and involves no physical/sexual contact. Similarly, the writer's wife did not compromise herself sexually with the Maharaja. The two French protagonists remain French and remain pure. The film ends with one more negative note for Alvina. She is shown with her husband, Tahar, in the beautiful Moorish villa, which has been transformed into a den with animals everywhere, a scandal for French people who would have then and still today interpret this behavior as gross and the mark of a lack of culture. But the message of the film is clear. Alvina is better off in her own country with her own people, and the French writer is better off with his wife in Paris. It is significant that Baker objected to not being able to play a role in which she would marry the French man or even the Maharaja. Notice that the film is about both class and race. The wife has a normal, nonpatronizing relationship with the Maharaja, her class equal, while her husband is patronizing and mocking of the low-class Alvina. But in the end race wins out over class, and neither White French person is defiled by contact with the dark Other. Once again, race matters.

Similarly in *Pépé le Moko*, Pépé (played by Jean Gabin) abandons the Gypsy Inez (played by Line Noro) for Gaby the French girl (played by Mireille Balin). Again the French woman is represented as someone with whom the French man fits naturally and normally, to whom he is immediately attracted and with whom he feels comfortable. In a moment of playful verbal dueling as they exchange names of Parisian streets and squares, Gaby and Pépé realize that they come from the same Parisian neighborhood and the same background; they are made for each other. As critics have pointed out, they both share a love for pearls, which they acquire illicitly, one as a mistress and the other as a gangster. As the French proverb says: "Qui se ressemble s'assemble" [Birds of a feather flock together]. Gaby rejuvenates Pépé; when they dance together in perfect fit, he thinks of le 14 juillet, whereas the Arabic music gets on his nerves. He tells Inez that she is a *régime* for him, i.e., a diet that deprives one of the food one likes—an obligation, not a choice or a pleasure. Inez is just a commodity for Pépé. She is portrayed as a hindrance, a suffocating and entrapping female. She is also associated with negative connotations, being part of the treacherous, dangerous Kasbah described as such by the French inspector to his Parisian counterpart, and out of jealousy she has become a traitor to Pépé just like Slimane the Arab informer and local policeman with whom she collaborates. In the end fate and jealousy make things return to the "correct," natural order. Pépé is not united with Inez, and Gaby stays with her rich older French man. Although this latter relationship is unnatural, it is tolerated and was even expected by French society at the time.

The clear and obvious message of *Princesse Tam Tam*, *Zou Zou*, and *Pépé le Moko* is that the French woman fulfills the fantasy of White men. Note that the names of the White women, Claire and Gaby, connoted Frenchness for spectators and still do, and that the names of the other women, Inez, Zou Zou, Alvina, and Tam Tam, connoted something exotic, a mixture of baby talk, African, and Spanish. These films not only project a positive image of the French woman, they also connect the Other with features and characteristics that had negative connotations in French culture at that time. The dysphoric representations of the non-French women and the rough treatment that they suffered from the French men can also be read as a displacement of European/French misogyny onto the Other woman, treated as object, despised, manipulated, used, and then discarded.

Social, racial, and sexual constructions, which came to life through popular culture, in films, in shows, and in literature in France of the 1930s, reinforced the prohibition and discouragement of the interracial unions that existed in the colonies. They underscored the notion of White identity and of Frenchness and participated in the colonial discourse that privileged the White individual over the dark-skinned Other. The interracial relationships were tropes that contributed to the legitimization of the colonial ideology and the feeling of superiority of the French.

THE SECOND WAVE OF COLONIAL FILMS: THE 1970S TO THE 1990S

La Victoire en chantant (Black and White and in Color, 1976), *Rue casesnègres* (Sugar Cane Alley, 1983), *Fort Saganne* (1984), *Chocolat* (1988), *Le Vent de la Toussaint* (1989), *Outremer* (Overseas, 1991), *L'Amant* (The Lover, 1992), and *Indochine* (1992) are the imaginings and refigurings of colonial life that appeared in a France traversed by various successive tendencies including deconstruction, feminism, postcolonialism, reflections on identity, resurgence of racism, and return to and nostalgia for the colonial past. Interracial relationships recur constantly in these films and raise the following questions: What do directors represent after decolonization? How are these representations inserted into and how do they participate in the discourse of their time?

As part of the re-presentation of colonial life, several of these films show colonial sexual exploitation with native women used as sexual objects. In *La Victoire en chantant*, Sargent Bosselet's boy knows his master's taste for two girls at the same time. In *Indochine*, Emile, Eliane's father, gets a crack at each new young servant hired in the kitchen; in fact, Eliane approves her father's latest conquest because he is happy. An indirect reminder of the sexual practices of the colonizers appears in *L'Amant* when the two French girls are seen in the dormitory and dining room surrounded by racially mixed girls. These children born from French men and Vietnamese women were rejected by both the French and the Vietnamese and kept hidden in orphanages so that there would be no overt shame and dishonor in the French community.[12] In *Chocolat* the coffee planter sneaks food to his slave/mistress at night. The films clearly show that these relationships were considered "normal," a legitimate right of the colonizer. Several films display or refer to sexual adventures or pleasure trysts that men can have in the colonies. In *Fort Saganne*, in a remote post in the desert, the captain receives the visit of a young girl, who comes spontaneously to spend the night with him. In *Le Vent de la Toussaint* the French doctor and the Algerian man, both ex-officers in the French army, remember fondly their fling together with two Vietnamese cousins during the Indochina war.

Such relationships are one of the topoi of life in the colonies and do not mobilize the attention of spectators. But several films present more complex and developed interracial love affairs that are a significant part of the diegesis. These love affairs are the sites at which fierce racism emerges and the rejection of the non-White is particularly blatant. These attitudes are thematized and highlighted in the dialogues and behavior of the characters. In *La Victoire en chantant* the French men and women talk with dismay about the relationship between Fresnoy and the Black girl, whom they refer to as a "négresse": "Bosselet on comprend, mais lui, une négresse!" [With Bosselet we understand, but him, a nigger!], "J'en digère pas le coup de la négresse" [I can't swallow that story with the nigger], say the women, and one of the priests explains: "La nature a fait en ce jeune homme des exigences bizarres" [Nature has endowed this young man with strange needs]. In *Rue cases-nègres* the most poignant moment of the film takes place when Léopold, the racially mixed child, hears his Béké father disown him and his mother because of their race, thus denying his mistress/ wife and child any status in French society. In *Le Vent de la Toussaint*, violent reactions to the relationship between the French doctor and Malika, the Kabyle girl, come from both sides. The French hotel director refuses to serve the couple once he realizes Malika is a native girl, and her Algerian father cannot accept that his daughter became the lover of a Frenchman. His resentment becomes embroiled with his nationalist aspirations.

L'Amant is often presented as the depiction of the sensuality and erotic experience of a young girl with her Chinese lover. While this reading is correct and is the cause of the success of the film, another important aspect of it is its emphasis on the violent reactions provoked by the interracial relationship. The conversations between the lovers mostly center on the impossibility of their relationship because of their race, and they both express the racism of their respective ethnic community. In addition, the negative reactions of the girl's mother, brother, and schoolmates and the equally negative reaction of the Chinese man's father are presented extensively.

Although they do not purport to document or truthfully render the past, these films stage and underscore aspects of colonial culture that have been studied by scholars of colonial culture, namely that interracial relationships are tropes that express other aspects of colonial life. They concretize how in these multiracial but highly segregated colonial societies interracial relationships were about sexual access and exploitation, class distinction, class demarcation, and identity and how they provoked violent reaction because they challenged and threatened colonial hierarchies.

These contemporary imaginings and refigurings of colonial life are also documents and comments on the mood and mentality of contemporary France, which makes it possible for cinematic discourse to present images different from those of the past. In colonial films and novels of the colonial era, White men, legionnaires, soldiers, and adventurers had love affairs with native women, but the possible attraction of a White woman for a native man was never even alluded to. Love with the Other in the contact zone was not tolerated for a woman and was not represented in films or novels. The films made by contemporary directors offer an interesting reversal of roles by overtly representing the White woman's physical attraction and desire for the Other, the non-White. In *Rue cases-nègres* Carmen mimics for his young friend José how his White mistress seduced him and explains that he is *le chéri* de Madame.[13] In *Chocolat* Denis displays subtly the potential for sexual attraction and desire between Aimée and Protée in the mirror scene when Protée is ordered to help Aimée zip up her evening dress. This is a redoing of the classic mirror scene of the woman looking at herself in the mirror in *La Souriante Madame Beudet*, or in *Gilda*, for instance, but what Aimée sees in her mirror is her gaze and that of Protée, their heads together, and the intimacy she shares with her Black servant, who is allowed in her room.[14] And Denis states explicitly that a French woman can be attracted by a Black man when Suzanne unambiguously tells Aimée: "Il est beau ton boy" [He is good-looking, your boy],[15] and there is a striking scene in which Aimée tries to have a physical contact with Protée and is spurned. Denis creates an atmosphere heavy with tension, innuendos, and frustrations because of the overt or covert movements of attraction and repulsion that develop between Aimée and Protée. Indeed, it is a question of limits, and of teasing these limits, that the film is about, and sexual and interracial limits go along with the limits of land, power, and domination that are played out in the film.[16] Annaud's rendition of Duras's novel focuses almost exclusively on the girl's attraction for the Chinese man's body, the pleasure and the torment they experience, and the sensuality of their evenings in the Chinese quarters. In *Outremer* Rouän presents the younger sister, Gritte, who rebels against the family, patriarchal pressure, and the colonial system, and has a love affair with an Arab and a revolutionary.[17] Rouän has Gritte reject all the French suitors but shows her in the company of the Algerian revolutionary in an intimate moment with her head on his knees, waiting anxiously in the night to meet him, and feeling intense sorrow when he is killed.[18] But note the ambiguity here: Gritte loves Algeria and accuses one of her French suitors of not understanding it. She listens intently as De Gaulle gives his famous Algérie Française speech in Algiers, saying, "Je vous ai compris" [I have understood you]. Gritte's behavior expresses a classic case of ambiguous nostalgia.

When France was a colonial power and during the Algerian war, such representations would have been censored because they would have undermined French superiority, racial policies, and the separation between ethnic groups. Now a particular mood permeates the culture. In the wake of feminism, women directors want to propose other roles and other images for women, and it is perhaps fashionable for Annaud to say that he wanted to represent feminine sensuality. Furthermore, it is now possible and desirable for financial reasons to titillate spectators with old taboos. Annaud could say about *L'Amant* that he wanted to "faire aimer l'image du désir, de l'amour, du contact entre deux races" [make spectators love the images of desire, of love, and of contact between two races]. And the producer of *Chocolat* saw it appropriate to request that Denis construct a love affair between Protée and Aimée, as Catherine Portuges reports in Chapter 5 of this volume.

In contrast to the films from the colonial era, in the films that I am discussing here the directors give a positive image of the personality, the looks, and the behavior of the non-French characters. They do not cast them in secondary roles or as mere shadows in the background. They do not portray them as childish, inferior, grotesque, or associated with animality. Rather they represent them as individuals endowed with sensitivity, feelings, pride, and determination. In *La Victoire en chantant* Fresnoy's beautiful Black companion presides with him at the military parade as would a French officer's wife accompanying her husband. In *Le Vent de la Toussaint*, Malika, the Kabyle girl from the Aurès mountains, wants to become a doctor. With the help of Doctor Hennuin and his French friends, she succeeds in becoming a medical student in Algiers. In *Indochine*, Camille, the Annamite princess pushed by the force of her passion, is determined to find the French officer she loves, and she musters the mental and physical strength she needs to survive in the maximum security prison. In *Chocolat*, Protée, the caring nanny, the protean boy who can do anything (including speak several languages), is attracted to Aimée but does not succumb to her advances. Denis thus avoids the stereotype of the Black man with powerful sexual drives. The Chinese man of *L'Amant* is particularly moving in his elegant and sincere sorrow. The colonized screen lovers or potential lovers are constructed as attractive and intelligent individuals and definitely not as preconceived racial stereotypes.

In addition, the directors' representational practices are in keeping with current filmic and media practices in displaying mixed couples in lovemaking situations and paying attention to the male body. But a postcolonial twist is introduced, because their camera focuses on the Black man's or the Chinese man's bodies, which are coded to have sexual appeal. The camera displays their bodies, half naked or naked and wearing different uniforms (Protée), or elegant clothing (the Chinese man). Protée and the Chinese man are the counterparts of Pépé the well-dressed gangster, showing off his body as he walked the streets and sang on the roofs of the Kasbah. A note of humor is introduced in *Chocolat* when one of the Black women servants watches the British man showering and makes fun of him. The White man's body is ridiculed for a moment—but note that he is British, not French.

And yet, as in the colonial films of the 1930s, the interracial relationships are not represented as viable. Transracial physical pleasure and attraction can exist, but the meetings have to occur clandestinely and in a marginal place where reality is suspended, and they do not lead to a durable relationship. Love is a fatal attraction for Camille and Jean-Baptiste, shown drifting in a junk, a doomed interracial Tristan and Iseult. Protée is expelled from the house after he has violently rejected Aimée. Gritte is reabsorbed into French society but at the end of the film is again about to refuse to marry a Frenchman. Malika becomes a terrorist working against the French. The French girl of *L'Amant* leaves the Chinese man and goes to France.[19] Furthermore, these lovers from the colonies emit a mixed message, for they do indeed share a particular feature. They are Europeanized, have lived in France, or have been taught French customs. They are not really Others, but between two cultures. They wear European clothes and use European gestures as well as native ones. Their undecidable status underscores the ambiguity of the representation. They can also be seen as representing the fulfillment of the French power fantasy. For instance, in *La Victoire en chantant* it is possible to view Fresnoy's accomplishments as having reorganized the army, trained his orderly, and shaped the Black woman into a White woman's role. She is then the result of a forced submission to the colonized and represents an assertion of White supremacy. Camille of *Indochine*, the young Annamite princess raised in French schools, heiress of French and Vietnamese rubber estates, represents the complicity of the native elite with the French colonial system.

It might also be the case that some spectators feel that these films offer a biased representation of the Other. For instance, in making Malika a terrorist the director of *Le Vent de la Toussaint* emphasized her lack of gratitude for the French colonizers who helped her. In *Outremer* one can see the Algerian approaching Gritte from behind with a knife, signifying violence and perpetuating the image of the dangerous Arab.[20] The scenario in *Indochine* is written in such a way that it is Camille who seems to be the cause of all the troubles brought to the French officer, and by showing her legend, which is enacted in theaters all over the country and which leads to insurrection, the interracial couple is indirectly blamed for the revolution. As Panivong Norindr states in Chapter 7 of this volume, Camille is made into a cold, feelingless communist leader abandoning her child. Finally, these are "films de Blancs."[21] They present the point of view of French men and women. And while they display more efforts to present the Other and their culture than colonial films do, with the Chinese wedding of *L'Amant* and the references to local customs in *Indochine* and in *Le Vent de la Toussaint*, these films do not put racial and cultural Otherness into circulation. Despite such ambiguities and biases, however, these films present interracial relationships that fit the tone and the mood of French culture in the last twenty years, during which a progressive recognition and acceptance of the Other as a human being rather than an object has taken place.

POSTCOLONIAL CINEMA: THE 1970S TO THE 1990S

Several social and political components of postcolonial France should be noted, as they constitute the backdrop against which films have been made since the 1970s. With the steady immigration from the former colonies,

France is becoming increasingly a multiethnic country. The populations that were formerly on the periphery are now making their way into the old metropolis. Mixed marriages are more frequent,[22] and often well-known public figures—such as Isabelle Adjani, Yannick Noah, and Harlem Désir—are celebrated as the products of such marriages. The former colonies have become independent countries with economic and political ties with France so that a fair number of French citizens live there as businessmen, advisers, and technicians. So again French individuals and Others are in contact, either in the former colonies or in France. How is cinema articulating these facts and in what ways do these representations fit the mood of France today and/or try to affect it?

Two films from the 1970s have as their main focus relationships involving a Black man and a White woman and the violent reactions provoked by such an interracial union.[23] In *Odeur de fauve* (1971), by Robert Balducci, a scandal reporter (Maurice Ronet) succeeds in photographing a Black man and the daughter of a prominent Ku Klux Klan leader lying together at poolside at a Paris private club patronized by African men and French as well as other White women. As a result, the reporter is beaten up by Americans and forced to go into hiding to save his life. The Black man, an African engineer living and working in Paris, is savagely killed. *L'Etat sauvage* (1978), by Francis Girod, is an adaptation of the 1964 Goncourt Prize–winning novel by Georges Conchon and features such famous actors as Marie-Christine Barraud, Jean Dutronc, Doura Mane, and Michel Piccoli, who was also the producer of the film. Set in an undetermined African country, it vigorously criticizes neocolonialist corruption as practiced by both the Africans and the French. But the centerpiece of the film is the interracial relationship between Laurence (Marie-Christine Barraud), the French woman, and Doumbé (Doura Mane), the African doctor who is also minister of health. This relationship is not tolerated by either the Africans or the French. Through the collaboration of the two, the minister is arrested, in a scene that in brutally distilled form brings together neocolonial politics and interracial relationships in that he is in bed with his White French mistress at the time. Soon after, he is killed, and the French woman faces the threat of being stoned, lynched, and raped by African and French men, but her first husband (Dutronc) and the chief of police (Piccoli) help her. The African girl forced to spend the night with Dutronc is killed by a Black mob. This particularly violent film, which victimizes both the White and the Black women, repeats the familiar Africanist topoi about Black men's sexuality, White women's hysteria in Africa, the accessibility of Black girls, and the right of White men to do as they please with Black girls. One of the French men states that White women get in an "état sauvage" in Africa because of the climate, and repeatedly it is implied that Laurence sleeps with Black men, any Black men. It is revealing that such topoi are also found in popular detective novels by French writers and involving African and French individuals, as is documented in the semiotic study *Le Nègre dans le roman français (1945–1977)*, in which the author, Sébastien Joaquin, notes the "interdit d'interracialité qui pèse sur le roman d'espionnage tourné vers l'Afrique" [the interdiction of interraciality that weighs on the spy novel set in Africa].[24]

As far as content is concerned, the message of these films is mixed. They convey very clearly that love is possible between individuals of different races, but they emphasize that society will not tolerate such relationships. They display mixed couples dancing very intimately in an exclusive Black club or mixed couples naked in bed, and they portray reciprocal attraction and pleasure. The Black men are not subaltern characters but are highly educated and qualified professionals working in jobs that connote success and achievement. But the female characters are constructed as unstable, unsatisfied, and troubled, in the case of the French woman in Africa, or a mixed-up American girl led astray in Paris and wanting to rebel against her racist father by sleeping with Black men. These films definitely do not seek to promote interracial relationships, and their very titles have extremely negative Africanist connotations, associated with animality and wildness.

The mid-1980s saw the emergence of the Beur movement, with many children of North African immigrant workers reaching their twenties, raised in France in mixed neighborhoods or ghettos. Two films present young French and Beur characters living in the margins of affluent French society. Poverty leads young French women to prostitution and young French and Beur men to pimping, stealing, and selling drugs in *Le Thé au harem d'Archimède*, by Medhi Charef (1985), and *Tchao pantin*, by Claude Berri (1985). One might expect the interracial relationships that are presented to be charged with negative overtones, but it is the contrary. Charef shows both Patrick and Madjid dancing and sleeping with French girls they meet in a disco without any incidents or remarks having to do with race. While in *Tchao pantin*, Berri, through Coluche, makes fun of the construction of gender and ethnicity,[25] the punk girl Lola is attracted to the Beur Bensoussan, and other French girls are seen in bed with Beur drug dealers. The characters do not pay much attention to the ethnic background of their partner, and the brief relationships seem natural, normal, untainted by racial issues.[26] The same casual attitude appears in the novels by Leila Sebbar, in which marginal young people living in tenements (*squatts*) are involved in interracial relationships.[27] These films and novels are renderings of the *culture de banlieue*, ethnographies of marginality that document a mode of life in which ethnic mixing is part of the culture of young individuals—French, Beur, or Black—living outside French society. Questions of ethnicity and identity were not yet in the forefront of current events. It was rather the fear of the Other, the spread of delinquency and drugs, and the feeling of insecurity that pervaded French society at the time, fueled by the rhetoric of Jean-Marie Le Pen. The two films participate in this discourse in opposite ways. *Le Thé au harem d'Archimède* underscores the automaticity of the stereotype by showing that even though the French youth (Patrick) does the stealing, it is the Beur youth (Madjid) who is suspected and accused, and *Tchao pantin* reinforces the stereotype of the Maghrebian drug dealer.

In the late 1980s and early 1990s and contemporary with the films on the colonies by Denis, Roüan, and Annaud, as the dominant society constructs immigrants in more and more negative terms and deteriorating economic conditions cause tensions and polarizations around issues of race, ethnicity, and identity, French cinema proposes contradictory images of these issues. Gérard Blain (*Pierre et Djemila*, 1987) and Cédric Kahan (*Trop de bonheur*, 1995) show the impossibility of interracial relationships, while Nicolas Ribouski (*Périgord noir*, 1988), Coline Serreau (*Romuald et Juliette*, 1990), Jean-Loup Hubert (*La Reine blanche*, 1991), and Mathieu Kassovitz (*Métisse* [*Chocolat au lait*], 1993) display successful if somewhat odd interracial relationships. *Pierre et Djemila* takes place in a multiethnic working-class neighborhood in the industrial town of Roubaix. Pierre, seventeen years old, works, and Djemila, fourteen years old, goes to school. Djemila's brother, Djaffa, notices the attraction of his sister for the French boy and kills him. Djemila drowns herself in a canal. *Trop de bonheur* is about Didier and Kamel going to parties and trying to sleep with girls. Brahim, Kamel's older brother, explains to his younger brother that it is all right to sleep with French girls but never to love one, because they will always consider you an outcast. The message of these films is obvious. Interracial relationships lead to tragedy; such unions are doomed to failure not because the individuals are mismatched but because society—Arab and French—does not tolerate or accept them. The same attitude that was prevalent in the 1930s surfaced again in colonial films of the 1980s and 1990s, such as *Le Vent de la Toussaint* and *The Lover*.

In *Périgord noir*, which was advertised in a TV magazine as "une histoire d'amour et un conte sur le respect du droit à la différence" [a love story and a tale about the respect of the right to be different], members of an African tribe arrive in France to work in an almost abandoned village in Périgord. After a year they go back to Africa with money to exploit their bankrupt plantation. One of the women brings back a French husband, and one of the men a French wife. The weddings take place in France and mingle both traditions. In *Romuald and Juliet*, Juliet, a French Caribbean woman janitor with five children from five different husbands, marries the French CEO of the company where she works after she has helped him fight the evil and greediness of his jealous colleagues. *La reine blanche* was the name given Catherine Deneuve in the film by the same name. As the plot goes, twenty years earlier she was elected queen of the carnival and paraded on a float decorated with snow and ice. At that time she chose to marry the character acted by Bohringer rather than the one acted by Giraudeau, who, deeply pained by this choice, emigrated to the Caribbean, where he married a Black woman. Now he is back in France with his wife and the children of this mixed-race marriage. His daughter is elected the queen of the carnival and parades on a tropical float, radiating her golden beauty and overcoming racism and jealousy. *Métisse* has been hailed as a mixture of Spike Lee (*She's Gotta Have It*) and Woody Allen (for his portrayal of the Jewish family). It is also reminiscent of Coline Serreau's *Pourquoi pas* (1977), in which one woman lives with two lovers, but instead of focusing on the sexual freedom of the 1970s, director Mathieu Kassovitz addresses the issue of ethnicity, of interracial relationships, with three characters—a poor Jewish rap singer/composer, a rich Black law student, and a light-colored Martinican girl. The characters constantly talk about ethnicity, sometimes in violent terms, sometimes in humorous ways—as when the girl's grandmother, who is definitely Black, says she likes the Black boy but he is a bit too dark.

Clearly these films are postcolonial fairy tales. It is highly improbable that French peasants from Périgord are going to sell their property and relocate in Africa out of love for an African man or woman or that a French CEO will get involved in such an ancillary relationship and marry his husky janitor, and it is not that easy for children of mixed marriages to be so readily accepted by the French, especially in the provinces or in the suburbs of big cities. And it is also unlikely that a girl from Martinique is going to be able to live with two men—one Black, the other White—who agree to share household tasks without knowing who is the father of the baby. That the directors made these films, however, and chose very popular and famous actors and actresses (such as Daniel Auteuil, Richard Borhinger, Catherine Deneuve, Jean Giraudeau, and Smaïn) who attract a wide public, and that the press hailed the beauty of Julie Mauduech, the beautiful girl from the Caribbean in Paris, are salient facts. It means that such a discourse is possible in the present climate and that the directors feel there is a need to raise the question of mixed marriages and of the re-actions of the French to these marriages and to make films that debate the issues facing France today, where French individuals and individuals from the former colonies live together. But even though these films do not overtly send a negative message, they do not yet and perhaps cannot yet propose representations of interracial relationships that challenge racial barriers and promote social bondings, biculturalism, and biracialism ful-filled through realist love.

France has had several waves of immigration since the turn of the cen-tury. Italians, Spaniards, Portuguese, Yugoslavs, Greeks, and Turks, as well as Europeans from North Africa, have settled in France. Mixed marriages have occurred, as they also have between Jews and Catholics and Catholics and Protestants. Yet marriages involving Europeans from different coun-tries have seldom been subject matter for past or recent films or even past or present literature.[28] These mixed marriages were not highly charged issues in French society, since the populations of European origin were quickly assimilated and thus did not represent the same degree of Other-ness that African Blacks and Arabs do and did not cause the same anxiety and fear of *métissage*.

Significant aspects of thoughts and feelings in France in the last fifty years concerning the construction of its ethnic identity and its attitude toward the Other, colonized and ex-colonized, appear in the films I have dis-cussed. These films have shaped and continue to shape the French experi-ence of the Other, of the colonies, and of the colonial past, and they reflect and express the shifting positions of masculinity, femininity, and ethnicity in contemporary France. They have determined how the Other was con-structed in the past, and they are determining how the Other(s) are con-structed today. And the recent appearance in France of several films deal-ing with the colonial past and with situations involving characters of different ethnic backgrounds is not merely a fortuitous phenomenon; rather, it is a set of statements and metastatements about issues arising be-cause contemporary France is becoming more and more multiethnic.

Understanding the relationship between France and its colonial and postcolonial Others requires attention to an intersection of social, cultural, political, economic, and historical factors. In this essay I have argued that gender, and especially interracial sexual relations, are central to this understanding and are often a trope of it, as expressed so poignantly in the films from the two periods that I examine. These films can have several simultaneous and often conflicting meanings and interpretations, reinforcing stereotypes or raising issues, thus revealing French—and, more generally, European—society's ambiguous, ambivalent, and changing attitudes toward race, ethnicity, class, gender, and interracial relationships. The films are complex and deal with many matters. Ultimately they demonstrate that with regard to France and its very significant Others, it is race that matters most.[29]

NOTES

1. I do not analyze the films that I have chosen in depth; rather, I examine how the interracial relationships are constructed in them and how they relate to and articulate aspects of the society and culture of the time.

2. Ann Stoler, "Carnal Knowledge and Imperial Power," in *Gender at the Crossroads of Knowledge*, ed. M. Di Leonardo (Berkeley: University of California Press, 1991), 51–101. I draw heavily on this excellent and thorough study.

3. See Aimé Dupuy, *L'Algérie dans les lettres d'expression française* (Paris: Editions universitaires, 1956), 83.

4. John Allen Stevenson, "A Vampire in the Mirror: The Sexuality of Dracula," *Modern Language Association* 103, no. 2 (1988): 139–149.

5. It would be interesting to speculate about why Dracula has recently reappeared on the screen. Fear of AIDS? fear of women's sexuality? fear of interracial unions?

6. Pierre Loti, *Le Roman d'un spahi* (Paris: Calmann-Lévy, 1925), 263.

7. This information can be found in the study of the life and career of Josephine Baker by Phyllis Rose, *Jazz Cleopatra* (New York: Doubleday, 1989). Here is the French text of *J'ai deux amours:* On dit qu'au delà des mers. Là-bas sous un ciel clair. Il existe une cité au séjour enchanté. Et sous les grands arbres noirs. Chaque soir, vers elle s'en va tout mon espoir. Refrain: J'ai deux amours. Mon pays et Paris. Pour eux toujours mon pays est ravi. Ma savane est belle. Mais à quoi bon le nier. Ce qui m'ensorcelle. C'est Paris. Paris tout entier. Le voir un jour. C'est mon rêve joli. J'ai deux amours. Mon pays et Paris. Quand sur la rive, parfois, au lointain j'aperçois. Un paquebot qui s'en va. Vers lui je tends les bras. Et mon coeur battant d'émoi. A mi-voix. Doucement je dis: "Emporte-moi." Au refrain. [People say that beyond the seas. Over there under a clear sky. There is a city which offers an enchanted life. And under the tall black trees. Every night, towards this city all my hope goes. Refrain. I have two loves. My country and Paris. For them my country is always ravishing. My savanna is beautiful. But why should I deny it. What charms me. It is Paris. The whole of Paris. To see it one day. This is my beautiful dream. I have two loves. My country and Paris. When on the shore, sometimes, far away I perceive. A ship which is leaving. Toward it I extend my arms. And my heart beating with emotion. In a low voice. Softly I say: "Take me away." Refrain.]

8. Several of these novels, which have now been reprinted, are discussed in Patrice Franchini, *Métis* (Paris: Jacques Bertoin, 1992).

9. Here are the words of "La Petite Tonkinoise": "C'est moi qui suis sa petite, son Annana, son Annana, son Annanamite. Je suis vive, je suis charmante. Comme un petit oiseau qui chante. Il m'appelle sa petite bourgeoise. Sa Tonkiki, sa Tonkiki, sa Tonkinoise. D'autres lui font de beaux yeux. Mais c'est moi qui l'aime le mieux." [I am his little, his Anna, Anna, Annamite. I am quick, I am charming. Like a little bird who sings. He calls me his little wife. His Tonkiki, Tonkiki, Tonkinese. Others look at him with loving eyes, but I am the one who loves him best.]

10. André Malraux, *La Voie royale* (Paris: Grasset, 1930).

11. See Phyllis Chester on this aspect of Baker's talent, which derived from her African American experience in the United States and became her trademark in France, connoting African wildness, energy, and eroticism.

12. Stoler and Franchini discuss the condition of the *métis* in Vietnam. Eliane tells Etienne about his past and at one point explains that his father's family never tried to get in contact with her to see him. The presupposed unsaid here is that with his Asiatic features he probably would have been a reminder of their son's tragic love affair with a Vietnamese woman.

13. At this point José notices a book on the night table. It is *Chéri*, by Colette, which is the story of the relationship of an older woman and a young man. Another such allusion occurs with the poster of the film *Cleopatra* in the hallway of the movie house. Cleopatra, the Egyptian queen and her Roman lovers Anthony and Caesar, formed interracial couples that echo and are variants of the couple formed by Leopold's parents, the Béké and the Black Martinican woman. With these various couples Palcy focuses on a set of women rebelling against conventions and transgressing the norms that shape gender roles and ethnic demarcations.

14. Palcy and Denis underscore the ambiguity of the domestic colonial arrangements in which the boy had access to and lived in close proximity to the White quarters and in particular to the White woman's intimate space and yet was denied any freedom or autonomy, and any identity other than that of boy, or servant.

15. In Alain Robbe-Grillet, *La Jalousie* (Paris: Minuit, 1952), A, the wife of the colonist, states that a White woman could sleep with a Black man.

16. Protée and Aimée are surrounded by other men and women equally attracted to each other. Denis achieves this effect by revealing the adulterous affair between Suzanne and Segalen, by showing the attraction of Jonathan Bushby for Aimée and that of Segalen for Aimée, by referring to the possible relationship that might have occurred between Marc and Bushby, and by establishing the fierce competition for Aimée that takes place between Segalen and Protée and ends with Protée expelling Segalen. For a postcolonial reading of this film, see Ien Ang, "Hegemony in Trouble," in *Screening Europe: Change and Cinematic Representation in Modern Europe*, ed. Duncan Petrie (London: British Film Institute, 1992), 21–31, and Stuart Hall, "Cinema on the Verge of a Nervous Breakdown," in Petrie, *Screening Europe*, 45–53.

17. Historically such a relationship would have been possible. The Gritte episode of *Outremer*, the relationship between Malika and Hennuin in *Le Vent de la Toussaint*, and the possible relationship between Aimée and Protée in *Chocolat*, as well as A saying to Frank that she could conceive a White woman sleeping with a Black man in Robbe-Grillet's *La Jalousie*, take place in the 1950s, when a younger generation of colonizers were less stridently racist than their predecessors and the perception of what was possible had shifted.

18. Roüan elaborates three variations on a complex set of intertwined issues, love, marriage, patriarchal and colonial oppression, gender roles, death, and separation. The sections are ironically framed musically by Glück's "The Triumph of Love" from his opera *Orfeo and Euridice,* where love does not triumph because the lovers live first in torment and then are separated by death, as in the three sisters' stories. The film ends with bittersweet children's songs that are also about failed marriage and bad relationships between men and women. In an ironic side comment, Roüan shows Zon, the older sister, perhaps the most racist of the three, trying on a belly dancer outfit, presumably to excite her husband with an exotic Arab touch.

19. Spike Lee's *Jungle Fever* and Bertolucci's *Sheltering Skies,* among others, display interracial relationships, but there too they are temporary.

20. This orientalist stereotype was pointed out to me by Salah Hassan.

21. I am using a remark of Claire Denis, who declared that *Chocolat* was "un film de blanche." See Jean-Michel Frodon, "Claire Denis: Une enfance africaine," *Le Point* 816 (1988): 75.

22. One such famous couple is the mayor of Saint Coulitz in the Finistère, who is originally from Senegal, and his wife, from Brittany.

23. These films were recently made available by Facett Video. Although I do not discuss them and although they might not be easily available, I would like to mention *Elise ou la vraie vie* (1970), by Michel Drach, which is about a French girl from the provinces discovering hard work in a factory and racism because her lover is an Algerian worker in a factory, and *Dupont la joie* (1974), by Yves Boisset, in which an Algerian is falsely accused of a rape and murder actually committed by a Frenchman. Both films denounced racism against North African workers.

24. Sebastien Joaquin, *Le Nègre dans le roman blanc: Lecture sémiotique et idéologique de romans français et canadiens, 1945–1977* (Montréal: Presses de l'Université de Montréal, 1980) 129.

25. This aspect is discussed by Steven Ungar, "L'effet Coluche: From Mec to Lambert" (paper delivered at the Twentieth Century Colloquium on French Studies, Dartmouth, March 1993).

26. *Diva* (1980) is another film in which race and ethnicity are not foregrounded, even though the film displays interracial relationships.

27. See Leïla Sebbar, *Shérazade* (Paris: Stock, 1982) and *Les Carnets de Shérazade* (Paris: Stock, 1985).

28. In Marcel Pagnol's *The Baker's Wife,* the wife of the baker elopes with an Italian farmworker, but the affair does not last and she comes back to her baker. A recent film, Eric Barbier's *Le Brasier* (1990), has a Polish immigrant's son working in the mines of northern France fall in love with a French girl. But note that this is a film of the 1990s, when notions of ethnicity and nationality are being debated actively in the country.

29. In *Race Matter: About Race Matters and How Race Matters* (Boston: Beacon Press, 1993), Cornell West notes that racial hierarchy dooms America to collective paranoia and hysteria (2). This is perhaps what is currently happening in France, where issues of ethnicity are polarizing both French and diasporic Third World peoples.

ABOUT THE AUTHORS

NANDI BHATIA is a doctoral student at the University of Texas at Austin and is doing comparative work on postcolonial Indian theater. Her forthcoming articles include "Staging Resistance: The Indian People's Theatre Association (IPTA)" and "Hindi Literature in the Twentieth Century." She published an article on Rudyard Kipling's *Kim* in the May 1994 issue of *SAGAR* (*South Asia Graduate Research Journal*) and has written articles on South Asia in *SAMAR* (*South Asia Magazine for Action and Reflection*).

MADELEINE COTTENET-HAGE is Associate Professor at the University of Maryland, where she teaches French literature and cinema. She is the author of *Gisèle Prassinos ou le désir du lieu intime* (J. M. Place, 1988) and is currently working on a biography of French poet and novelist Lucie Delarue-Mardus. She has published articles on Marguerite Duras's films in *The French Review* and *Post-Script*, on Audiberti's film reviews in *Europe* (special issue on Audiberti), and on Godard's *Le Gai Savoir* (with Robert Kolker). She has also written on French and Caribbean writers in various journals and reviews, such as *Callaloo*, *Francofonia*, *Avante-Garde*, *Dada and Surrealism*, as well as on cultural features in *Contemporary French Civilization*. She is coeditor with Christiane Makward of *Dictionnaire critique des écrivaines de langue française* (forthcoming), of *Regards sur la France des quatre-vingt: Le roman* (Stanford French and Italian Studies 80, 1995) (with Joseph Brami and Pierre Verdaguer), and of *Penser la Créolité* (Karthala, 1995) (with Maryse Condé). A critical anthology of short stories by Francophone women writers is also forthcoming (L'instant Même).

JOHN D. H. DOWNING is in the Department of Radio-Television-Film at the University of Texas at Austin. He teaches courses on cinemas of the Third World and is editor of *Film and Politics in the Third World* (Autonomedia, 1987). He has also published *The Media Machine* (Pluto Press, 1980) and *Radical Media: The Political*

Experience of Alternative Communication (South End Press, 1984), and he has co-edited *Questioning the Media* (Sage Publications). He is the author of research articles and chapters on a variety of topics, including racism, ethnicity and media, and media in Eastern Europe.

NAOMI GREENE is Professor of French and Film Studies at the University of California at Santa Barbara. Her major publications include *Antonin Artaud: Poet without Worlds* (Simon and Schuster, 1971); *René Clair: References and Resources* (GK Hall, 1985); a translation of Marc Ferro's *Cinéma et Histoire* (Wayne State, 1988); and *Pier Paolo Pasolini: Cinema As Heresy* (Princeton University Press, 1990).

MARTINE ASTIER LOUTFI is Professor of French at Tufts University. She is the author of *Littérature et Colonialisme* (Mouton, 1971) and coauthor of *Récits d'aujourd'hui* (Holt, 1989). She has also written numerous articles on French cinema in such journals as the *French Review*.

PANIVONG NORINDR is Associate Professor in the Department of French and Italian at the University of Wisconsin–Milwaukee. He has contributed articles and reviews in such journals as *Differences, Sub-Stance,* and *French Cultural Studies.* Norindr is the author of *Fantasmatic Indochina: French Colonial Ideology in Architecture, Cinema, and Literature* (Durham: Duke University Press, 1996) and essays in such anthologies as *Displacements: Cultural Identity in Question,* ed. Angelika Bammer.

CATHERINE PORTUGES is Professor and Graduate Program Director in the Department of Comparative Literature at the University of Massachusetts, Amherst, where she also serves as Director of the Interdepartmental Program in Film Studies. Her articles on French women writers and filmmakers appear in *Yale French Studies, L'Esprit Createur,* and *Dalhousie French Studies and Massachusetts Review;* she is coeditor of *Gendered Subjects: The Dynamics of Feminist Pedagogy* (Routledge, 1985). She has contributed chapters for *French Women Writers* (Greenwood, 1991); *Life/Lines: Theorizing Women's Autobiography* (Cornell University Press, 1988); and *Essays on Marguerite Duras* (Peter Lang, 1990). Her recent work on postcolonial French and East European cinema will appear in *Genders* and *Discourse,* as well as in collected volumes, including *Cultural Sitings* (Stanford University Press, 1996) and *Re-Writing New Identities: Nation, Gender, and Immigration in New European Subjects* (University of Minnesota Press, 1996). She is the author of *Screen Memories: The Hungarian Cinema of Marta Meszaros* (Indiana University Press, 1993).

MIREILLE ROSELLO teaches literature and culture in French at the University of Nottingham. Her major publications include *Littérature et identité créoles aux Antilles* (Karthala, 1993), *L'In-différence Chez Michel Tournier* (Corti, 1990), and *L'Humour noir selon André Breton* (Corti, 1987).

DINA SHERZER is Professor of French and Comparative Literature at the University of Texas at Austin. Her books include *Structure de la Trilogie de Beckett* (Mouton, 1976) and *Representation in Contemporary French Fiction* (University of Nebraska

Press, 1986). She has written on Duras, Beckett, Genet, Sebbar, and the New Wave. She teaches courses on French cinema and is currently researching various facets of postcolonialism.

PAUL STOLLER is Professor of Anthropology at West Chester University. His main fieldwork was carried out among the Songhay of Niger, where he met Jean Rouch. In fact, he is known as the "son of Rouch" in Songhay country. Stoller's books include *Fusion of the Worlds: An Ethnography of Possession among the Songhai of Niger* (University of Chicago Press, 1989), *The Taste of Ethnographic Things: The Senses in Anthropology* (University of Pennsylvania Press, 1985), *The Cinematic Griot: The Ethnography of Jean Rouch* (University of Chicago Press, 1992), and *Embodying Colonial Memories: Spirit Possession, Power, and the Hauka in West Africa* (Routledge, 1995).

STEVEN UNGAR is Professor of French and Chair of the Program in Comparative Literature at the University of Iowa. He is the author of *Roland Barthes: The Professor of Desire* (University of Nebraska Press, 1983) and *Scandal and Aftereffect: Blanchot and France since 1930* (University of Minnesota Press, 1995) and coeditor with Tom Conley of the forthcoming *Identity Papers: Scenes of Contested Nationhood in Twentieth-Century France* (University of Minnesota Press). He is completing a study with Dudley Andrew on the cultures of the Popular Front.

INDEX